THE MAN BEHIND
THE SOUND BITE

THE MAN BEHIND THE SOUND BITE

◆

THE REAL STORY OF THE REV. AL

SHARPTON

MICHAEL KLEIN

Castillo
INTERNATIONAL
NEW YORK

Castillo International, Inc.
500 Greenwich Street, Suite 201
New York, New York 10013

Library of Congress Catalog Number: 91-74101

Klein, Michael.
The Man Behind the Sound Bite: The Real Story
of the Rev. Al Sharpton

Includes bibliographical references and index.

ISBN 0-9628621-1-8

Grateful acknowledgment is made for permission to reprint portion
Speaks. Copyright © 1965, 1989 by Betty Shabazz and Pathfinder Press. Used by
permission.

COVER PHOTO BY JEFF CONNELL COURTESY OF THE NATIONAL ALLIANCE NEWSPAPER.
TYPOGRAPHY BY ILENE ADVERTISING
BOOK DESIGN BY DAVID NACKMAN AND DIANE STILES
PHOTO CREDITS ON PAGE 295

94   93   92   91   5   4   3   2   1

Manufactured in the United States of America

Dedicated to *everyone* who supported Tawana
because
it was the right thing to do;
and to Moses and Diane,
for giving themselves.

Contents

Acknowledgments

Thanks to the following:

In the shop:

My editors Gabrielle Kurlander, Jacqueline Salit and Phyllis Goldberg for help in shaping this biography at every stage;

My fellow editors at the *National Alliance*, Mary Fridley and Dan Friedman;

Diane Stiles and the production department of the Castillo Cultural Center;

Kate Henselmans, Rachel Massad, Richard Ronner, Freda Rosen, Dan Kaplan, and Sarah Russell for research assistance;

Margo Fletcher Grant and her extraordinary proofreading team;

David Nackman and the Castillo design team;

The staffs of Castillo Communications and Castillo International.

In the field:

To everyone on the streets who made this story happen and shared it, including the Reverend Al Sharpton; Kathy Jordan Sharpton; Moses Stewart; Diane Hawkins; Alvaader Frazier and Alton Maddox, Jr. and all the people's attorneys; Dr. Lenora Fulani; Dr. Rafael Mendez; Lorraine, Jamela and Shameka Stevens; John Beatty; Thelma and Phillip Pannell; the youth of the African Council; Ada Sharpton; Joy Sharpton; Glenda,

Juanita, and Tawana Brawley; Ralph King, Jr.; Mary Davis and family; Ricardo Burgos and family; the families and friends of the too many dead, who have chosen to fight for the generation to come; various unnamed sources in the strangest places who in a fair and decent world could be named proudly; Gloria Klein and Matty Regina for early admonitions to do the right thing and everyone at home for putting them into practice.

•

And to Dr. Fred Newman, without whom this and much else would not be thinkable, let alone possible.

Preface

HOLLYWOOD, June 1991. Here in LA, it seemed just like the old days: the stars, the photo opportunities, the parties, the power lunches and the autograph hounds. Back in the heart of the gold-studded world of Black show business, Rev was soaking it all up and loving every minute.

The biggest thrill of all was the Godfather's return to the stage. A pay-per-view TV audience of millions watched the long-awaited comeback of James Brown after his years locked away in a South Carolina jail cell on some nonsense thanks to a bunch of trigger-happy redneck cops who still can't stomach the sight of a sharp-looking Black man in a fancy car cruising down the highway.

It was also the return of the Reverend Al Sharpton to James Brown, the man who took Rev in as his son, and then took him around the world. And introduced him to the casinos of Vegas with flamboyant millionaire promoter Don King, the stars of Hollywood, the record company execs and everywhere, big, big money flying around, practically for the grabbing, especially for a sharp, street-smart character like Reverend Al Sharpton.

Over the past two years, Rev had waged an often lonely crusade to get the Godfather sprung while an industry with a short attention span and a bad habit of not taking care of its own let him fade from sight.

But the Godfather wasn't bitter about it all, so Rev, no party-pooper, took it in stride too for this trip to the coast. He let the aura envelop him, the smell and taste and feel of success everywhere. Occasionally, his mind would wander back a decade, to the day he and his soon-to-be bride Kathy Jordan, a talented, church-trained singer in James' band able to melt an audience in its seats, flew the Brown nest in the middle of the night in Augusta, Georgia to make it on their own in New York.

For Rev, it was a decision to return not only to the streets and the movement, but also to years of abuse, vilification, indictments and his own near-assassination. To have all the work land him nothing more than the honor of being called the "master of the sound bite."

Looking around now in Hollywood at the fortune and glitz he left behind, he wondered: Why? Was he committed? Crazy? Was it some childhood experience long buried in his subconscious? Something he ate?

Tonight, anyway, he was relaxing.

•

"Rev, there's a Miss Mayse, from Newark, on the phone. She's gotta talk to you."

The post-show festivities were barely underway and the stage not even broken down yet before the sobbing voice of a mother who had tracked Rev down in Tinseltown from across the continent came through the wires to his hotel room. The bright Hollywood lights began to dim as she told her story; in minutes Rev was barking instructions to his assistant to cut short the hoopla and get them on the red-eye going east.

Damn.

•

Hours later in Newark, New Jersey Rev listened intently as the 14-year-old girl told her story. "Reverend, they shot, shot, shot and stopped, and told all of us to stand up in the van." The horror of the night still hadn't fully sunk in, and she spoke with the quick coolness of a person in shock.

"All of us who could, stood up and they only started firing again. Then they dragged me by my hair out of the back window. I was shot in the shoulder. The cop looked at me and said, 'We should have blown your fucking brains out,' and stomped me in the face as I was lying on the ground holding my bullet wound."

Two of her friends were dead, including 15-year-old Tasha Mayse, who was expecting her first child later this year. Seven unarmed young people were joy-riding in the van that night through Newark; only one 13-year-old escaped the rain of 43 police bullets when they were pulled over in neighboring Hillside after a chase through the streets.

Rev listened to the story of another teenage girl, also dragged bleeding from the van with a gunshot wound in her back, and then was kicked and beaten so violently in her vaginal area that she needed stitches to close the wound.

Still weary from the flight home, Rev tried to maintain his composure as he listened to the young survivors' stories. Before the night of terror was over, his extended family would have new members, a family drawn together in a common bond of pain and suffering and a burning need for justice.

Rev readied himself to face the press and the public as he prepared to march on Newark's City Hall, meticulously gathering all the names and facts and events, comparing them with the police version, finding all the holes and contradictions in the official story, and figuring out what the families' next moves should be.

In the middle of it all he broke down, sobbing — screaming, really — uncontrollably. He had cried often enough before, with Moses Stewart and Diane Hawkins, as they talked about their son Yusuf, and what it must have been like by that dark Bensonhurst schoolyard as a frenzied white mob stood him up against the wall and shot him through the heart while an entire neighborhood watched. And with Thelma and Phillip Pannell, Sr., as they looked at pictures of their child, Phillip, Jr., who pleaded for his life with his arms stretched high over his head, a tiny figure in an oversized down jacket, right before a cop shot him through the back.

How could you not cry?

It wasn't the first time that Rev heard himself say: Enough is enough. This can't go on any longer. But the stories of these children in Newark snapped something in Rev's heart. He thought about the press that had gathered for him at City Hall as he approached with hundreds of angry citizens, demanding justice from the mayor. They were waiting for the sound bite they could put on the six o'clock news.

His eyes still red, Rev looked over at the reporters, their video cameras spinning and pads at the ready. He thought about the silence that had followed the almost unthinkable horror which had taken place on the streets of this community, and how the press and even the official Black leadership, including Newark's Black mayor, Sharpe James, had said nothing.

"They want a sound bite, I'll give 'em a sound bite!"

"We are here because there was a massacre," he bellowed. "Not an accident, not police business, but a massacre occurred in Hillside. We cried in Teaneck, we cried with Rodney King in Los Angeles. *I have no tears left.* These police have no humanity. It looks like we have to go from being activists to being animal trainers.

"I warn you that you and your silence will seal your own doom. You can move now or you will be moved later!"

There. They had their "sound bite."

The casinos of Las Vegas, the glitter of Hollywood, and the smell of money. He had indeed left it all behind, and for what? Rev thought about his two young daughters, Ashley and Dominique, three and four years old, playing together just 20 minutes down the road at their modest little home. "They're growing up the same color and in the same social circumstances as Tasha Mayse," Rev thought. "And there's a van waiting for them and there's a consortium of savage, insensitive, senseless police waiting for that van. If I don't march now, I'll mourn later."

•

"For anyone who thinks progress has been made, they need to look at my appointment book," Rev had said 18 months before. At the time he was standing in the funky halls of the Brooklyn Supreme Courthouse, where he was monitoring the trial of some of the Bensonhurst hoods who had shot down Yusuf Hawkins in cold blood on a hot summer night the year before. "It shows you that racism is alive and well — you can go from one case to the next."

He was racing off from there to City Hall to deal with New York City's new police commissioner, Lee Brown (late of Atlanta and Houston), to see what would be done about the police officers accused by the city medical examiner of murdering 28-year-old Dane Kemp of Brooklyn while he was in their custody. And off to Yonkers to battle segregation, and on and on.

On the steps of the Brooklyn courthouse, after the sound bites had been recorded and the press packed and gone, the people of Brooklyn stayed to press notes into Rev's hands about this case or that; a son who died in jail, supposedly a suicide; an employer who fired a college-educated Black woman because she blew the whistle on her white superiors; an illegal eviction; a struggling block association; a church that needed him to rouse the congregation.

No money for a child's funeral. No food on the table. No books in the classroom. No doctors in the hospital. No room at the shelter. Long after the cameras were gone the community lingered on, asking what they could do about the endless problems and heartbreaks that millions live with in places where the TV cameras never go.

"No justice, no peace," said Rev, taking down phone numbers, and the addresses of those without phones, and giving out phone numbers to those without phones or addresses.

•

Who is the man behind the sound bite?

When I first started covering the Reverend Al Sharpton for the *National Alliance* newspaper three years ago, it wasn't my intention to find out the answer to that question. I was assigned to cover the movement that was happening out on the streets of New York, and Rev was clearly one of the movers and shakers of it.

I first got a chance to hear the man who was just then making headlines by jumping on subway tracks and desktops in 1983, when Rev was a panelist at a "Religion and Politics" forum sponsored by the New York Institute for Social Therapy and Research, which at the time was holding a regularly scheduled speaker series on a whole range of topics. The panel was made up largely of folks who were advocates and practitioners of "liberation theology," which teaches that the role of the church is to serve the poor. Liberation theologians were being violently persecuted in places like Latin America and Africa, and the speakers mostly talked about their experiences in far-off places working among the poor.

Then Rev got up to speak, and I don't remember much other than that the much-maligned minister not only impressed the multi-racial audience of 300 or so community folks and people who were decidedly leftists with his intellect, but had them rolling in the aisles.

Then came Howard Beach. About midway through the trial I began covering the case, getting a closer look at the movement and its key players; it didn't take long to realize that the keyest was Reverend Al Sharpton. Still, the focus was the movement, which continued to snowball on the streets right up until December of 1987 and the Day of Outrage. I descended with a sea of people into the catacombs of the Borough Hall subway station for one of the most daring acts of civil disobedience in modern times.

Then came the court trials, and the backlash from the powers-that-be, and what was perhaps the most difficult story of all to cover — the almost successful attempt to wipe out this new and vibrant movement which was becoming a vehicle for power for a community that hadn't any.

For the crime of putting pressure on the judicial system of the State of New York Reverend Al Sharpton was about to become the target of a vicious (and, many believe, illegal) onslaught by the state.

I began covering the Tawana Brawley case for the *Alliance* soon after it happened; once again, Rev was at the center of it. But unlike Howard Beach, this wasn't going to be a story about the dogged and ultimately successful movement to secure justice in a case of racial violence.

From the start the "Brawley team," made up of Tawana and her family, Rev and attorneys C. Vernon Mason and Alton Maddox, Jr., was on the defensive, facing down a hostile press pummeling them with questions about a supposedly lying Tawana.

I have never been able to pinpoint the moment that the story of a brutal racial assault on a teenage girl became transformed in the white corporate-owned media into a vendetta against her and her supporters. That transformation was the product of the evil genius of a ruthless politician named Mario Cuomo (a master of the sound bite, "Magic" Mario's sorcery had been familiar to me since my childhood in Corona, Queens, where he perfected his art of spellbinding oratory that left only those with enough street smarts checking for their wallets) and New York Attorney General Robert Abrams, a man of mediocre talents but boundless ambition (*Alliance* editor Mary Fridley had described Bob Abrams as the high school nerd who grew up to become a powerful, and vindictive, adult).

But somewhere along the line everything changed. In a blinding sequence, Rev and the little girl he was defending found themselves up against brute power. Hundreds of Rev's supporters backed him in that fight with their bodies and countless more with their hearts, but it became painfully clear that "they" were gaining the upper hand, at least in this case. Rev, a man of the cloth, insisted always that their victory was unimportant, often quoting Dr. Martin Luther King, Jr.'s dictum that "truth crushed to earth will rise again."

Most painful of all to me, someone who grew up enmeshed in "the movement," was watching *this* new movement, made up of ordinary, extraordinary people whom I had gotten to know over the course of the fight, be beaten down. As a student of previous governmental and extra-governmental attempts to destroy previous movements, it was depressing to see history repeat itself.

For as long as anybody could remember, middle class white leftists from unloving families took out their frustration by standing on street corners to screech about revolution and were politely ignored (or occasionally encouraged) by the powers-that-be. But when real, living African American people took on the struggle for justice and a better life, they were ground into the dirt by the State of New York, in particular, a governor who was the national spokesperson for the "party of the people."

And there was the raw racism of the press, and the manipulations of members of the coalition by outside forces, bringing to mind images of the often bloody internecine warfare within the Black Panther movement of the '60s that the FBI was able to orchestrate with such success.

I spent 1988 alternately traveling the streets with Rev and the road with Dr. Lenora Fulani, now the chairperson of the New Alliance Party, covering her history-making Presidential run. Fulani led a march of hundreds of women of color through Poughkeepsie, New York early on in the Brawley affair, and made Tawana's case a centerpiece of her campaign.

Sometimes I covered them simultaneously, like in Atlanta during the Democratic National Convention, when Rev, Fulani and Louis Farrakhan were among those who descended on a sweltering city besieged by CNN and politicians to press the case of the people before, among others, Mario Cuomo.

It was thrilling to watch as Rev and Fulani began to work more closely together, seeing how the whole was even bigger and badder than the sum of these talented and committed parts. A high point was the extraordinary coming together of Rev and Dr. Fred Newman, my own political and spiritual and social mentor, who has meant the same to me as James has to Rev, at an historic forum on Blacks and Jews where they made a powerful and unified-in-action statement on what is perhaps the key (and the most explosive) issue in New York City today.

•

If these sound like the notes of a less than disinterested chronicler and biographer, that is because there is no way one can be anything other than that in monitoring and reporting on the life of someone like Al Sharpton. For any honest writer it couldn't be otherwise, and that contention has been borne out by three years of experience on the Rev "beat."

In the course of covering that beat, I've witnessed reporters spar with Rev and (particularly during the Brawley affair) have every one of their arguments (mostly fed to them by the Cuomo crowd) shot down one by one, only to watch these same reporters take their places before a camera or a computer keyboard and twist the very words that were spoken moments before.

I have watched as reporters (of all races and genders) commented — with disdain — on how lovely and lively Tawana was starting to look, seeing that as further proof of some complex forgery she had concocted to pull the wool over the eyes of the sharpest reporters on the planet. To them, Tawana was not acting like a proper rape victim. In actual fact, this remarkable young woman was doing something other than being a *victim*, even as these reporters made themselves accessories to the rape being perpetrated against her (and her supporters) daily by Albany.

Tawana was regaining her dignity in the only way possible for a Black woman in these United States, circa 1988. She was *fighting*, and as such she was a constant source of inspiration.

I had seen more than one of these reporters grapple with the ethical implications of their behavior; I saw how the only way they could find to deal with it was through a sort of weird group psychology, reassuring each other that it was OK, just a job, and drowning their moral misgivings in the amoral security of the collective media beast.

And the meanness of the opposition; I went down a flight of stairs with ordinary people (many of them quite elderly) when Brooklyn court officers rioted right in the courtroom and charged a group of supporters who were waiting for Rev and Vernon Mason outside; I saw the look of contempt in Robert Abrams' eyes when, during an otherwise celebratory press conference on his plans to lock up Tawana's mother for resisting his paper grand jury, I asked him if he thought there was anything fishy about the fact that the only arrests made since Tawana was first found were of members of his own staff.

I sat Rev down on more than one occasion to ask him point-blank what the deal was with all these stories about him doing this and that, even when I knew them to be so much nonsense. Just to see what he said.

In the course of it all, I met and came to know the man behind the sound bite.

Rev had set out as a civil rights leader at precisely that point in history when all the heroes were dead, the movements destroyed, the ideologies in shambles. All that remained was the pain of a community of millions, living and dying in almost unimaginable poverty, in the very shadows of the equally unimaginable wealth of the nation's greatest metropolis.

Dr. Newman always insists that the only way you can build things is with the materials at hand, whatever they may be and no matter how damaged they are. Rev had seen the materials at hand, including the media empire which had made its billions in part by selling an evil picture of his people.

Now some angry leaders might simply try to ignore that reality, or toss a rock through a window in Rockefeller Plaza, or call for a boycott. Rev had other ideas.

Reverend Sound Bite was born, and so was a new movement.

An ordinary man doing extraordinary things. Behind the sound bites, and the mountains of media, the trials, the marches, was a rather ordinary guy from Brooklyn, with the pulse of the streets in his veins. He wanted nothing more than to be a preacher, bringing the word to his people.

And to raise a family. The better part of the past dozen years has been spent with singer Kathy Jordan, whom he first met on the road with James. Church-raised just like Rev was, Kathy brings to the stage the same power, fire and rare ability to seize an audience at the roots of their soul that her husband does.

Most recently, Kathy has been dazzling fans with her Monday night performances at John Beatty's legendary Cotton Club on 125th Street. Beatty has been a quiet but devoted supporter of the movement from the beginning, one time putting up the club as collateral for Rev's bail. Kathy's shows have become a Harlem institution, weekly capturing the spirit, power and beauty of half a century of Harlem's cultural creativity.

Kathy and the internationally known man behind the sound bite live in a modest garden apartment in New Jersey, with two of the most adorable offspring ever to sit in a courtroom and watch their daddy on trial for his life, the above-mentioned Ashley and Dominique. He owns no car, has a couple of suits and the most extravagant thing a search of the house would unearth is a closet full of more jogging suits than perhaps the average person might own.

•

The stabbing. January 12, 1991. Reverend Al Sharpton had not only used his body and his being as a lightning rod for the anger of his people, but for the anger of the forces of evil as well. On that day, on the streets of Bensonhurst, that evil plunged a knife in his chest much too near his heart.

Within an instant the press — in particular, New York's "newspaper of record" — was proclaiming a "new Al Sharpton" who would be a moderate, conciliatory voice working within the body politic.

That tickled me no end, since from what I saw Rev was quite sedated and recovering in Coney Island Hospital during the whole time the story was going to press.

"What's the new Al Sharpton have to say?" I asked him after the line of politicians finally made their way out of his little recovery room.

"Tell them the new Al Sharpton will be marching on Gracie Mansion Saturday."

PROLOGUE

January 12, 1991

The face hovering over the bed at Coney Island Hospital was familiar, but it seemed very different from the dreams and the passing visions that swept through Rev's mind during the night. Older, more mature, fatherly. In the dreams, the Afro was bigger, the suit jacket a suede vest, and sideburns ringed the boyish face of the Reverend Jesse Jackson, who now stood over the bedside of Reverend Al Sharpton, assuring him, 22 years after they began their journey together, that it was not over yet.

A fact which was not very clear to Rev over the past 18 hours; from the hospital bed, the events of the previous afternoon in the Bensonhurst schoolyard were still a confusing blur. January 12 at PS 205 on 20th Avenue started off unceremoniously; the scene of hundreds of Black-led, multi-racial demonstrators waiting anxiously to begin a protest march through the all-white Brooklyn enclave had been rendered routine by the time of this, the 29th such excursion.

It was the 18th month of marches through Bensonhurst since the hot summer night when 16-year-old Yusuf Hawkins was gunned down by one of a gang of more than 30 white youths as he walked with three friends past this schoolyard on their way to inquire about a used car one of them had spotted in the classifieds. The murder of Yusuf Hawkins was to be the spark that would ignite a Black revolution on the streets of New York City; within months, the entire city government that three-term

1

New York Mayor Ed Koch headed — a government that to many symbolized the racial indifference and outright hostility towards America's largest and poorest African American community — would be swept from power in the wake of the marches that Rev and others would lead. And New York would even elect its first Black mayor ever.

Eighteen months later, the honeymoon would be over. The marches through Bensonhurst had temporarily resulted in a truce that was consummated when Rev brought 200 supporters to Saint Dominic's Catholic Church on 20th Avenue for Sunday services and reconciliation. The deal: no more marches in exchange for an agreement that Bensonhurst's civic and political authorities would do all they could to revive the maladroit efforts of the Brooklyn district attorney's office to bring all those involved in the murder of Yusuf Hawkins to justice and to obtain convictions against those already charged.

By January, 1991 the agreement was in shambles, done in by the failure of the DA's office to secure murder convictions against any except one of the defendants (accused triggerman Joey Fama, whose flight out of the city made him a sitting duck for a conviction despite the prosecution's flimsy case) and the failure of local politicians to take any action following the historic handshakes at St. Dominic's.

What Rev often called "political laryngitis."

In January two more of the accused killers, John Vento and Joseph Serrano, escaped with wrist-slaps. Serrano, a bear of a fellow with the alias "Joey Babes," received no time at all. To Rev and Yusuf's family, the Vento murder acquittal was particularly galling. Vento had initially confessed to being one of the killers in exchange for an agreement to testify against his fellow gang members, but, no doubt suspecting that life in Bensonhurst (or anywhere) would be unpleasant for a snitch, backed off and made tracks for Ohio, where he remained until his capture weeks later. Yet although he had virtually confessed to the crime, once again a shaky prosecution was unable to land a murder conviction.

As a light snow fell outside, the press gathered for the thousandth time in the lobby of the Brooklyn Supreme Courthouse; cameras, boom mikes, tape recorders, pads and their operators stood at the ready. Seconds after Supreme Court Judge Thaddeus Owens, the eccentric 70-year-old African American magistrate who presided over the series of disasters on the fourth floor known as the Bensonhurst case, announced his sentences of one and a third to four years for Vento and three years' probation for Serrano, word reached the lobby that the Hawkins family and their advisor were heading down in the specially reserved elevator. It was time for what the TV news producers call the "reaction shots."

Their path to the door blocked by the media army, Sharpton and Yusuf's parents Moses Stewart and Diane Hawkins came to a stop in front of the wall of reporters and their hardware. The tapes began to roll and Sharpton, fuming, denounced the verdict; Stewart maintained a superhuman composure as one reporter badgered him for a response, as if the pain and heartbreak and exhaustion etched in all of their faces wasn't reaction enough. For countless months, in each instance of thwarted justice, the reporters and their producers had become used to obtaining a response from Rev that could be edited for a quick sound bite, which would then be counterposed with the provoked anger of Moses, portrayed as the vengeance-obsessed father calling for the blood of his son's assassins, offset by Diane's tears.

On January 11, the press would get none of that. The rage and tears of the family of Yusuf Hawkins and the Reverend Al Sharpton, who had become as kin to Yusuf's family in the cataclysmic months since the murder, would not be shed waiting passively for justice that was not forthcoming.

The deal was off by default of the other side; the patience of this side was exhausted. The promises of politicians and DA's were just that. It was time to turn the heat up again.

We're going back to Bensonhurst.

•

Clouds filled the sky again on January 12 as the buses and cars arrived from the Slave Theater in Bed-Stuy, New Alliance Party headquarters in Harlem, and other points around the city. The steely gray skies lent a calmness to the afternoon; inside the schoolyard, within the police-designated "secure area" ringed by a phalanx of police officers, 500 marchers, many of them veterans of dozens of such protests, were lining up. Nearby Rev, also in the "secure area," emerged from his car and surveyed the scene, a black leather coat and a scarf over his trademark running suit as protection against the nasty weather.

At the gate to the schoolyard, 27-year-old Michael Riccardi moves among the sea of police officers — 300 altogether — who are on duty that day. A street peddler living in a basement apartment on a nearby street, Riccardi had a record of violent racial crimes stretching back close to a decade. Among them was an arrest for the murder of Leon Lindsey, who died in the early morning hours on the Fourth of July, 1987 on a Brooklyn street after a confrontation with a drunken Riccardi. Mysteriously, the Brooklyn DA voided that arrest, concluding that Lindsey's death was the result of his falling and fatally hitting his head on the ground with "no criminality" on the part of Riccardi.

So Michael Riccardi remained free despite the ceaseless terror spree (he would be arrested again in 1988 after tearing up a Greenwich Village McDonald's while hurling racist slurs at patrons); on January 12, 1991 a drunken Riccardi moved effortlessly among the blue wall deployed that Saturday to keep the peace.

Earlier, before Rev's arrival, Riccardi had gotten into an argument with one of the Community Affairs officers on the scene, and was told to leave after cursing about how he was not allowed in a schoolyard in his neighborhood. But despite this noisy altercation, Riccardi was allowed to walk unimpeded through the "frozen area," circling the block and making his way past the lines of standing demonstrators, where he would linger, waiting for the moment to strike.

Shortly after 1 pm, Riccardi decided the moment was right. He grasped at the five-inch kitchen knife under his baseball jacket, and charged full steam toward Rev, shouting his name as he ran; it was eerily reminiscent of how, in 1958, Dr. Martin Luther King heard his name uttered a split second before a woman plunged a letter opener into his chest.

The blow came with such force it sent Rev reeling; he looked down and saw that what he thought had been a punch was in fact a knife, stuck square in his chest. Cursing, he yanked it out and threw it to the damp ground of the schoolyard. The hazy Saturday afternoon became a blur around him, and as he slid slowly to the ground chaos took hold of the schoolyard. Around him, none of the officers on the scene made a move to assist.

Riccardi broke loose, running madly and violently in a desperate escape attempt. An attempt that would seem futile, except that still, the cops continued to stand by. Angry demonstrators took off in hot pursuit of Riccardi, and when he was captured, the police finally sprang into action — administering a beating to Moses Stewart and Sharpton security aide Henry Johnson.

"Somebody call an ambulance!" Sharpton associate Lenora Fulani yelled, and yelled again, sensing that there was no reason to think anyone in this police-controlled "secure area" was doing just that. Dr. Jessie Fields, a New Alliance Party activist and physician from Chicago who had just flown in to New York, administered first aid. Fields — on the scene by sheer luck of history — and a helpful Community Affairs person with medical training would be the *only* medical personnel to attend to the injured Sharpton until he arrived at Coney Island Hospital, driven there in a private car by supporters.

The police had not requested any Emergency Medical Service vehicles for the demonstration, and none were in sight as Rev sat crumpled on the schoolyard pavement, attended to by supporters while scores of police stood silently or dashed aimlessly about. With the minutes ticking away, Rev was lifted into a car for the trip to Coney Island Hospital. Rev's people all but took over the hulk of a building that loomed over the desolation of what was once America's most fabled playground, filling the vacuum of authority suspiciously relinquished by the New York City Police Department back at the schoolyard, and which remained absent here at the hospital.

•

Would this be the end of the long journey, here on a cold, rainswept street in Bensonhurst just miles from where it began 36 years before, in the back seat of a car silently clutching his chest? The images dashed through Rev's mind: Brooklyn, 1969, the first meeting with the imposing man with the Afro and sideburns. Those were chaotic days too; across the movement and across the world, the words of Nina Simone's song rang in the hearts of millions: "What's gonna happen now that the King of Love is dead?" For the teenage "wonder boy preacher" Reverend Alfred Sharpton, the response to the loss of Dr. Martin Luther King took shape from a fateful handshake with the young firebrand Chicago minister Reverend Jesse Louis Jackson; soon Rev's crew cut and suit were replaced with an Afro, sideburns, vest and medallion of his own.

In the course of two decades, he would be a first hand participant in history in the making, a time which would see a spark that lived amidst the ashes of the movement that died with the King of Love be nurtured and grow. The promises of a "Great Society" evaporated from the hot pavements of poor communities across the land as a new generation grew up without a dream. From the streets, Reverend Al Sharpton was among those who struggled to keep the dream alive in the harsh and brutal realities of post-'60s America.

By the onset of the '80s, he would be more than a participant; Reverend Al Sharpton, brought up in the streets of Bed-Stuy, coming of age in an America of shattered dreams, would become a shaper of history. One becomes a shaper of history only by becoming fully grounded in it, and for Rev, this meant planting himself solidly within the ground of the African American community, in the grassroots. It was a position left vacant by the murder of those who had filled it earlier.

Malcolm X, cut down as he was moving from his training ground in the mosques of Elijah Muhammad's Nation of Islam to become an international spokesperson for the downtrodden of the earth. The teenage Rev devoured Malcolm's *Autobiography*, inspired by his un-compromising passion for the despised and locked-out, and learning all he could about leadership.

And then King, whose murder was the final shattering of the dream.

Both men had prophesied their own deaths (Malcolm had prophesied both his *and* King's) at precisely the point when they became fully aware of the fact that their goals of civil rights and human rights and an end to injustice came into irreconcilable conflict with the very fabric of American society. A complex fabric, much, much deeper than southern redneck sheriffs and courts and jails. It stretched into every pore of society, from the most caricaturish cracker racist to the most liberal of institutions. And when the system was threatened by the demands of those who, like Malcolm and King, would not compromise even if it meant a total overhaul of *everything*, the system — a rich, white male creature — struck back. Liberal and conservative alike joined together in their condemnations of Malcolm and King, even as streets were being dedicated to them in the safety of their death.

And the Black Panther Party — young, Black and vibrant — would fall too, as it reached a political maturity a mere three years after its birth and began to universalize its struggle. Chicago Panther leader Fred Hampton was murdered in his sleep soon after laying plans for a broad-based Rainbow Coalition. The Panthers, who came of age in the wake of the murders of King and Malcolm, did not prophesy their own deaths. They fought. But in their youth, they could not prophesy the tragic treachery of "the movement," which had brought millions out to the streets to oppose a war that threatened to send white youth to a pointless death, but stood silently by (at best) as J. Edgar Hoover launched his systematic destruction of the Panthers.

By the onset of the '90s Rev had moved to fill the dangerous leadership vacuum. James Baldwin has written of how African America supports and respects its politicians the way it does its sports heroes and others who have "made it," because, simply enough, they made it in a hostile world. It just doesn't expect a goddamn thing from them.

The deep-seated love of the community is reserved for the Kings and the Malcolms and the Sharptons, those who proved their dedication to their community, putting their lives on the line for the simple yet profound cause of making their lives better. It is these leaders who are the most beloved — and the most vulnerable.

In the back seat of the car, Rev silently scanned the course of the history he had shaped and been shaped by, weighing the victories and defeats, calculating how much had been accomplished and how much was to be done. "When we started we were at the back of the bus," he thought. "Now we're at the front of City Hall."

A Black mayor in City Hall in New York. And Reverend Al Sharpton, the *bête noire* of a decade-plus of Ed Koch, standing on the steps of City Hall with the new mayor, whose very job was almost a by-product of the unfinished revolution Rev had led on the streets a year before. The long road to a Black mayor in City Hall said much about where we had come from and where we needed to go. "Now we need the *right* Black mayor," Rev thought to himself, his mind temporarily off the throbbing in his chest.

Coney Island Hospital loomed in the distance, and events became more of a blur; soon anesthesia would block out further wrestling with the very issue Malcolm and King had grappled with: could the leadership position be filled without murder striking yet again?

Lying in his hospital bed, a cold fear swept through Rev. Not a cowardly kind of fear, but that particular kind of fear that afflicts someone who always operates from the vantage point of knowing every precise detail of every situation they are in. Rev was *definitely* in a situation here. But what was it? Was he dying? He needed to know.

As the sedatives took effect, all contact with the mortal world faded; if anyone was nearby who could answer some questions, Rev could neither see them nor bring the words to his lips. Semi-conscious, the images of others who had fallen passed through his mind. More fear.

A week later, at a packed Bethany Baptist Church in Bed-Stuy for a homecoming, he recounted that fearful night. "I could see all of the people who suffered like this, and I said "God, *please* send some help." And round about midnight, God sent an angel."

Something about the angel, Rev told the overflow crowd, looked a little funny. "I said, 'This angel don't look right. You don't look clean enough, you don't look well kept enough.' "

Rev pressed the angel for answers, a dialogue of the subconscious, carried out somewhere between a room at Coney Island Hospital and history. Between death and life. A wave of raw emotion swept through every pew in Bethany Baptist as Rev preached, recounting the conversation with the midnight visitor in the hazy darkness of Coney Island Hospital.

"What about the bites in your hand?" the young Brooklyn minister asked this funky looking angel.

"Oh, that's because of a young man like you named Daniel, who fought the government in his day, and I had to wrestle with lions all night in the den."

"Why are there those thorns sticking in your head?"

"I had to stop by Calvary one day, and pull a pile of thorns off Jesus' head."

"Well, why are your shoes so muddy?"

"There was a woman called Tubman, who helped to build an underground railroad."

"Why do you got that towel in your hand?"

"Well, not long ago I left Memphis, and I put a towel under Martin's head and ushered him on home to rest."

Rev was now close to an answer, and pushed on in his questioning of the angel.

"And I said, 'Why is that fresh blood on your hands?' And he said, 'I just left the schoolyard, and they was getting ready to go for your heart, but I grabbed the knife!' "

And he spoke of meeting the angels of goodness and mercy that night, who told him they had signed a contract with his mother when he was a boy preacher, stipulating that if he would stand up for what was right, they would follow him all of his days.

Well, for *now*, perhaps, Rev thought as he awoke to the worried gaze of Reverend Jesse Jackson, towering above him and Kathy's reassuring smile. But there wasn't time to think about that at the moment. The voices around him confirmed that the journey wasn't over yet.

And there was work to do.

PART I

I've been screamin' ever since the doctor slapped me.

— Rev

ONE

African America, 1954

1954 was supposed to be the year that would make it unnecessary for a Reverend Al Sharpton, or anyone for that matter, to have to holler anymore. There would be no need for a Dr. Martin Luther King, upon arrival in Montgomery, Alabama, to do anything other than that which drew him to the pulpit in the first place: the drive to be, simply, a great preacher of the gospel. And the second child, a son, born to Alfred and Ada Sharpton of Brooklyn, New York would look forward to a life free from the shackles of racism and likewise pursue a love of ministering.

History would demand otherwise. The year that little Rev let out that first scream in the pediatrics ward at Kings County Hospital was a decisive one in the history of the far-from-ended battle for justice for the African American community. In the southern town of Montgomery, Alabama the future Al Sharpton — his life and his character — was being shaped. And what was happening in Montgomery would form Sharpton into the single most important figure shaping (and still being shaped by) that movement.

From the heart of Bedford-Stuyvesant in Brooklyn, New York to Little Rock, Arkansas and far beyond, the year 1954 was one filled with promise for America's African American community. A little girl in Topeka, Kansas who had been forced to attend a segregated school took the case to court, backed by the NAACP, demanding to be allowed into the "white" school. The Brown family of Topeka and their attorney, Thurgood Marshall, who would later become the first Black member of the Supreme Court, took their case against the city's board of education all the way to the Supreme Court.

It wasn't the first time segregation — which was instituted in post-Reconstruction America following the federal pullout from the South, enforced by the terror of the Ku Klux Klan and institutionalized with the 1896 *Plessy v. Ferguson* decision establishing the doctrine of "separate but equal" — had been challenged. America's apartheid was repeatedly confronted throughout the first half of the 20th century, but it wasn't until post-World War II that a concerted assault was made on the centuries-old "race problem."

In 1954, the South was ready to rise. Centuries of slavery, terror, and segregation had reached one of those points in history when change was unstoppable. Civil rights had split the Democratic Party in 1948, as that institution wrestled with the complexities of how to bring the southern Black vote into the fold without fracturing the racist status quo too badly in the region of the country that had already seceded once in the past century; Strom Thurmond's States Rights Party of 1948 was one such result.

Gradual change was to be the watchword.

But there was an underside to it all. The liberal establishment's tentative advance along the path towards racial reform was to be carried out under the most controlled of circumstances, and that meant the absence of "radicals." It was the era of McCarthyism, witch-hunts and the "red menace," and any overt voices shouting for civil rights were to fall victim; in some southern states, the NAACP was declared subversive and illegal. So a new movement took root, underground as it were, north and south.

In the South, the churches became the sanctuary of the struggle, a refuge that the witch-hunters dared not violate. Elsewhere, a movement would grow in the most underground of locales, behind the concrete and steel of America's prisons where the former Elijah Poole, who as a child had watched his father strung up from an oak tree before his eyes and subsequently became known as Elijah Muhammad, was gaining adherents among the most despised and dispossessed for a new African American religion, among them a man known as Malcolm Little.

•

"This is a great day for the Negro. This is democracy's finest hour." Congressman Adam Clayton Powell, Jr., Harlem's long-time representative on Capitol Hill and the elder statesman of African American politics, spoke for millions the day the nine white men of the Supreme Court of the United States returned with their decision in *Brown v. Board of Education.* Segregation was wrong, the court ruled, but in keeping with the spirit of "gradualism," the order would be stayed for a year to give the South and the country time to prepare for desegregation.

In 1955 the federal desegregation order officially went into effect, the court's mandated one year preparation period over. But in Montgomery, as in cities and towns across the South, progress stood still; in fact, the danger to the African American community deepened yet further. A new terror was begun, blocking any attempts at school enrollment or voter registration. The forces of reaction retrenched, with tens of thousands of "respectable" community leaders joining the White Citizens' Councils and the Klan night riders stepping up their raids.

In Montgomery, Alabama, 30 years before a young Reverend Al Sharpton would first make world headlines by leading non-violent marches through all white communities that had taken the lives of Black children, a young reverend named Martin Luther King, Jr., who only wanted to be a great preacher, would take charge of shaping and leading a movement that would challenge America to uphold the principles of equality that were being announced as official federal policy.

King was pressed into service as the head of the Montgomery Improvement Association, which embroiled itself in the Rosa Parks case in 1955. The on-the-bus rebellion of Parks, a seamstress, was not quite the spontaneous act of defiance that has become common lore, no doubt in an attempt to recast the history of the civil rights struggle in the form of moderate, white liberal America's coming to the rescue of a helpless people symbolized by a tired woman on a bus. Parks, in fact, was a former official in the NAACP, and the Montgomery movement itself was a well-organized, grassroots *African American* movement. Black-led. A challenge to, not a client of, white mainstream America. And its organizers had gauged many factors in the decision to press ahead with this challenge, among them being the fact that many, many African American people in the South were *tired* and ready to move — if leadership was provided.

Montgomery, a modest sized southern city, would be the first proving ground for King on his journey toward becoming the most important world leader of his time. In the course of the struggle in this one small part of the world, King would discover universal truths about the country he lived in. "The future of America is bound up with the solution of the present crisis," he would write afterwards. "The shape of the world today does not permit us the luxury of a faltering democracy. The United States cannot hope to attain the respect of the vital and growing colored nations of the world unless it remedies its racial problems at home."

African America, north and south, and the whole world, watched closely. In 1954 Jim Crow was alive and well in all its deadly forms, deeper than mere separate schools. In 1954, the median income of Black families was scarcely more than half that of whites. Health care, education, employment and housing were abysmal, and the constant threat of violent injury or death — at the hands of sheriffs, lynch mobs or northern policemen — was omnipresent.

In the North, in places like Brooklyn's Bedford-Stuyvesant and East New York, it was illegal to maintain segregated schools and housing or discriminate in the employment arena on the basis of race. But that mattered little, because in the North segregation took a deeper form. The races were separated, not by law, but by deep-rooted economic and social forces. *And* by careful, self-conscious design on the part of the city fathers.

A look at the history of urban planning in New York City in the 20th century shows that far from being a "melting pot," the city was designed with excruciating attention paid to race and class. From its highways, to its playgrounds, to its housing plans for its laboring classes, the design of

New York ensured that the better off, white New Yorker was kept safely away from the darker masses (including those of European background darkened by the soot of industry), an intricate design that was a less overt but no less real version of the southern "other side of the tracks." The planning was epitomized by the works of the "master builder" himself, Robert Moses. The key power broker of 20th century New York as well as the personification of the entrenched, institutionalized corruption of New York's one-party rule, Moses rarely hid his contempt for New York's people of color and its poor in general; of the scores of playgrounds that he designed, you could count on the fingers of one hand (even with a few fingers missing) those that went into Black or Latino neighborhoods.

And then there was Brooklyn.

When the devastated slums of Harlem could no longer contain the African American poor of New York, and poverty spread onto the benches of white neighborhoods, Moses — using his dictatorial powers — embarked on a massive plan of "urban renewal" that rivaled the housing policies of South Africa. In the first seven years after World War II — at the same time apartheid was being institutionalized in South Africa by the victorious National Party — 170,000 (by official estimates) mostly Black and Latino New Yorkers were forcibly evicted from their homes as part of Moses' "slum clearance" programs. Or as the official terminology put it, "relocated."

To where? City officials didn't know and didn't care. Robert Caro's biography of Moses, *The Power Broker*, notes that up to half of those "relocated" had files that were officially discharged with the disposition "Disappeared — whereabouts unknown" in a blatant cover-up of the fact that people by the tens of thousands were being dumped in far-flung parts of the city into wretched housing. At the same time, developers raked in huge legal profits from the projects and huger illegal ones skimmed brazenly from the top.

In the 1950s New York City's monstrous and corrupt political machine, made up of developers, finance wizards, mobsters, labor unions, police, a huge bureaucracy and Democratic Party officials, exerted such a stranglehold

that even the small white reform movement — shocked by the reloca-
tion policies — was crushed under its weight. The African American
community of Brooklyn, New York where Alfred Sharpton, Jr. would
grow up was still a community coming-into-being without yet a voice,
standing in opposition to the brutalities being committed against it by
the powers of domination.

Many families, like the Sharptons, looked to the South from which
they had recently migrated, watching what was happening in Montgomery.

Twenty-six-year-old Dr. King was fashioning his two decades of
training as a spiritual leader into tactics in his new and slightly reluctant
position as head of the Montgomery movement. He weighed carefully
both theoretical and practical forms of resistance — violent and pacifist
alike. His academic and theological training (an intellectual path that
Rev would follow a generation later, with King himself one of Rev's
teachers) led him to develop the practice of non-violent civil
disobedience. King gave much credit to Gandhi, but it was, like the
southern Black church, distinctly American, with King seeking to avoid
what he saw as the moral logjam created by the passive acceptance of
injustice and a violent resistance that produced a destructive and self-
destructive hate.

"The non-violent resister agrees with the person who acquiesces that
one should not be physically aggressive towards his opponent; but he
balances the equation by agreeing with the person of violence that evil
must be resisted," King wrote in his first book *Stride Toward Freedom*, his
own account of Montgomery. "He avoids the nonresistence of the former
and the violent resistance of the latter. With non-violent resistance, no
individual or group need submit to any wrong, nor need anyone resort to
violence to right a wrong."

•

Many of those watching the historic events in the South from Brooklyn
were southerners themselves. Ada Richards of Dothan, Alabama was
one. A two-hour drive southeast of Montgomery, Dothan, in Houston
County on the Florida border south of Alabama's Black Belt, is small by

any but Alabama standards. The second congressional district where Dothan sits has sent a Republican to the House of Representatives for the past 30 years. Dothan, like the rest of Alabama, is a complex mix of populism, poverty, right wing racism, Black militance and Black conservatism. Alabama was the cradle of the confederacy *and* the civil rights movement; Black voters supported both the independent, Black-led National Democratic Party of Alabama *and* the return of George Wallace to the statehouse in the early '80s. The Communist Party maintained a strong base going back to the 1930s with the militant Alabama Sharecroppers Union; neo-Nazi paramilitary groups trained in Alabama, while the Nation of Islam operated a farm.

But for a century poverty has been the overriding characteristic of Alabama. Since the abolition of slavery the state has stagnated (as has Mississippi), an underdeveloped region of America, missing out on much of the country's industrial development in the 20th century, and relying on such military support as Fort Rucker outside Dothan, or such scattered projects as the Sony VCR plant there.

Post-war America saw a new wave of migrations from the Deep South and the Black Belt get underway. Ada would be on board.

Mr. Richards died shortly after Ada was born; she lived with her mother in the house in Dothan which Rev visited during some eye-opening trips (she passed on while Rev was a teenager). Ada was a teenage bride back home, wed to John Glasgow, with whom she had two children, Thomas Jefferson "Sonny" Glasgow, and then a daughter, Ernestine. John and Ada lived in Eufaula and Abbeville, where Ada had inherited property passed down through her parents, who were the children of slaves of wealthy slaveowners. For as long as they remained together in Alabama, Ada and John were working farmers.

But things didn't work out for Ada and John, and she came north with her sister Redell, settling in Brooklyn. Like Rosa Parks, Ada went to work as a seamstress for a major manufacturer based in Brooklyn, and joined the Cornerstone Baptist Church. Cornerstone was pastored at the time by the Reverend Sandy Ray, who among other things was a political confidant of Republican Nelson Rockefeller, and the New York governor's closest contact in the Black community. Redell married a Navy man; Ada, her divorce finalized, began to court Alfred Sharpton, Sr.

Like Ada, Alfred, Sr. came north in the migration, from even deeper South — Wabasa and Vero Beach, Florida. Today Vero Beach, up the coast from Miami, is a growing retirement community with a steady influx of northerners; in Alfred's time, it was a quiet southern town with a substantial Black community. Alfred, Sr. was one of 17 children born to Coleman and Mamie B. Sharpton, who owned the country store in Wabasa.

Like Ada's, Alfred, Sr.'s first marriage didn't work out, and he headed north practically the same year as Ada to start anew in Brooklyn. He went into construction, starting his own contracting company, dabbling in real estate, and making a relatively good income as a subcontractor. By the onset of the '50s, Ada and Alfred were preparing for marriage and what looked like a relatively comfortable life in Brooklyn.

In November, 1951 their first child, Cheryl (she would change it to Joy as a teenager), was born. The Sharptons owned a four-family home at 542 Logan Avenue in the East New York section of Brooklyn, renting out the other three apartments. Logan Avenue was then a mixed Italian American and African American community, stable working class along with those, like the Sharptons, who seemed safely on the road to the middle class. Around the corner on Belmont Street, Alfred, Sr. owned a grocery store and newsstand.

Poverty, of course, was rife not far from this community, and even within it, but it was still the 1950s and Ike was in the White House; it was a good decade before the streets of Brooklyn and the rest of African America would explode in rebellion, as the defiant rumblings in Montgomery in 1955 spread into open revolt across the country. Political activity, outside machine politics, was close to nil. The working people of East New York took refuge in neighbors, family and the omnipresent churches. These ranged from the gracefully staid Cornerstone Baptist to the countless storefront, basement and backroom revival halls, where the poor and kicked around Black community transformed into a mighty people in exile awaiting redemption and justice, singing the praises of a just God who would be casting judgment soon.

And it was a decade before nefarious and shadowy forces would infiltrate a steady and ever-deadlier supply of drugs onto urban streets like those of East New York.

By early 1954, with the eyes of millions watching closely as white men in black robes in the nation's capital deliberated the case of a little girl in Kansas, Ada gave Alfred the news that they were expecting their second child that autumn.

TWO

Adventures of a
Wonder Boy Preacher

Things were going well enough for the Sharptons soon after Rev came
out hollerin' — good enough for Alfred Sharpton to close the store and
newsstand around the corner and devote himself full-time to running his
two companies, Nuncio Construction and Alada, the latter company's
name being a composite of his and his wife's given names. Alfred and
Ada Sharpton had achieved the most important qualification for success
in this town — they were property owners. In addition to the construction
and subcontracting and plumbing work, Alfred was buying up apartment
buildings as well.

For little Alfred, things were going well too; the comforts of a
successful family filtered down to provide the kind of stability, mixed
with love, that made for a happy three-year-old. In this very ordinary
early childhood, one thing stood out — church, church, church.

No amount of success, however, could get the Sharptons away from
one fact of life in mid-'50s Brooklyn, New York: segregation. The
neighborhood was pleasant enough; four- and six-family dwellings
intermingled with mom and pop stores, friendly neighbors who were
always available for babysitting, safe streets, a good community spirit.

But the ever-present reality was that anywhere and at any time one
could be maimed, beaten, arrested, insulted or murdered because of the

color of one's skin. Dr. W.E.B. DuBois, Harvard-educated a century ago and from an upstanding Boston family, often pointed out that being Black, no matter what kind of Black, meant that the spectre of violence always loomed.

The Sharptons wanted to move. Segregation was a reality everywhere, with the substantial and growing African American and Latino communities of New York confined by deep, institutional pressures to neighborhoods where *everything* was substandard. But there were always places — Sugar Hill, Strivers Row — where an aspiring Black middle class family could find some comforts. And newer places, like Hollis and St. Albans, Queens.

In the meantime Ada, a Baptist up until then, left her church, and with Alfred went Pentecostal. They did so in style, joining the Washington Temple Church of God in Christ, located in Bedford-Stuyvesant and one of the biggest Pentecostal churches in the country.

Washington Temple was pastored by the legendary Bishop Frederick Douglass Washington, the man who would be the biggest influence in the life of the young Al Sharpton and literally shape him right through to his teenage years. The son of a Little Rock, Arkansas minister, Washington was a "boy preacher" at the age of four, a not uncommon phenomenon in the Bible-thumping, holy rolling Pentecostal movement. Washington came north and started a church in Montclair, New Jersey; eventually he took his crusade into Brooklyn, where he set up a tent, steadily building his flock at the revival meetings.

An inspired preacher, Washington saw his congregation grow by leaps and bounds; they moved into their own building, a former Loew's movie theater that could (and often did) seat up to 3,500 congregants. There were four services during the week at Washington Temple, and the church would be packed all day and all night Sundays.

Occasionally, the Sharptons would be among the crowd.

Music is as deeply a part of the history and fabric of the African American church as the Scriptures; so deeply rooted, in fact, that much of what is characterized as American popular music can in one way or another trace its roots to the Black church. The church has always been a sanctuary, not just for the often suppressed struggle for equality, but for an entire culture. Music, dance, poetry, improvisation, art — all were cultivated and flourished in the church. Whitened-up histories of African American cultural forms obsessively focus on the whorehouse and speak-easy as the "birthplace of the blues," clearly an attempt to discredit the integrity of the art forms that pervade all of American culture. Otherwise, cultural historians would have to grapple with the question of why America's most creative geniuses — from Eubie Blake to Lady Day to James Brown — had to create and refine their art in "dives."

The church was as much about performance as spirit, and in that respect, no one could touch the show Bishop Frederick Douglass Washington directed in Bedford-Stuyvesant. Key to the performance was the Bishop's wife Ernestine Beatrice Washington, who was one of the most popular gospel singers of her day. The combination of these two was a crowd-pleasing phenomenon, rocking the walls of the old Loew's Theater. Bishop Washington knew that the more the Holy Ghost could be summoned forth from the pulpit and stage, the better able he would be to bring his teachings to the flock.

Late one Sunday night, the spirit took hold of the Sharptons. Bishop Washington had preached a particularly rousing sermon, and gospel singer Emily Bram got ready to sing. Suddenly Ada Sharpton burst into tears, sobbing uncontrollably. She ran down the aisle with little Alfred, Jr. and Cheryl right on her heels. Minutes later, Ada Sharpton was the newest member of Washington Temple Church of God in Christ. Bishop Washington baptized the entire family.

•

For as long as there have been movements and leaders, innovators and followers, audiences and performers, there have been those who are possessed with the drive to step into the spotlight. The reasons for that drive (as powerful a force as the sheer terror that fills the average, stage-frightened person) are as complex as the times in which such persons live, but it is almost always there.

Bishop Washington had it, and from an early age. But even in maturity,

Bishop Washington must have retained those characteristics that led him to preaching as a mere toddler in Little Rock, because 40 years later, another four-year-old named Alfred would be inspired by *him*.

Before he was in kindergarten, in May of 1959, Alfred joined the Junior Usher Boys at Washington Temple. There was always lots to do at the church, for young and old alike. And every year the church held an anniversary program, with Ms Hazel Griffith serving as the anniversary coordinator for the young folks.

A good 50 of the kids were gathered together for one of the planning meetings when Ms Griffith went around the room, posing a question to each of the children: "What would you like to do for the anniversary program?"

Cheryl Sharpton wanted to read a poem. Her little sweetheart, Ronnie Dyson, wanted to sing. Ronnie was still a few years away from pop stardom, an early pioneer of Brooklyn's cultural renaissance who would top the charts with hits like "Why Can't I Touch You?" a decade later. Others volunteered to do the readings and all the other tasks for the anniversary celebration.

"What would you like to do, Alfred?" Ms Griffith asked.

"I would like to preach the sermon," Alfred, Jr. replied, deadly earnest.

Forty-nine giggles resonated through the room. Ms Griffith quickly cut that short, however.

"Now, don't laugh," she advised. "Bishop Washington started preaching at Alfred's age." The room quieted down. "Maybe this is his calling."

She turned to Alfred. "Do you feel that you have been called to preach?" she asked.

"Yes."

Ms Griffith noted that for the anniversary program, Alfred Sharpton would be preaching.

The first sermon of Alfred Sharpton, Jr., four years old going on five that October, was scheduled for July 9, 1959.

Ever since the Sharptons first started to attend Washington Temple, little Alfred had been captivated by the art of preaching. It had little to do with firing and inspiring a congregation on the path to justice; the role models and the experiences which would inspire that stage of development were still a ways down the road. At age four, it was Bishop Washington and the community he created in Bedford-Stuyvesant that seized the heart of a four-year-old boy.

Frederick Douglass Washington was not an "activist priest" and Washington Temple was not an activist church, at least not in today's sense. Washington was a civic activist, with deep ties to the community. The bishop was a "big" Republican, even bringing then Vice President Richard Nixon to the church. His Republicanism was rooted in adherence to the "party of Lincoln," mixed with a healthy dose of pragmatism.

But first and foremost, Washington was a preacher, and a mesmerizing one. Enough so that a four-year-old was ready to follow in his footsteps. So much so, in fact, that in his own mind Rev already had his own church. Every day, after coming home from Washington Temple, Alfred would line up Cheryl's dolls, and preach from memory whatever sermon Bishop Washington had preached that morning. His own congregation!

He began preparing for the big day. Thomas and Ernestine, Rev's older half-brother and half-sister from Ada's first marriage who had moved to New York also, helped out. There was no point writing anything down — Rev wasn't even in kindergarten yet and didn't know how to read! Instead, Ernestine and Thomas rehearsed Rev over and over.

Rev agreed with Ms Griffith: this was definitely his calling. The excitement of the crowd drew him like a magnet. He couldn't wait for the day to arrive.

And soon enough, it did. Sitting in church, waiting to be called up, Rev looked around. These were not his big sister's dolls sitting quietly and listening attentively to his sermon. There were a good 800 congregants in church on that warm July day for the Junior Ushers' services. And one four-year-old with a flock of butterflies fluttering in his stomach.

But the nervousness only lasted for as long as he waited for his moment. As the service drew to a climax, Rev was called up to give the sermon. Not up to the rostrum, because the four-year-old was too short.

A box was found, and Alfred, wearing the gold robe with the black lapels Ada and Ernestine had made for him, climbed up behind the offering table. As soon as he stood up the butterflies were gone, and Alfred commenced a 20-minute sermon, "Let not your heart be troubled," from John 14.

Tears welled up in many eyes as Rev moved easily and naturally through the sermon. In front of the crowd, he felt at home. Ada and Alfred Sr. were thrilled, as was Bishop Washington, the former boy preacher.

•

Meanwhile, the Sharptons had found the home they were looking for out in Hollis, a middle class Queens community on the way to Long Island. They bought a ten-room house at 100-50 199th Street, renting out the top floor, living on the bottom, and with a finished basement to boot. Alfred Sr. bought a brand new Cadillac that year, and another one for Ada the following year.

It was still segregation, but this time the Sharptons were segregated among a relatively well-to-do Black middle class, in a community surrounded by Jewish and Italian middle class families. Among their neighbors were African American artists, athletes and business figures. William "Count" Basie, originally from Red Bank, New Jersey via Kansas City and the whole world, settled a few blocks away. So did legendary r&b singer Brooke Benton. Shortly — and prophetically — the Godfather himself, James Brown, would be a neighbor.

Rev was halfway through kindergarten when he transferred to PS 134, a mostly white, predominantly Jewish elementary school; probably none of the students or teachers had been at Washington Temple in Brooklyn that July day when he dazzled 800 churchgoers.

Rev would make sure they knew. He arrived at PS 134 every day in a suit and tie, just like a minister. He turned in his homework with "Minister Alfred Sharpton," or "Reverend Alfred Sharpton," signed across the top. One time he signed "Bishop Alfred Sharpton."

It was cause for mild concern on the part of teachers with little first-hand knowledge of the Black community. Boy preachers were not an everyday phenomenon, but they were not unheard of. Mrs. Sharpton, who often got calls at home, would patiently explain that, yes, her son was indeed a boy preacher.

Back in Brooklyn Bishop Washington, deeply moved by little Alfred's performance, took an immediate interest in his development. Every few weeks he called on his young apprentice to deliver the sermon at Washington Temple, where the Sharptons remained members in good standing even after setting off for Queens. Soon, young Alfred found himself appointed junior pastor of the church; from the age of seven until he was 18, he conducted the Friday services.

And by the time he was seven, Rev found himself constantly on "the circuit," an invited preacher at churches all around town. That was Sundays. Fridays, as a junior pastor, Rev conducted services just like any true minister would. Junior ushers, junior missionaries, junior trustees to take up the money — everything the "senior" church had, Rev had. A junior choir, junior officers. Everything.

At seven years old, Alfred Sharpton, Jr. became known as "the wonder boy preacher."

At home Ada Sharpton was a strict southern parent, indeed, a disciplinarian: homework had to be done; TV could be watched only during certain hours; bedtime was non-negotiable. The firm regimen at 199th Street matched that at the church; the discipline imposed a measure of control and dignity in a hostile world; it also provided some shelter from the hostility.

Down south, in the wake of Montgomery and a string of subsequent victories and defeats for Dr. King and the now regional movement he was leading, more and more people were moving from passive rebellion into open revolt. At lunch counters, on buses and in bus stations, in department stores, thousands of students, based in the "Negro" colleges, were slowly shattering the century-old institution of segregation with sit-ins and freedom rides.

The old civil rights groups like the NAACP, which had led the court victories against desegregation, were now being superseded by newer organizations: King's Southern Christian Leadership Conference

(SCLC), the Congress of Organizations for Racial Equality (CORE) and the Student Nonviolent Coordinating Committee (SNCC). These groups took the struggle beyond the legal strategies of the NAACP's often brilliant but confined-to-the-courtroom tactics and out onto the streets, highways and back roads of segregated America.

And it wasn't confined to the South. The new civil rights movement took the battle north, too. There were demonstrations in support of the southern movement, such as the protests at Woolworth's and other national chains that maintained segregated operations in the South, as well as direct challenges to the de facto segregation of the North. In New York City, lawsuits were filed against school boards to bring about open admissions. African American students in New York and other northern cities were not barred from better equipped "white" schools by law (as in the South) but by neighborhood. You went to the school in your neighborhood, and if you lived in an underserved and underfunded ghetto, you went to an underserved and underfunded school. Housing policies, employment discrimination, police brutality and other issues were being taken on in the North as well.

By the onset of the '60s, America was still a few years away from the cataclysmic upheavals that were approaching; the blazing ghetto rebellions in the North and the bloody freedom summers in the South, when the forces of white reaction unleashed a pogrom against the Black community that summoned forth images of Nazi brownshirts on the march.

The world was in upheaval. It was only a matter of time before the turmoil would burst through the rich, though sheltered, world of the young Rev.

That day came in 1961.

By this time, Rev had become accustomed to the middle class mores of his Hollis community; despite the segregation, he attended a mixed, predominantly white school. Friends were white and Black. Racism was of the refined, middle class sort, the kind that doesn't hit you in the back of the head with a baseball bat, but slowly wears away at the soul. Rev, as an apprentice theologian, took shelter in the teachings of the Bible and the comfort of community. But the four-year-old who had advised 800 members of his community not to let their hearts be troubled would find himself shaken to his young soul just a few years later.

•

In 1961 Alfred, Sr. made plans for a car trip south to see his parents in Florida; he decided to take his two young children. The car trip was pleasant enough — until, that is, they got past the nation's capital. South of the Mason-Dixon line, Rev saw something he had never seen in his young life, something along the highway that shook him deeply.

"Whites only."

Little Alfred turned to his father. "What is all of this? What does that mean, 'whites only?' "

"Black people can't eat in those restaurants, can't stay in those hotels and can't use certain water fountains," came the reply. Alfred Sharpton, Sr. tried to contain his anger as he explained segregation to Cheryl and young Alfred. But he couldn't for long. He would have to do something more than just explain it, passively. As if it were OK, as if it were acceptable.

Alfred, Sr. and the kids stopped at a restaurant in North Carolina, a restaurant with one of *those* signs. He first asked for, and then *demanded,* a hamburger. Alfred, Sr. was no civil rights activist, but he was going to demonstrate to his children that he was a *man,* and that this evil thing in the world called segregation was not something that he took lying down. The white store proprietors humiliated him, right there in front of his children, but he had to make his point (just like *his* father had, 30 years earlier — Coleman Sharpton had once been ordered off the curb in Wabasa and into the street; when he refused, the gang of whites slapped him and threw him into the road, where they left him bleeding).

They continued their drive straight through, because in America, 1961 there was no hotel where this middle class African American family from a good neighborhood in St. Albans, New York could stop to rest on the way to visit their loved ones in Florida.

•

It was a far cry from the comforts of home in Queens, this awful southern racism. In just a few years, family misfortune would wrench Ada Sharpton and her children from such comfort, and a whole new world of injustices and pain would be opened up for the young reverend. It would be both an eye-opening education into how the majority of his people, here in New York City, were forced to live, *and* first-hand proof of DuBois' painful axiom that being Black meant always living inches or seconds from disaster.

But in the meantime, there was still the leisure and comfort of Hollis. Young Rev and Cheryl had their own rooms, and shared a series of pet dogs, which would frolic on the huge family lawn. It was a series of dogs because Rev was less than diligent in his dog-walking duties, opting instead to open the front door and let them run around. On more than one occasion, the family pet did not return, the young Rev having long since forgotten his responsibility as he hopped on down to the basement.

Down there Rev had a den all to himself, a quiet and comfortable space where he passed many an hour snuggling up with his second love, after preaching.

Books.

When the lunch bell rang at PS 134, Rev went off with the other kids to the local pizzeria. After a slice or two, he would stroll next door, where a Black nationalist bookstore had opened up.

By this time, Rev had received strong encouragement in his studies from a teacher at PS 134, Jerry Greenberg. Mr. Greenberg took an interest in young Al's development, sensing early on both his talent and the need for the kind of strong support that talented young folks are rarely able to get. In particular, Jerry Greenberg encouraged his student to read, read, read. Which Rev would do, stretched out on the couch in the basement when he got home each afternoon.

One day in between pizza and punchball (his third love), Rev was browsing through the bookstore when something caught his eye. On the cover of one of the books was a picture of a minister. Most folks probably first noted the stately and urbane face on the book cover, but the first thing Rev noticed was the cleric's collar and robe. A preacher.

"Wow! They're writing a book about a Black minister!" he exclaimed to no one in particular.

At that time, most people knew of Adam Clayton Powell, Jr. the politician. Rev probably wouldn't have paid him no mind if it hadn't been for the collar staring at him from the bookshelf. But from that moment on, Al Sharpton — until then a preacher from the fundamentalist, Bible-thumping school — would harbor a life-long fascination with Powell and politics.

Rev now had two seemingly incongruous sides to his life's experience. On the one hand was the insular and all-consuming world of the church fraternity, a source of warmth and community, where he had found a home and a calling. And there were the evils of the world, the "whites only" signs and the humiliation of his father, and grandfather and grandmother. Generation after generation, his whole family, his whole *people*, unable to live and walk in dignity. Was this to be the future of this promising young preacher, and of his generation?

Reading about Powell, and about another hero, Black nationalist pioneer Marcus Aurelius Garvey, helped Rev begin to put the disturbing trip to Florida in some perspective. Up until the time Rev picked up the book on Powell at the bookstore, his perspective revolved totally around the Washington Temple Church of God in Christ.

Powell, like Rev, was a preacher, a prestigious Black preacher, living in this same, humiliating world. He had style and flair, the kind that Rev was working extra hard — with a fair amount of success — to acquire. But there was something more.

Power.

This was no ordinary Black preacher. As Rev eagerly raced through the pages of the book, he learned about a Black preacher who was tearing down the whites-only signs that dotted the highways and byways of America, those awful symbols of the subjugation of his people. A man who grew up in the church, and who made headlines as a very young man by bringing thousands of people into the streets of Harlem, threatening to boycott *any* institution that discriminated on the basis of race, segregation or no segregation. Hospitals, subways, the phone company, all of the thousands of indignities brought against people of color; *this* Black preacher fought them all.

And right into the halls of Congress. This Black preacher went in representing the people of Harlem, USA, going nose to nose with his esteemed southern redneck colleagues who defended the "whites only" signs on the floor of Congress. To Rev, the sight of a Black preacher tearing down those signs was nothing short of a revelation.

But that wasn't all that attracted Rev to Adam Clayton Powell, Jr., just as it wasn't simply the teachings of God that had brought him under the sway of Bishop Washington. Powell was, to say the least, *flamboyant.* Outrageous. He not only maintained an ostentatious lifestyle, he flaunted it. But Powell had no desire whatsoever to disassociate himself from the folks on the street who made up his base of support.

It was a political gamble, and for decades it was a successful one. Powell knew the community trusted politicians as far as they could throw them, so why not put all your cards on the table? The strategy had the effect of putting any would-be challengers on the defensive, guilty of the one thing no one accused Powell of — hypocrisy. Campaign opponents who attacked Powell's ostentatious ways would often be shouted down by the crowd. "Quit your wailing, Jack," a slightly inebriated Harlemite yelled to one contender against Powell. "The Cat's only livin'!"

All that attracted Rev deeply. Powell was a man of substance *and* style, and both were important to a "wonder boy preacher," a job which was, almost by definition, part faith and part showmanship.

•

A year after the trip to Florida to see Alfred, Sr.'s family, the kids set off for the South again, this time to see Ada's mother in Dothan, Alabama. They took a slightly different route to Dothan, but the signs all along the way were still there, as they had been the year before, and the year before that, as far as Rev could tell. What could be done?

In August, 1963 Alfred, Sr. told his son he was going to Washington, DC. "Why?" asked the son.

"There's going to be a big march down there," said Alfred, Sr.

"I want to go!"

"You can't, Alfred, there's no kids allowed." That wasn't quite true, but the thought of having to keep an eye on a precocious nine-year-old while marching through the streets of DC on a hot summer day was enough to make Alfred, Sr. stretch the facts a bit.

"Why are you going?"

"Because of all of those 'whites only' signs you saw going down south."

Which only made Rev want to go more. But he would have to wait until his father returned to find out what happened. When Alfred, Sr. — one of the quarter million people who descended on the nation's capital that summer day pressing for civil rights and voting rights — returned from the historic 1963 March on Washington, Rev devoured all the papers and miscellaneous items he brought back.

There were pictures of gospel great Mahalia Jackson, with whom Rev was already acquainted from the preaching circuit. And headlines of a man who had captivated an entire nation with the words "I have a dream." It was the first time Rev had heard of Dr. Martin Luther King, Jr.

Soon after, Rev would see him in person, when he came to speak at Washington Temple. Of course as the junior pastor at the church, Rev got a personal introduction. But despite that, the actual encounter quickly became a blur, so taken was the young preacher by the awesome presence of King.

And not only was King there speaking before a packed church. The Freedom Riders were there, too.

Freedom rides were first initiated in the late 1940s by a courageous grouping of activists who set out to challenge the segregated facilities at bus stations across the South. A decade later the Supreme Court would rule that such facilities were illegal, but, as in the case of *Brown v. Board of Education*, the law did not conform to reality. Starting in 1960 the Freedom Riders took off in earnest, with thousands participating in rides that criss-crossed the South, challenging segregation.

The Freedom Riders came up with King that night, and Reverend Al Sharpton had his first direct contact with the movement. Now things were definitely beginning to fall into place. Not only was Rev traveling to new and exciting places — Bishop Washington would take him on tour as far as the Caribbean — he was learning about the world and what an up-and-coming young preacher could look forward to. He had met Dr. Martin Luther King, Jr. — in the flesh — and through his studies, men like Garvey and Powell.

But at the cozy Hollis home of the Sharptons, things were beginning to come apart as fast as they were coming together for Rev. One morning, Ada Sharpton went to her son's room and woke him up, quietly telling him some fearful news.

THREE

Adam

Early in the morning ten-year-old Rev was stirred awake by his mother, who was crying softly.

"Alfred, your father is gone and isn't coming back," she said. "And I don't know how we gonna make it."

Ada, Cheryl and Alfred, Jr. joined hands and prayed together. There was nothing else to do.

But even the praying could not fend off the mounting anxiety of the situation that the Sharptons found themselves in after that morning. Ada Sharpton's friends and family convinced her to check into the hospital for a while, because she just *had* to rest her nerves if she was going to carry on with what she had to do. The kids moved in with a woman from the Washington Temple community three doors away, who took care of them while Ada rested.

But no amount of rest would prepare Ada for the simple fact that without Alfred, Sr. around, there was no way to continue in the life to which they had so recently grown accustomed. It was Alfred who brought in all the money, and Ada had settled down to the work of being a housewife and raising the children. A full time job to be sure, but not one that would pay the bills.

As Ada explained to the children, their father was not coming back —

not even to bring any money. Soon, the electricity, the gas and the lights were off; winter approached, and a dark chill swept through the Sharpton household. A large fancy house in a comfortable middle class community, darkened like a fancy cruise ship crippled in the middle of the ocean.

They stayed there as long as they could — three months to be exact — before mounting bills forced a change and a sudden, catastrophic tumble from middle class "respectability" to the uncertainties of poverty.

The Sharptons, for those three months, lived in two worlds. A big house, with no lights and no gas, all the trappings of comfort with no money to make it run. Behind the walls, the family sat shivering from the cold; when the big blackout hit New York City that year, the Sharptons were already blacked-out. It was a sad irony that when all the lights in the city went out, kids from across the street who had laughed about the big dark house now had to come knocking on its doors to borrow candles.

Alfred, Jr. did his best to keep up a strong spirit at home; suddenly he was, at the age of 10, the "man of the house." He was, after all, a "wonder boy preacher," and no small part of that job was to minister to those whose hearts were troubled. Young Rev was in no position to ponder some of the deeper issues involved here, particularly the fact that being "the man of the house" was a duty that Alfred Sharpton, Sr. and many thousands more were unable to handle, despite having been able to achieve relative financial security.

But Rev had not learned yet from more seasoned professionals like Bishop Washington how to navigate the emotional minefields of ministering to the pain of loved ones (and oneself). And he was still a long way off from developing the avenues for channeling the pain and rage that are inseparable from being a citizen of African America in ways that served the common good. At home, young Rev remained as solid as a rock.

But he needed an emotional outlet, one in particular that would not put any more strain on Ada than there already was. He could only manage so well keeping his many troubling and confusing feelings at bay while at home watching over his mother and sister.

That release came during the day while he was at PS 134. Periodically little Reverend Al Sharpton broke down, and Mr. Greenberg would take the young man out of class for talks. During this time, Mr. Greenberg became Rev's counselor, providing him with an outlet for the pain of watching his mother veer close to a nervous breakdown — pain which he dared not express at home for fear that it might add to her burden. Mr. Greenberg's help proved to be invaluable to a ten-year-old who had already achieved in his own community no small measure of celebrityhood and had now fallen quite unexpectedly into crisis.

But soon enough, Ada came to terms with the troubling fact that, in her current circumstances, she would never be able to catch up with the expenses of the house. Ada Sharpton was not at all helpless; in fact she was a strong and able woman. Once she had recovered from the initial and overwhelming shock, she began to make the moves necessary for the family to continue on.

The Sharptons packed up what they needed and headed back to Brooklyn, moving in with close family friends in the Albany Projects in the heart of Bedford-Stuyvesant. From there, Ada began looking for work and for a new and permanent home for herself and the children. With the family breadwinner suddenly gone, she had to figure out a steady income for the family; Ada began doing domestic work and put in an application for welfare.

After about a month, Ada found an apartment for the family in Crown Heights at 1169 Lincoln Place, where she and Alfred and Cheryl — now on welfare — moved.

There was no more basement, but Rev still kept at the books, which, along with preaching, remained his passion. School was a ways down the list of the things that he got excited about, although his friendship with Mr. Greenberg and natural talents kept him always hovering around a respectable "B" average. English and social studies classes were where he excelled because they meant the always delightful opportunity to consume more literature and history books.

●

"If you applied yourself more, Alfred, you could do much better."

Certainly the teachers at PS 134 thought they had the best interests of the young Rev at heart when they gave him (as they often did) that bit of advice, but it was only Mr. Greenberg who really took the time to notice that this young man was indeed applying himself as much as any ten-year-old you could find. It just wasn't in the standard sort of ways.

The House at 12 Mona Road

Rev was already well known and popular on "the circuit" when at the age of ten Bishop Washington decided he would take him along for a three-week barnstorming tour of the Caribbean.

Bishop Washington, little Rev and the entourage covered the islands from practically one end to the other, spreading the gospel in Barbados, Trinidad, Puerto Rico and Haiti, where Rev preached with an interpreter translating his teachings into Creole.

And a week-long revival in Kingston, Jamaica, where Rev's thirst for knowledge and the precociousness that landed him the position of boy preacher led to a new adventure.

Rev had already been through the biography of Adam Clayton Powell, Jr. by the time he got to Jamaica. From that book he learned that one of Powell's heroes was a man named Marcus Garvey, a pioneer Black nationalist, whose Universal Negro Improvement Association at one time had hundreds of thousands of followers and members in Harlem and around the world. Garvey had come to the United States from Jamaica, part of the early 20th century migration of West Indians to Harlem.

Rev read about how the United States government went after Garvey — who built the first mass membership Black nationalist organization in the history of the US — with a vengeance. Garvey had combined his nationalist organizing with building business enterprises, including a steamship company, and organized political clubs that allowed the African American community to use their vote (at least in the North, where they had a vote) as a bloc.

Garvey was largely a spiritual leader whose main objective was to organize African America into a competitive economic and political force and to instill cultural pride in the hundreds of millions of people of African heritage around the world. The term "Back to Africa" had a spiritual connotation; the notion of a mass migration to Africa was a concoction of the white establishment, which hoped to discredit a movement that sought equal opportunities for all citizens as "unpatriotic."

White America saw a threat in Marcus Garvey, and federal prosecutors used his business enterprises as a pretext for going after him. He was convicted of using the mails to defraud, and locked up in the federal penitentiary in Atlanta on February 8, 1925. After serving almost three years Garvey had his sentence commuted by President Calvin Coolidge, but in December, 1927 he was deported as an "undesirable alien." Rev remembered reading that Garvey returned to his native Jamaica after his deportation before eventually moving on to London, where he died in 1940.

The pace of the week-long revival in Kingston was intense, with people coming from miles around to "hear the boy preacher!" But while he was in Jamaica, Rev had to find the time to learn more about his new-found hero Garvey, which would also, he expected, give him more insight into the still-living, larger-than-life object of his admiration, Adam Clayton Powell.

Rev tracked down Garvey's widow, Amy Jacques Garvey, at her home at 12 Mona Road in Kingston, and promptly called her.

"Mrs. Garvey, this is the Reverend Al Sharpton," said Rev in his biggest ten-year-old voice. "I'm a minister from America, and I've studied your husband's life, and I would like very much to have the opportunity to meet you." Mrs. Garvey politely agreed to make an appointment with Reverend Al Sharpton from America while he was on the island.

Rev put on his Sunday best, and caught a ride with one of the fellows along on the tour. He hopped out in front of number 12, made his way briskly up the path and rang the bell.

Mrs. Garvey looked through the peephole, which was a good foot higher than the top of Rev's head, and seeing nobody, turned to walk back to the sitting room.

Rev pushed the bell again, hoping Mrs. Garvey hadn't forgotten their appointment. Again she approached the peephole and looked through, straight out to Mona Road.

Rev rang the bell one more time. Mrs. Garvey opened the door angrily, convinced by now that someone was playing a practical joke. "Who's there!" came a woman's cross Jamaican lilt. Mrs. Garvey glanced left and right and saw no one — until she looked straight down at the slightly startled young visitor on her porch.

"Hello, I'm Reverend Alfred Sharpton," said the boy looking up at her.

It took a while for Mrs. Garvey to get over the fact that the distinguished Reverend Alfred Sharpton she had been expecting from the United States and the pudgy little fellow in the suit on her porch were one and the same person. But with that temporary confusion cleared up, the two generations spent the next couple of hours on the subject of Marcus Aurelius Garvey, Mrs. Garvey the teacher and the young Rev the breathless student. Rev peppered Mrs. Garvey for hours with questions about her husband's life; she happily obliged, supplementing the lesson with pictures from her photo album.

As the time wound on, Mrs. Garvey took a close look at the chubby young man sitting with her.

"You're going to be a big leader like Garvey," she told the Rev, who was flattered and astonished. "You have a big head, just like Garvey." The nationalist pioneer's widow explained that her husband had been chubby, too.

The hours passed quickly; soon it was time to get back to the revival, and then back to Brooklyn. But from that day Rev would carry on a correspondence with Mrs. Garvey, treasuring the letters she sent and saving them for his children to look at one day.

Not long after the revival returned home to Brooklyn, Bishop Washington helped set up what was to be the biggest triumph yet of the still ten-year-old Rev's remarkable career.

After a 25-year absence, the World's Fair had returned to New York City. The fairgrounds were spread across acres of former swampland and industrial dumpsites in Queens, adjacent to where Shea Stadium, the new home of the New York Mets, had just been constructed.

At the futuristic-looking New York Pavilion, gospel great Mahalia Jackson was lined up to perform before 5,000 people. And in between sets, there was to be a sermon by none other than the wonder boy preacher himself!

After the World's Fair date, the Queen of Gospel took the Rev on tour with her around the country, through the South, out to the Midwest and as far as Seattle, Washington. She would sing, and during the breaks Rev would deliver a stirring 15-minute sermon. From that point on, Rev toured regularly with Mahalia as part of the gospel road shows that she put together.

By this time, Ada Sharpton had found a job as a domestic, and was getting up every morning at five. Rev left the house on Lincoln Place with her each day and walked her to the bus stop. As the bus arrived with the morning sun, he kissed her goodbye and then climbed up onto the "el" train all the way out to Queens. Rev wanted to continue on in school in Queens after he graduated from PS 134, even though he was now living in the heart of Brooklyn, and took the old yellow train all the way out to Junior High School 109 all by himself.

"Ladies! This is the wonder boy preacher!"

While the Sharptons were still living on Lincoln Place, Rev finally convinced his mother to instruct Cheryl to take him up to Harlem to see his idol, Adam Clayton Powell, Jr. Rev would have gone by himself, but Ada was not going to let her son travel all the way up to Harlem alone.

One Sunday morning, Cheryl and Rev made their way uptown on the A train, getting off at 145th Street and walking over to the stately Abyssinian Baptist Church where Powell had taken over the ministering duties from his father, Adam Powell, Sr., three decades earlier. But it was a bit of a disappointment, because Rev's hero, who was by then also a twenty-year veteran of the US Congress, did not show up.

Not to be deterred, Rev and Cheryl tried again at the next opportunity. There was enough of a buzz in the church for them to know that this time, *he* was here. After all the preliminaries, a side door opened at the front of the church, and a man who was the most majestic sight young Rev had ever seen strode gracefully to the pulpit, his long black robe flowing smoothly along with him.

Adam Clayton Powell preached that day on love, a simple, ordinary theme to which this complex man often returned throughout his tumultuous career. From the congregation seats, an awestruck 11-year-old Reverend Al Sharpton earnestly wondered if he was seeing God himself there behind the pulpit of the elegant, historic Harlem church.

He wasn't quite sure, but Rev did know that as soon as the sermon was over he would have to meet this man. He knew that he was *going* to meet him.

Rev and Cheryl made their way back towards Powell's office, where he had retired after the sermon. Rev calmly presented himself to Powell's secretary.

"Ma'am, I would like to meet with Reverend Powell, please."

The secretary eyed the 11-year-old young man and 14-year-old young lady dressed in their Sunday best with a mixture of amusement and suspicion.

"And *who-o-om* shall I tell the congressman it is that wants to meet with him?" she responded, with more than a touch of arrogance. But that sort of thing never particularly bothered Rev.

"The Reverend Alfred Sharpton," he responded without flinching, mimicking her *very* proper enunciation.

"*Reverend* Alfred Sharpton?"

"Yeah, *Reverend*." Rev proceeded to write out a note to Powell for the secretary to bring to him.

The secretary reluctantly took the note, no longer amused by this young person who was now (because he was still standing there) becoming a bona fide nuisance. She disappeared into Powell's office, returning in about two minutes with a startled look on her face. The office had the kind of doors that open in halves, and she opened the top half, looking down at Rev, who made it all the way up to the top of the bottom half.

"Follow me, *Rev-er-end*. The congressman will see you now," she said, the shocked look still on her face.

Rev and Cheryl followed her into the huge office. Powell was standing there, minus his shirt and undershirt, chatting with a couple of elderly, female members of the church. In all, a good 15 people were mingling there in the colossal office.

As Rev and Cheryl came into the room, Powell cut his conversation short.

"Ladies! *This* is the wonder boy preacher!"

Rev nearly fell over. Adam Clayton Powell knew who *he* was! In fact, the congressman had heard Rev a number of times on his friend Bishop Washington's Sunday radio broadcasts.

"Have a seat, Reverend!" Powell said amiably, treating his visitor like a fellow big-shot minister. Rev and Cheryl took seats in the office, while Powell continued his conversations with the church ladies.

Finishing with them, Powell put on his shirt and clergyman's collar, the one that had jumped off the cover of the book Rev had seen in the bookstore back in Queens. Once he was fully dressed, he turned his attention back to Rev.

"You want a drink, Reverend? I'm going down to the bar."

"A *drink?* I'm 11 years old!" the shocked young guest replied.

"Alright, we won't hold it against you," Powell replied, a twinkle in his eye.

And then Powell, his bodyguards, assistants, and two young visitors from Brooklyn trotting along behind made their way down to the Red Rooster, a popular Harlem club in the neighborhood. Powell pulled out a long cigar, lit up, and ordered Rev and Cheryl a Pepsi-Cola. Even Cheryl, by then a rebellious teen who had drifted away from the church, was enthralled with *this* preacher.

After a while, the two exhilarated kids got back on the subway for the trip home; they couldn't wait to tell their mother all about their adventure. She was very impressed, but any time Rev wanted to go back, he would, for now, still have to take Cheryl along with him. Despite those instructions, Rev was soon "running" with Powell, coming up to see him every time he was in town. Rev also began hanging with some of the guys around Powell, who was always surrounded by a large and loyal posse. There was his driver, Jack Packet; Hassan Donald Washington from the Nation of Islam, who served as a bodyguard; and the man Rev would get to know best, Powell's chief of staff, Odell Clark, who would call on Ada now and then just to check in on the impetuous young Rev.

It was the mid-'60s in New York City. The city and the world were becoming more complex by the day. In addition to Powell another African American leader, Malcolm X, was touching the lives of many young people like Rev and his friends at school and in the neighborhood, especially after Malcolm's assassination at Manhattan's Audubon Ballroom in 1965.

Barely two years earlier, politics had little effect on Rev. One day in November of 1963 Rev's teacher, tears in her eyes, had come into the classroom to tell the students that President John F. Kennedy had been shot in Dallas, and that everybody could go home. Rev was moved by his teacher's tears, but the assassination didn't mean much more than a sort of holiday.

Not so when Rev and his friends opened the *Daily News* one day two years later and saw the pictures of Malcolm lying mortally wounded on the floor of the Audubon. It was different. Things were different. *They* all were different. Rev and his circle of friends began reading *The Autobiography of Malcolm X*, which came out that same year, and studied up on Martin Luther King as well.

By 1966 Dr. King was seeing the world very differently from the days just a short decade before when he earnestly believed that the moral power of the African American community non-violently resisting an unjust system would inspire the good people of America and the world to correct injustice.

But by 1966, injustice seemed more entrenched than ever. The civil rights movement which King led had won some important legislative victories — the Voting Rights Act, the Civil Rights Act — but across America, for millions of Black people life was becoming increasingly desperate.

Although he was passionately committed to the tactic of non-violent resistance (some critics felt too much so), Dr. King was in no way committed to any particular analysis of the problems facing African Americans if that analysis did not stand up to the light of his substantial experience as an activist. King had marched thousands of miles, braved dogs and waterhoses, jails and lynch mobs. He moved north to Chicago, where he found an entrenched, institutionalized racism which made southern-style segregation look primitive. And with each passing day conditions worsened for the African American community, which was now, literally, in the flames of rebellion.

"It is time for all of us to tell each other the truth about who and what have brought the Negro to the condition of deprivation against which he struggles today," King wrote in *Where Do We Go From Here: Chaos or Community?* his last, posthumously published book. "In human relations the truth is hard to come by, because most groups are deceived about themselves." Discounting the view popular among both liberal and reactionary academics that the Black community was to blame for its oppression, King wrote that "to find the origins of the Negro problem we must turn to the white man's problem...in short, white America must assume the guilt for the Black man's inferior status."

King went on, through a rigorous historical analysis, to show that racism, rather than being an aberration in the body politic, was deeply embedded in the very fabric of American society and thoroughly interdependent with the economic exploitation of the poor. It was that entire society that needed to be overhauled — including the elimination of the institution of poverty — if there was to be racial equality. King extended his analysis to the world, and US foreign policy, concluding that the war in Viet Nam was but an extension of the economic exploitation of people of color.

King was no doubt prodded to his new analysis not only by his own experience, but by pressure from those in the movement who were taking a more "radical" tack and achieving a following. King also hoped that his new approach would outpace that of the "Black Power" movement, which had overtaken his own SCLC. He did not live long enough to find out.

In the meantime, Rev had transferred from Junior High School 109 in Queens to JHS 252, right in front of his new home in East Flatbush. In the course of her search for new lodgings after giving up the house in St. Albans, Ada ran into Rose Williams, an old friend who used to babysit for Rev when he was an infant back at their first home on Logan Street in East New York. Rose told Ada about a nice apartment in East Flatbush where, among other benefits, her son could again have his own room. Despite the ongoing hardships since Alfred, Sr.'s sudden abandonment of the family, Ada was doing all she could to make the family as comfortable as possible.

Their new building at 1107 Lenox Road was Rev's home for as long as he lived with his mother; she stayed there until returning to Alabama in 1988. The apartment was one of 40 in the building. The Sharptons were among a handful of Blacks who lived there, and the first "welfare family."

Not many African Americans lived in East Flatbush itself, although it was, at the time, a "changing" community. A Jewish gang called "The Calves" roamed the neighborhood, beating up anyone who wasn't wearing a yarmulke after 7 pm. As might be expected, Black kids were their primary target. Young Rev avoided the dilemma of either having to submit to the gang by wearing a yarmulke or getting beaten up; he stayed in the house at night.

The struggles on the streets and the debates about the direction of the movement had made their way into the halls of JHS 252 and many other schools. Rev, always a natural leader among his peers but until then confined strictly to the theological aspects of life, dove into the debates. Among his debating partners were adults like his English teacher Joe Tabb, as well as other students. The leading figures in the civil rights movement at the time took life in the students at JHS 252.

"Hey, Adam!"

"Hey, Stokely!"

And so Rev and his friends greeted each other, in all seriousness, in the hallways between classes each day. Rev, of course, would be "Adam Clayton Powell," since everyone by then knew Alfred was running with the controversial Harlem congressman. A more mild-mannered young man named Randy would transform in the hallways into "Martin Luther King." Dennis Neal, who disclaimed King's non-violent approach, became "Stokely Carmichael." Richard Farkas, a white companion, was "Robert Kennedy."

But while politics raged in the hallways of JHS 252, back at home church still took centerstage for Rev and his family. In the middle of Rev's junior high career, his sister Cheryl and a friend of hers got into some trouble with the law; she would be gone for three years. That left Rev — now barely a teenager — and Ada to figure out how to get by.

FOUR

Ada and Alfred in Babylon

At the heart of the deterioration of the fabric of Negro society is the deterioration of the Negro family. It is the fundamental source of the weakness in the Negro community at the present time.

—*The Negro Family: The Case for National Action,*
**Department of Labor, Office of Policy Planning and
Research, compiled by Daniel Patrick Moynihan.**

White America's officialdom sounded loud and clear what its attitude and policy towards the masses of African American poor people would be with the publication of the infamous Moynihan Report in 1965. It became a "bipartisan" statement (Moynihan served as an advisor to both the Johnson and Nixon administrations) that set the tone of the times, blaming the poor for their poorness, and paved the way for the subsequent attacks on the civil rights gains of the '60s almost as quickly as they had been won.

LBJ, who launched the "Great Society," took the report to heart; he seized upon Moynihan's "findings" that the African American family was a "tangle of pathology" and declared that the collapse of the family was to be given the utmost priority (it wasn't).

It was just a short policy step for Moynihan to declare five years later (and working for Nixon) that "the time may have come when the issue of race could benefit from a period of 'benign neglect.' The subject has been too much talked about. The forum has been too much taken over by hysterics, paranoids and boodlers on all sides."

In sharp contrast to the official policy statements and actual programs of white America via its government, folks in the community knew that pseudo-social scientists like Moynihan and Company had gotten it upside down, as always, to serve their own purposes. Broken families did not cause and perpetuate poverty. Poverty — and racism — were destroying families! It was a set-up from the start, and the raw statistics that documented the havoc which scarcity and destitution were wreaking on the African American community — particularly its young — proved with each passing day that LBJ's "War on Poverty" was a fraud.

•

While Daniel Patrick Moynihan was gathering the "data" for his report, Ada and Alfred, Jr. set out together, if not to make their mark on the world, then at least to figure out how to negotiate its perilous waters.

Ada was from the beginning unconditionally supportive of her young son's enchantment with the call to preach and Bishop Washington's tutoring in that profession. She combined the roles of mother and manager, doing everything possible to make sure Rev got to his gigs and back safely.

It meant a lot of sacrifice on Ada's part, with her already grueling schedule as a domestic for white folks and a single mother. Once Rev got back from touring with Mahalia Jackson, the requests for the wonder boy preacher came rolling in. Churches would call the home base at Washington Temple, and Bishop Washington would pass along Ada's phone number.

On some Sundays — in fact most of them — there were two or three requests for the Rev at different churches. Ada would put together a little traveling money, take her son by the hand, and climb down into the subway, most of the time heading up into midtown Manhattan to the

Port Authority Bus Terminal at 42nd Street. From there they took a bus across the river to one or another little town in New Jersey.

Ada made sure Rev got to every engagement unless she was just too tired — in which case she would enlist Cheryl, while she was still living at home, for the job.

As a rule, Ada did not charge the churches a fee for her son's sermons; instead, the local preacher passed the plate around. The congregation never failed to be aroused by the Rev's preaching, and showed their appreciation: depending on the size of the church and other circumstances, the Sharptons would take home $20, $30, maybe $50 for an engagement.

They discovered that even the church was not free from the nastiness of the world; the Sharptons got ripped off on more than one occasion, sometimes openly, sometimes quietly. One afternoon, Rev heard the preacher announce proudly that over $300 dollars was raised from the congregation after the sermon. But later in the back room of the church, the preacher took a different approach.

"You're a young kid, Alfred. You wouldn't be needing more than ten dollars." And he peeled a ten-dollar bill off the roll of bills that had been collected, handed it over, and sent the bewildered boy preacher on his way.

Reverend Alfred Sharpton, Jr.'s first encounter with the American judicial system

Strangely enough, it was the young Rev's preaching that landed him in front of a judge when he was still barely a teenager.

Ada had not sat idly by after the sudden abandonment of the family by Alfred, Sr. Eventually she sued him for child support. But Alfred, Sr. was ready when it was time to appear in court, telling his honor that among the reasons why he shouldn't have to pay was that his son was making a decent income as a preacher. Young Rev was indeed preaching, on a regular basis, and he was making money doing it. There was no denying it.

So his honor decided that if the Sharptons were going to receive child support, Rev would have to give up the profession of preaching. Thus the Reverend Al Sharpton heard, for the first time (but not the last), a judge order him to cease and desist. It was still a good 20 years before the words "No justice, no peace!" would come from Rev's lips.

The judge said he wanted an update in a month.

A month passed, and the Sharptons returned to court.

"Alfred," the judge said sternly. "Did you preach this month?"

"Yes."

"Are you still doing those Friday services at the Washington Temple?"

"Yes."

The judge took young Rev and his little sister (even though she was older, Cheryl was always quite a bit smaller than her younger brother) aside. In the back alone with the youngsters, his honor began a gentle but firm cross-examination.

"Why do you preach, Alfred?"

"Because I believe in it. God called me to preach."

And that was the end of the private cross-examination. The judge took Rev and Cheryl by the hand and walked out. "Mrs. Sharpton is not making your son preach for money," he told Alfred, Sr. "He is doing it because he is sincere in what he believes."

It was Rev's first legal victory, and a strange one indeed. A judge had lifted a court order barring Rev from preaching!

As it turned out, the money that Rev was making on the preaching engagements, while certainly no windfall, was pretty much indispensible for him to follow his calling. At the end of each month, the money that the family had raised was divided up. Some would go towards the house and helping out Ada and Cheryl, but the lion's share was re-invested in the young reverend, who needed a supply of suits to preach in, and the bus fare out to the little towns in New Jersey or wherever else he was called. Ada would never have been able to manage on a welfare check, particularly when she wasn't working.

Whatever spare money there might be Rev took on down to the bookstore, barely able to satisfy his voracious appetite for books, books, books. In addition to Powell and Garvey, Rev read the works of contemporary theologians and in particular the ones who had influenced Bishop Washington — Tillich, Toynbee and Spurgeon. Tillich and Toynbee in particular fueled Rev's relentless quest for a way to reconcile the strong religious conservatism learned in the Pentecostal church with the uncompromising activism of an Adam Clayton Powell, Jr. The search led him to the greatest theologian of his time, Dr. Martin Luther King, who grappled with that very dilemma and came out on the other end with the theory and practice of non-violent resistance. Each new book opened up more doors to more learning; from King's books, Rev was inspired to read everything he could on Gandhi and non-violence.

Many took an interest in the development of the young Rev, some very famous men among them. They all had their own reasons for doing so. Some tried to fill the role of the missing father. Others wanted Rev to fill the role of a missing son. Spiritual leaders saw in him a young disciple, as did civil rights activists, entertainers and businesspeople. But in each case, they all recognized in the young man a powerful intellect, a boundless drive, natural leadership qualities and the potential for greatness.

At this stage in his life, those who took Rev under their wing were people like Walter H. Banks, who had joined Washington Temple after coming from an Episcopal church.

Most of the folks in the Washington Temple community were decent, God-fearing, and largely uneducated.

Walter H. Banks was one of the exceptions. Banks, a businessman, held a degree in accounting. He came to Ada Sharpton one day, inquiring about her son. "I'd like to come by and see him," he told her. "Take him around and help round him out."

That was fine with Ada — a respectable gentleman such as Mr. Banks "rounding out" some of the edges on her talented son. Mr. Banks would come pick up the Rev on weekends, often for the whole day on Saturday. They'd head into Manhattan, strolling leisurely down Fifth Avenue, hopping from bookstore to bookstore and museum to museum. Within a square mile area, you could, with a Mr. Banks to guide you, take in the finest cultural offerings the great metropolis of New York City had to offer.

Sometimes they spent half a Saturday browsing through Brentano's (*the* bookstore in New York at the time), then took off to a museum, then went on to Barnes and Noble for some more book-browsing, and then another museum. In the course of the afternoon, Mr. Banks would buy some of the books that caught the Rev's eye. They weren't simply gifts; after Rev had gone through them, Mr. Banks would test his young charge on his understanding of what he had read. Many men subsequently took Alfred Sharpton under their wings, but he owed much of his early intellectual development to Walter Banks.

At this time, the first inklings of Rev's political development were showing themselves. It was only a matter of time before the intense rumblings of the 1960s began to penetrate the conservative religious consciousness of Reverend Alfred Sharpton, then 12 years old; in 1966, even 12-year-olds were being drawn into the struggle. Alternative student newspapers were being produced, civil rights demonstrations were hitting the high schools and even the junior high schools, and many young folks had parents active in the movement.

Rev's entry into the civil rights struggle eventually came about through his older friends and mentors at Washington Temple. What might have delayed that entry was his continued enchantment with Adam Clayton Powell, Jr., who was now approaching the twilight of a rich career as the dean of African American politics.

As the civil rights movement heated up in the '60s, the veteran congressman sprang into action on Capitol Hill. While the movement in the streets and country roads swelled, Powell — who became chairman of the House Committee on Education and Labor in 1961 — was a veritable whirlwind in Congress, serving as the legislative counterpart to the battle on the streets.

"Powell's committee produced significant public policies beneficial to Blacks, the aged, the handicapped, women, poor whites, and Hispanic Americans," notes author Martin Kilson in his essay *Adam Clayton Powell, Jr.: The Militant as Politician.*

Kilson records that in his first five years as chairman,

> Powell's committee generated nearly sixty pieces of significant social legislation, forty-nine of which were bedrock bills and eleven were amending bills. These bills covered such crucial areas of social legislation as fair employment practices, elemen-

tary and secondary school aid, manpower development and training, vocational rehabilitation, school lunch program, war on poverty, federal aid to libraries, barring discrimination in wages for women, and increasing the minimum wage.

But these successes and the support they had garnered for him in his Harlem district and nationally notwithstanding, by the latter part of the 1960s war had been declared on the civil rights movement and its leaders. Malcolm X had been shot dead in what was in all probability an assassination engineered by any or all of America's intelligence agencies (the CIA had consistently violated the legislative ban on the agency's domestic activities); J. Edgar Hoover was already years into the dirty war against Martin Luther King, Jr. that would end with King's murder; thousands of FBI agents and recruits they hired or pressed into service by other means were infiltrating and disrupting every level of the movement. Out in Oakland, California police moved against a new and militant young organization that called itself the Black Panther Party for Self Defense (which took its name from the panther symbol of the Black independent political party that had formed in Alabama), successfully baiting them into a three year-long shooting war which would seal the party's fate.

Not even a veteran congressman like Powell (he was first elected to the House in 1944) was safe from the racist backlash against the movement. For a generation Powell had withstood criticisms of his free-wheeling lifestyle with his sheer productivity, brilliance on the House floor, and plain old-fashioned charm. He had also managed to build a strong political machine capable of weathering the vicissitudes of New York City politics (Adam was one of the few Black politicians to survive a split with the "Silver Fox," Black Tammany Hall boss J. Raymond Jones). Racists in and out of Congress stepped up the attacks on him, escalating the perennial criticisms into an outright attempt to destroy his career.

In 1960 Powell had accused one Esther James of being a "bag woman" who carried bribes to corrupt New York City cops. The Knapp Commission and the *Serpico* book and movie that showed corruption was rampant among "New York's finest" was still a decade away, and when James sued

Powell for defamation of character he was hard-pressed to find a cop willing to break the "code of silence" and testify in his defense. Powell had steered clear of New York up until the time of Rev's fateful visit to his church in order to keep from having to pay damages to James (the case was finally settled in 1967 with Powell giving her $46,000).

The heat was stepped up in 1966, when racists in the House accused Powell of receiving money meant for his staffers. Ohio Democrat Wayne Hays chaired an ad hoc committee that found Powell guilty of the charges (Hays himself would become enmeshed in a sex scandal in the '70s) and the House voted to strip the Harlem congressman of his committee chairmanship. When Congress opened for business the following January, Powell was not allowed to be seated — even after he was re-elected in a landslide three months later.

By then, Rev had already been up to see Powell and drink Cokes with him at the Red Rooster, and was hooked for real.

Watching the news on the night of January 10, 1967 the 12-year-old Rev was madder than hell. He sprang into action immediately. Rev's plunge into politics that year, when he formed the Youth Committee for Powell, was mostly a matter of loyalty to his hero. The committee hit the churches and the streets to collect petition signatures, which they sent off to Speaker of the House John McCormack demanding that he reinstate Powell. It was Rev's first feat of activism.

After a number of fights in the House which saw him reinstated and then barred again, Powell — after taking the case all the way to the Supreme Court — won his seat back.

In those days, Powell would show up in Harlem about twice a month, and Rev would hang with him on about half those occasions: the wonder boy preacher would hop into the car and accompany his idol to appointments, often not leaving the car but waiting patiently for Powell to return. But just as often Rev came in to the speeches and rallies and church appearances (including, of course, the home base of Abyssinian Baptist) as well as coming along when Powell appeared on the big TV talk shows of the day, Dick Cavett and David Frost. And there were visits to a doctor friend on Manhattan's Upper West Side and stops at

Powell's apartment over the Duncan Funeral Home on 135th Street and Seventh Avenue (now known as Adam Clayton Powell Boulevard).

With Powell the Rev listened, taking in every sentence, word and utterance. The words ranged from talk of all the people Powell planned to get even with (and there were, justly, many) to what always seemed to be deep philosophical stuff. And sometimes the philosophical moments would be shared with the young Rev.

"There will come a time in life when you will grow to be a great man, Alfred," Powell told him once in a quiet moment. "The key to greatness is to do things in your generation that seem unusual, but are really on time. And once you do that, *then* you can remove yourself from the scene. You don't have to push it until they kill you. You have to know when to hit it and know when to quit it." Adam knew that his time was coming, and coming soon.

FIVE

The Haunted House

It was at Tilden High School in Brooklyn that the Reverend Al Sharpton began to come into his own as a leader outside of the church. Soon after his arrival at Tilden, Rev began to move beyond the oratory of the pulpit and into organizing and advocacy. He had been taking a serious and painful look at what was happening around him in East Flatbush and elsewhere.

Being Black in America was hell for sure, and the misfortunes of the Sharpton family often made every day a struggle, but young Reverend Al Sharpton was, by the time he entered Tilden High School, in a position to go just about anywhere he wanted to in life. Call him a member of the "talented tenth," or an example of pulling yourself up by your bootstraps, or place him in any of the countless sociological categories that were popular. Rev was in a position to "make it," and he knew it.

But that wasn't all he knew. East Flatbush, like many "mixed" communities, was transitioning into an all-Black neighborhood. And it began to change, practically overnight. Out on the street, Ada and Rev would see and experience dangerous, terrible things. Practically every day they would hear of yet another house being robbed, of someone getting ripped off, beaten or worse.

Rev talked Ada into buying a police lock, the kind you had to slide open and closed every time you went in or out of the house. But even that would not guarantee safety. Ada's bag was snatched one day, and Rev and his friends spent the whole week stalking the streets trying to catch the culprits — unsuccessfully.

Certainly there had always been crime and drugs in the community. But now something new was happening, and it shook Rev deeply. Once he got past the initial anger of, say, his mother being violated on the street, he would be struck by the gnawing reality of what was happening to his community and his people.

In his powerful book *The Fire Next Time*, James Baldwin describes the anguishing personal hell that he found himself in at this same age in life (psychologists have a ridiculous term for it — "identity crisis" — but both Baldwin and the young Rev knew that their pain went way beyond the confines of their active minds).

Baldwin describes how his awareness of what was happening in Harlem drew him violently into the refuge of the church. He saw the brothers and the sisters on the street — gangsters, pimps, whores — and came to realize that they were out there because America had condemned them to *death*:

> Crime became real, for example — for the first time — not as *a* possibility but as *the* possibility. One could never defeat one's circumstances by working and saving one's pennies; one would never, by working, acquire that many pennies, and besides, the social treatment accorded even the most successful Negroes proved that one needed, in order to be free, something more than a bank account. One needed a handle, a lever, a means of inspiring fear...

Repelled by America's dictum that he could not be as good as a young white boy at whatever he chose to do, and turning away from the street life, Baldwin temporarily took refuge in the life of a boy preacher on his way to becoming a master chronicler of the collapse of Western civilization from the perspective of African America. Like his contemporary and fellow humanist, the Martiniquan psychiatrist Frantz

Fanon, Baldwin issued a warning to the white Christian world:

"If we do not now dare everything, the fulfillment of that prophecy, recreated from the Bible in song by a slave, is upon us: *God gave Noah the rainbow sign, no more water, the fire next time!*"

For a teenager named Alfred Sharpton, Jr. in the ghetto of East Flatbush, Brooklyn the pain and horror that Baldwin wrestled with were startlingly real, and personal. Older guys he knew were coming back from a place called Viet Nam to wind up on a corner or in an alleyway; he saw them nodding their lives away. The same with guys who never even thought about Viet Nam and had never left. Their eyes were glassy too, their moods erratic, and every day they seemed one day closer to death, destroyed by a gun or a needle, or at the hands of the police.

Rev, who always had an eye for the girls in the neighborhood (and they for him), saw the same awful transformation in them. He might have his eye on a young lady in the springtime, then not see her maybe for the whole summer. Until the fall, when school rolled around again. There would be the same girl, but thin, sick, an otherworldly look in her eyes. A junkie.

A plague was sweeping through East Flatbush, killing men and women, boys and girls, nice people and not so nice people. *His* people. Friends and strangers.

Like Baldwin, Rev was not a disinterested observer; he wondered, despite his skills and smarts — would *he* be next? He had the church, and his family. He was becoming an activist. But would that save him? There was an evil at work here much bigger than he was, he was realizing, and bigger even than his intentions to survive. He was in a prison, or worse — a haunted house. America.

Night after night, he dreamed about it: it would begin after his Friday night services, a dream of going out afterwards with the guys, then coming upon and entering a haunted house.

Each of the guys would peer in, and then find himself drawn into one of the rooms — rooms like "drugs," and "Viet Nam," and "police brutality" and "suicide."

Death in every room. Rev would gaze in horror, just like in one of those grade B fright movies, at his best friends, one by one, lying dead. Some had needles in their arms, some had a bloodstained Black Panther Party beret by the side of their heads and a gun in their hands where a cop had placed it as "evidence," some had been murdered by one another.

Emilio, Ronald, Dennis, Carol, David. All of them, in one way or another, gone. Carol had a few kids before she died of an overdose. David, who was with the Black Panther Party, went to jail, as did Emilio. The cops shot Ronald dead when they caught him sticking up a check-cashing spot.

Years later, as a national figure, Rev yearned to go back to the old neighborhood, to sit with his friends and talk about what he had done, and how he had made it. But they weren't there. All he could do was try to get a message through to the world about the haunted house, and about his friends — to let the world know that they weren't bad kids, they were not "born" junkies or criminals or stick-up artists. They were born just like him, wanting what he and millions of people in the African American community wanted — to live a normal life. "They, the blacks," James Baldwin wrote, "simply don't wish to be beaten over the head by the whites every instant of our brief passage on this planet."

Rev would be the only one to escape. Like in the movies, he would run to warn the other kids about this house, because he knew they were planning to go there *next* Friday night. By virtue of having escaped, he owed it to those who were killed and those who were in danger to tell them that this house — America — had evil, murderous intentions.

•

Another man came into the Rev's life around this time, a gentleman Ada had begun dating. Robert Owens (later a minister) was at the time a deacon at Charity Baptist Church; Rev used to preach there during Easter week to a big congregation.

All during Easter week, starting on Sunday and going right through to the next weekend. Deacon Owens — who also took the young Rev around town — was a member of Operation Breadbasket, a project of Dr. King's Southern Christian Leadership Conference.

The Politics of Pressure

Adam Clayton Powell pioneered the modern day use of the boycott in the early 1930s. In 1937 he formed the Greater New York Coordinating Committee for Employment, which used boycotts to force bus companies, bottling and bread firms and New York's utility companies to hire and promote African American workers. In its heyday the Greater New York Coordinating Committee for Employment comprised hundreds of organizations and had close to a quarter of a million members; it worked closely with radical white groups and the Communist Party, which was also then in its heyday and had a strong following in the white and Black communities.

In 1959, the Reverend Leon Sullivan (who while he was a board member of General Motors authored the influential "Sullivan Principles" that served as a guideline to corporations for divesting from South Africa) brought together hundreds of Philadelphia ministers to organize their congregations to participate in "selective patronage" programs, directed against companies that practiced discrimination. Sullivan claimed to have created 5,000 jobs for Blacks in the City of Brotherly Love and brought millions of dollars into their pockets as a result of consumer boycotts against Pepsi-Cola, Tasty Cakes, Gulf and Sun Oil.

Dr. King was particularly impressed with Sullivan's use of the network of ministers and their congregations as a base from which to operate — and to win. Dr. King and the Reverend Ralph Abernathy summoned Leon Sullivan to Atlanta in 1962 to set up a similar program, which would be the economic arm of SCLC. In September of that year Operation Breadbasket was set up, with the Reverend Fred Bennett, Jr. serving as director. The program was, as Dr. King would describe it a few years later, "a simple one, in which Negro ministers put pressure on employers to hire and upgrade more Negroes, especially members of their own congregations."

In its first years, Breadbasket reportedly won thousands of jobs for Blacks in Atlanta and selected Southern target cities. Dr. King took the program north with him and in 1966 established a Chicago branch of Breadbasket. An energetic and ambitious young minister who had arrived on the scene a few years earlier and quickly caught everyone's attention became the leader of Chicago Breadbasket.

Whoever may have criticized or questioned the leadership style of the new director, no one could deny that young Reverend Jesse Jackson was making Breadbasket (and lots more) happen in Chicago. Jackson took the simple principle of Breadbasket and developed it into the "Kingdom Theory," insisting that economic empowerment was central to the struggle. From a wing of SCLC, Jackson developed Breadbasket into a sophisticated boycott and negotiating instrument, as well as a power base in both Chicago's African American *and* business communities. By the time Dr. King took Breadbasket national in 1967, Jackson was there to replace Bennett as national director.

•

On a Thursday night in April 1968 Rev was at home in front of the TV with his mother and sister, watching Raymond Burr as a wheelchair-bound San Francisco detective named Ironside, a family favorite. The first time the message flashed across the bottom of the screen, they almost missed it, so unbelievable was the news.

"Dr. Martin Luther King was killed in Memphis."

When the news sank in, Ada Sharpton and her two children cried and cried, and cried some more.

As did millions across the country. In many inner cities, sadness and anger exploded into rage and rebellion, with the community putting a torch to the "haunted house" from Harlem to Watts.

Rev was, however, still a fervid disciple of Adam Clayton Powell, who had not been on the best of terms with Dr. King. Rev had seen Martin a few times when he came into town and stopped over at Washington Temple, and was aware that he was in the presence of greatness. But Adam was still the Rev's homeboy, and after the initial shock of the murder was over, Rev hadn't thought so much about the implications of his death.

Then one night a year later Deacon Owens took Rev out to see a movie about Dr. King's life and the movement he led. Rev sat on the edge of his seat through the entire film; it stimulated not only his love of history, but something deeper.

That nightmarish dream, the terror of having escaped the haunted house and the guilt and urgency and uncertainty that went with it.

"What's gonna happen now that the King of Love is dead?" The passionate voice of Nina Simone (who had sounded the same alarm as Baldwin and Fanon in 1964 when she sang, "This whole country is full of lies/You're all gonna die and die like flies" in "Mississippi Goddamn") filled the theater. Tears filled Rev's eyes.

It was the end of a dream, and everybody knew it. In a little over a decade Dr. King had grown from a local activist preacher in Montgomery, Alabama to a world figure. And more; by the time of his death, King had concluded that nothing short of a radical restructuring of the foundations of America — if not the world — would be required to deal not only with the "Negro question," but the survival of the human race. As Baldwin had pointed out, then there would be no more Negro problem, because it wouldn't be necessary.

The haunted house. The dead friends and neighbors. And those who would die. He knew they would continue to die, just like Dr. King had died, if something wasn't done. The guilt pangs swept like nausea through the Rev.

"Damn! Martin Luther King is dead and we're not doing nothing!" Nina's words stung like an indictment handed down by his people. He got hysterical. By this time, Rev's hero Adam Clayton Powell was fading quickly from the scene; he had practically stopped coming around, reeling as he was under the unrelenting blows of the enemy. The wonder boy preacher had no more heroes.

•

The morning after the movie, Owens took Rev down to Breadbasket with Reverend Wharton, a pastor friend of his. The director of Bread-basket in New York was the Reverend William C. Jones, later the pastor of Bethany Baptist Church (his brother Clayton is a prominent civil rights attorney). A tall Kentucky native whose deep baritone voice resonates off the back wall of any church, he was then minus the shock of gray hair and beard that he has today.

By this time, Reverend Jones had established a track record by winning jobs and other concessions from Canada Dry, Wonder Bread, Sealtest and the now-defunct May's department store; now he was preparing to go up against a company even tougher than any Breadbasket had yet confronted in its local and national drives: the Atlantic & Pacific Tea Company, the mighty A&P, America's biggest and baddest supermarket chain, whose corporate headquarters were in the Big Apple.

A&P's board chairman William Kane, who had a rep as a heartless so-and-so even among his fellow corporate types, was holding fast against Jones' efforts to bring him to the negotiating table.

At Breadbasket's office, Rev was introduced to the New York City director. The occasion was reminiscent of his first meeting with Adam Powell.

"*Of course* I've heard of the 'wonder boy preacher,' " Reverend Jones boomed. "Glad to have you with us!"

With us? Rev thought.

Breadbasket was getting ready to open its new office upstairs over the Carver Federal Savings Bank, the only Black savings & loan bank in New York. When Rev went over for the opening a week later he met another of the town's "big" preachers, Reverend Taylor of Concord Baptist, who led the prayer.

Then Reverend Jones took Rev to the back of the office to meet Breadbasket's national director. Sitting behind a desk was a very tall, muscular fellow with a big Afro, thick sideburns, and a fringed suede jacket. All the other preachers in the room had on suits and ties.

Rev's own hand was lost in the huge hand extended to him by the Reverend Jesse Jackson.

"This is the wonder boy preacher, Alfred Sharpton," came Reverend Jones' introduction. "He's 14 years old, and we're making him youth director of the chapter."

Reverend Jackson looked the young man over, and said, "Choose your targets carefully, and kick ass!"

They all went over to the Friendship Baptist Church, where close to 20 years later Rev would start the United African Movement. At a rally upstairs Jesse spoke, Mahalia Jackson sang...and the Reverend Jesse Jackson became the most exciting person Rev had met since Adam Clayton Powell.

"What's gonna happen now that the King of Love is dead?" The song kept going through Rev as he thought about Adam no longer being there. Jesse Jackson certainly had the same charisma as Adam, not to mention the flamboyance. And his youthful style was irresistibly appealing to Rev, a young teenager.

Overnight Jesse Jackson became Rev's mentor. The new youth director's style changed overnight too; he went from a suit-and-tie, crew-cut, holy-roller boy preacher to an Afro-ed, sideburned, vested (just like his new hero) civil rights activist, with a Greenwich Village-purchased medallion on a chain around his neck.

SIX

Breadbasket

There seemed to be nothing Ada Sharpton could do to prevent her son's entry into the civil rights movement. Although many, many of the adults in charge of the movement were preachers or otherwise deeply involved in the church, Rev's mother — coming from a religious, non-activist background — was not convinced it was the thing to be doing.

But this was clearly what her son intended to do, and she knew she couldn't possibly stand in his way.

Nor did she want to. Although concerned about her son's inexperience and the inherent dangers of such activity — they had, after all, wept together over Dr. King's murder and seen other day-to-day acts of violence as well — she was truly proud of Rev. If this was her son's choice, Ada Sharpton would simply take whatever precautions she could.

Which meant paying a visit to Dr. Jones to ask that he look out for young Alfred. If this was to be Rev's career, she would in effect simply have to hand Alfred over to him. He agreed, and that satisfied her; Ada sensed that her son was in good hands and that she would not have to have anything more than a mother's ordinary worry for a child (20 years later, Dr. William Jones was still looking out for Rev — in 1990 he sat in the front row of the courtroom as the now quite adult Reverend Al

Sharpton faced off against the fullest fury of the New York State judicial system).

•

So when Reverend Al Sharpton signed on as the new youth director of Breadbasket, he did so just at the time Reverend Jones was leading the organization into its biggest battles. A&P board chairman Kane was continuing to give Reverend Jones the slip. Tenuously holding on to the company's position as number one among supermarket giants, the conservative Kane did not want to risk looking weak against either Jones or Jackson in the eyes of his stockholders.

Reverend Jones stepped up the street heat, and so did the Rev.

It was at Breadbasket that Rev first learned the art and science of putting "troops" on the street. Already a masterful orator, Rev took the leap from organizing young folks to put stock in the Lord to putting their behinds on the street. He developed an "army," roughly 500 kids he could call on to come out to wherever it was that Breadbasket was boycotting — 23 companies in New York City between 1969 and 1971, the period when Rev was there.

In a short time Rev became, among the youth, the undisputed master of the streets. Sit-ins, direct actions, pickets — the teenage Rev did not merely participate in them, he was in charge, following his directive to get and keep the kids in the street. The army was recruited from the neighborhood, from the churches where he preached, and from his primary political base among his fellow students over at Tilden.

Every Saturday there were rallies at Reverend Jones' Bethany Baptist, where Rev warmed up the crowd for the minister, or for Reverend Jackson himself if the national director was in town. At 15 he was introducing the leading civil rights activist in the country and bringing him out to the podium!

Meanwhile, a whole lot of shaking was going on in the public school system.

It had been a decade and a half since the Supreme Court's momentous *Brown v. Board of Education* decision abolished school segregation. But in

New York City the public schools — where Black and Latino students were now becoming a majority (in 1966 "minorities" made up 75% of Manhattan enrollment) — were still segregated. In places like Harlem and Brooklyn's East New York, the conditions for hundreds of thousands of children of color were nothing short of horrendous.

The teachers were still overwhelmingly white and Jewish, and organized in a strictly business union — the United Federation of Teachers — headed by a volatile and shady character named Albert Shanker.

In the '60s a "community control" movement came into being, often with militant Black leadership, which demanded that communities of color have control over the public schools. This simple demand put the community into direct confrontation with the union. Although the UFT had a positive record on civil rights issues, the move by the community to have more Black and Latino teachers for Black and Latino students led to a racial showdown that exposed the limits of liberalism.

The community no longer needed well-intentioned liberals to take care of helpless poor children. Now, the issue was power — Black power. When a new junior high school with a white administration and staff (which had been chosen specifically from among those deemed "sensitive" to racial issues and familiar with the Black community) was opened in Harlem, the community rebelled. The Board of Education was forced to replace the administration at IS 201 and undertook "demonstration" projects of community control in selected neighborhoods.

As tensions heightened, the liberal Lindsay administration went into action, appointing Ford Foundation president McGeorge Bundy (a longtime fixture in America's military-industrial complex) to head a panel that would make recommendations on how to reorganize education in the city.

When a local experimental school board in the Ocean Hill-Brownsville section of Brooklyn began replacing teachers, the UFT undertook a series of polarizing and often dangerous strikes. Much has been written about the bitter fight that ensued, with Shanker and the UFT ultimately regaining control of the schools thanks to the use of police force and political cave-ins by Lindsay. Decentralization and community control experiments were abolished. All that was left of the promising community control movement was 30 local boards, which degenerated into little more than patronage plums.

Out of the school strike as well came a new generation of African American political leaders who moved into Brooklyn Democratic Party politics, or set up power bases outside of the electoral arena. Albert Vann, who at that time was president of the African American Teachers Association, and Roger Green were both community-control leaders; both are now Brooklyn state assemblymen. Leslie Campbell, then a school teacher who became notorious when he read a student's poem on WBAI radio that was attacked as an example of Black anti-Semitism, is now the activist known as Jitu Weusi.

Rev was in his first year of high school when the teachers' strike hit.

"Hey Rev, you joining the Afro-American Club?"

With all the action on the streets of the community, that was the thing to do. By his sophomore year Rev, of course, had become president of the Afro-American Club, and would remain so until graduation. The club met almost daily at the Sharpton home.

He also became associate editor of the *Gadfly* newspaper, vice president of the Forum Club and Debating Team and head of the Martin Luther King Memorial Committee, which hung the first portrait and plaque in remembrance of Dr. King in any high school in the city (it's still there). Tilden High School, like many others, was the scene of riots and rebellions, just as was the surrounding community, although Rev kept his activities strictly within the context of Breadbasket and avoided the more heated (and unorganized) fights on the streets. By Rev's senior year he was enrolled in a city-sponsored intern program, in which students were taken out of classes for six months of work (eager to get him off campus, the school administration had happily signed him up).

Rev the teenage activist also joined a group called Panel of Americans, whose offices were on West 72nd Street in Manhattan. Panel of Americans — a legacy of the Lindsay years, which were characterized by numerous attempts to create vehicles for using individuals to "cool out" hot situations — brought together Black, Latino, Asian and white kids who traveled the streets speaking about race relations. Rev spent about two years with the organization.

One can imagine why the administration of Tilden High School was so eager to get the Rev out of its hair. The young preacher had by now developed his speaking style and skills to such an extent that he not only could mesmerize the crowds at Bethany Baptist, but he held a tight grip on the student body too. Once in a while Rev, who had begun to develop the devilish streak that is now an indelible part of his character, would use those skills for less than altruistic purposes:

"Mrs. Sharpton? This is Alfred's principal. How is he feeling today?"

"Oh, just fine."

"Do you think he'll be coming to school today?"

"Yes, he will."

"Oh, good. Thank you, ma'am."

As little as they cared to have Rev around, the administration knew that not having him at school could be even more treacherous. For the simple reason that Rev might wake up with a headache and get on the phone to his network of organizers:

"Let's have a boycott. No school today."

And, after maybe ten calls, there'd be no school.

But mostly, Rev's actions at the school involved some grievance the students may have had; in fact, *any* grievance. As youth leader with Operation Breadbasket, one of the biggest and most successful civil rights groups in the country, to Rev a school protest was a piece of cake.

The morning after leading a sit-in, or meeting with the chairman of a major department store like Robert Hall, or sitting alongside Jesse Jackson as he told A&P bigwigs, "Gentlemen, we will shut your stores down all over the country," it was no big deal to negotiate with the chairman of the history department at Tilden.

Freshman year in high school saw Rev's first involvement in an election campaign (Adam Powell, of course, was then so strong among his constituents that he hardly had to campaign at all). Volatile civil rights veteran James Farmer launched a run for Congress in Brooklyn as a Republican, going up against the widely respected Shirley Chisholm. Rev got involved on Farmer's behalf; it was a losing effort.

The following year, with Rev now at Breadbasket, Ms Chisholm approached him. After some chatting, she said, "Boy preacher, you got to check out your record. You're on the wrong side with James Farmer." When she came up for re-election the following year, Rev was among her campaign workers, taking her through the streets of the community and introducing her to folks on the block. And the most memorable experience of all — carrying her pocketbook when she stopped to chat. Thus began an ongoing political relationship.

•

In addition to firing up the crowd at the Breadbasket rallies every Saturday in the basement of Bethany Baptist, Rev conducted youth meetings on Wednesday nights at Reverend Jones' church. Rev and his crew would put up flyers in all the churches whose pastors were involved in Breadbasket, making sure the youth in those churches came out.

That built up to about 500 kids pretty quickly. The 16-year-old Rev gave lectures on the operating principles of the organization:

"Let me tell you what we mean by *economic reciprocity*," Rev would say from behind the lectern. "These corporations are making substantial profits, and they owe them to the Black community. The Black community is their *margin of profit*, yet these corporations do not do business with *us*.

"They don't return *any* of those dollars to our community. It's *our* future that is at stake, and so we have to *fight*."

And right there in those meetings, Rev took the names of those who were going to picket, those who would sit in and go to jail, and those who would volunteer at Breadbasket's offices.

Rev dived right into the boycotts Reverend Jones was leading against A&P, Robert Hall, Macy's, Pepsi-Cola, Coca-Cola, Wonder Bread. They hit a good dozen or more corporations in succession, one right after another. As Rev explained to the young folks at his Wednesday night meetings, the demands were simple: deposit money in Black banks; use

Black service contractors, as well as accountants and lawyers; bring the Black community into every aspect of the business, across the board — including, of course, employment.

Once a company signed an agreement with Breadbasket (these agreements were known as covenants, a term coined by Jesse Jackson), they moved on to the next target. Starting off with Wonder Bread, about 15 companies signed up in the course of Rev's stay with Breadbasket.

Rev was almost arrested for the first time during a picket at one of the Robert Hall stores. He was taken off the picket line and didn't get booked because he was a kid.

The next close call came in February of 1971, during the A&P battle, when Reverend Jones and 33 ministers went to the corporate headquarters in the Graybar Building at 420 Lexington Avenue in midtown Manhattan. They arrived at around 6 PM, demanding to see chairman of the board Kane.

But the corporate ducker and diver was nowhere to be found. So the group took over Kane's office, staying for two days. Eventually they were arrested; Rev was almost among those hauled off to jail, but the SCLC lawyer wouldn't let him go with the rest. "He's a minor," the lawyer explained. "It would just add aiding the delinquency of a minor charges to the charges against Reverend Jones."

That night, Reverend Jackson called Rev to say he was flying in to take charge of the drive in New York.

The following day Jackson led a march with Rev's youth division, held a sit-in, and got arrested for trespassing and disorderly conduct. Reverend Jones was still in jail and didn't even know what was going on; as he got out, Jesse was on his way in. That last time was the closest yet that Rev got to being arrested, but he still managed to participate in all of the sit-ins.

Good-bye, Adam

By 1970 Adam Clayton Powell had firmly established himself as a hero, but the war against him (aided and abetted by younger, rival Black political forces) was nearing victory.

The final blow came in the 1970 Democratic primary, when State Assemblyman Charles Rangel was pegged to go up against the legend. Rangel — of Black and Puerto Rican parentage and a product of Manhattan borough president/entrepreneur Percy Sutton's political machine — was greatly aided by new district lines, which took away some of Powell's working class base and added a segment of middle class Jewish constituents on Manhattan's Upper West Side.

Rev worked peripherally on Powell's 1970 primary campaign; he was more involved with Breadbasket and, in any case, Powell — who had always won by general acclamation — hardly campaigned.

But when the votes were counted on primary night, the results showed 7,804 for Rangel and 7,599 for Powell — a margin of 205. Rev was convinced the election had been stolen; he and Powell's other supporters urged the congressman to stay on and fight.

In fact, Rev was among those who went down to Powell's hideaway in Bimini after the primary, urging him to come back, but Powell held fast.

Rev caught up to him at the pier, where his boat was docked.

"Why won't you fight?"

Powell looked at the Rev in a fatherly fashion.

"I told you the day will come when it's time to quit," he said. "And when it's time to quit, don't push it. Have a fishing pole somewhere ready with bait and just go fishing."

With that he took his fishing pole and, accompanied by his wife, boarded the boat and sailed off. That was the last time Rev saw Congressman Adam Clayton Powell, Jr. until his funeral in Harlem in April of 1972.

Reverend Jackson had gone to see Adam at the hospital shortly before his death, and he and Rev talked about the older man often. There was, much to Rev's pleasure, quite a bit of mutual admiration between his two heroes.

The 1970 election marked Rev's first encounter with Charles Rangel, now a senior member of Congress. The election stirred all kinds of emotions in Rev: Sutton, the force behind Rangel, had a strong reputation (he had once been Malcolm X's attorney) and was a respected political figure. Most troubling was that he was very close with Reverend Jackson and a strong Breadbasket supporter. Rev, of course, was now Jackson's protegé.

So while he disdained Sutton's role in the downfall of his idol Powell, he also liked and respected Sutton because of his involvement in the cause to which he was committed.

It was the kind of conflicted relationship that Rev would have with many figures of the day, as complex and often competing political loyalties clashed on a regular basis; they soon did within Breadbasket and the SCLC itself.

It took Rev quite a few years before he could broach the subject of Powell's final defeat with his friend Sutton without the words getting stuck in his throat.

"The only thing I've got against you is that Adam should have died in office," Rev told the Harlem business magnate one day.

"I know you'll always resent us beating Adam, but you've got to remember there was no one else to beat," the seasoned politician replied.

The preacher in Rev couldn't accept it; what Sutton was saying went against all the moral absolutes of the church's teachings. But the more he thought about it, the more clearly Rev realized that even Adam would have understood the logic, and in fact was trying to get Rev to accept it.

"Well, Adam would probably want me to deal with whoever is here," Rev thought to himself. "I have to deal with what's real. That's what Adam would want."

For now, Rev was spending practically every day with Reverend Jones, traveling with him to see SCLC chief Ralph Abernathy, and meeting all the SCLC dignitaries who came into town: Coretta Scott King, Hosea Williams, James Bevel, Andrew Young.

It was quite an education. Rev was not merely a student of the civil rights movement — he was living it. At night, Reverend Jones would drop Rev off at home, where he still lived with Ada; home was his protection from the dangers of the streets.

Many, many people who later became leading figures in the Black political world came through Breadbasket. Rev met them all.

The Kid

Reverend Jones brought Rev along to a lot of the SCLC meetings, which proved particularly educative to the neophyte civil rights activist.

One such meeting took place at the New York Hilton in Rockefeller Center. With Reverend Abernathy chairing, a slew of dignitaries — including Reverends Jones and Jackson and veterans Bayard Rustin, Wyatt T. Walker and Hosea Williams — were in attendance.

At one point Williams, a crusty activist from an impoverished background who had taken numerous beatings at the hands of southern crackers, came in and asked for the floor. Abernathy refused. Suddenly Williams, known for his erratic temper, grabbed a chair and sent it crashing through the hotel room window. Rev watched in amazement while chairs and glass flew everywhere.

"Damn! This is a non-violent organization?!" Rev thought, shocked.

But young as he was — and the veterans of the movement took to calling him "the Kid" — Rev was soon taken into the leaders' confidence. While many young people were sitting in classrooms learning about the movement (at least those classrooms that taught such things), Rev was sitting at the knees of Hosea Williams and Ralph Abernathy and Jesse Jackson, who in quiet moments shared thrilling stories about Dr. King and the movement.

Selma. Birmingham. Montgomery. Stories that no one else could tell. Reverend Al Sharpton was, while still in high school, getting the best first-person education that any African American leader ever got. Which is why when he eventually was graduated from Tilden High School he quickly lost interest in college.

Rev studied political science, but no teacher could tell him much about the civil rights movement that he didn't know. He *knew* the guys in the books. He had talked to them. He was their friend, their protegé. He knew what really happened in Selma and Montgomery, having heard it from Ralph Abernathy. He knew what Dr. King did at night, and what it was like to walk across the Pettis Bridge in Selma — he heard it from Hosea Williams.

And because he was "the Kid," young Reverend Al Sharpton was trained to lead the generation ahead.

At Tilden High School, Rev got into the same debates with friends that were taking place between the leaders of the civil rights movement in which he had immersed himself and those who searched for a more militant approach to the struggle. One of his friends, David Conyers (whose sister Rev had been dating), gave him a copy of Mao's *Little Red Book*. Soon Rev and the whole crew were wearing denim caps with red stars and had *Red Books* tucked under their arms.

Rev debated hard with those who had joined the Panthers and were following the road of Mao. Rev was fascinated by the radicals' mobilization efforts and adhered philosophically to what he described as democratic socialism. He had no problem with the leftist outlook; his problem was with the dictum that a violent revolution was needed to effect any real change in the haunted house of America.

"I just don't think it's feasible," he told his friends. "You can't gain the sympathy of the overwhelming majority of the country for that kind of thing, and my study of revolution tells me that you need the general sympathy of the public to accomplish a violent overthrow of the government. You can only do that through a long political process."

And of course Rev fought with them about religion. Not in a hostile way; even though most of his friends were not at all religious, they *had* been. Panther David Conyers had come out of the church, and so had many others. David's mother was even a regular at the Rev's Friday night services.

Friendly arguments:

"Rev, don't you know that religion is the opiate of the people?"

"Well, you grew up in the church, and it didn't kill *you*!"

And so on.

Rev's militant buddies knew that their preacher friend was very much *involved* in the struggle. He was so unlike the typical, apolitical preacher that there was nothing hostile in their barbs; he was, after all, leading marches and sit-ins after school!

But despite his tactical disagreements with friends who had gone into the Black Panther Party and other militant groups, he was in complete agreement with what he felt were their common goals. "You're on the right track," he told them. "It's just the wrong tactic."

As for the Panthers, Rev adored the free food program they developed, providing breakfast for hundreds of kids in the community. That love only made the pain worse as, in practically no time, one after the other, Panther friends of his were set up and sent to jail; David Conyers for example, did three years.

For Rev, the effect of the arrests and beatings and killings was not only political, it was *personal*. David Conyers and the others were his friends.

Even while he was still in high school, Rev was deep into theological studies, defining what would become his mature theological perspective. And that would be *political*. Reverend Jones had Rev read Reinhold Niebuhr and other social theologians, and he more and more adopted the activist perspective. Still, unlike his friends his location was not in the "radical movement" but in the Black church movement. It was a different environment with different politics.

SEVEN

The Kid

The year 1971, which he spent honing his skills and refining his activism, was Rev's last year as youth director of Breadbasket.

Percy Sutton, who headed up a group called Capital Formation, and his associates were eager to see Rev go national with the youth work; they sent him off to Chicago, the home base of Jackson's Breadbasket, to attend the annual Black Expo which Jackson had organized.

At Sutton's expense Rev spent the whole week there, chatting with his hero Jesse and meeting his kids. After Rev came home, he took regular trips back and forth to the Windy City, coordinating the youth work in the two towns. Rev got tighter with the younger Jacksons, and became increasingly established as the protegé of the man who himself was recognized as the frontrunner in the battle for succession to the leadership position of the martyred Dr. King.

That battle had deep repercussions not only for Rev's future, but for the movement as a whole.

•

It was no secret that intensive warfare within King's SCLC broke out practically minutes after the fatal shots ripped through the beloved leader's skull on the balcony of Memphis' Lorraine Hotel in the spring of 1968.

While officially the leadership mantle was passed to the Reverend Ralph Abernathy, Jesse Jackson did not hesitate to put his own claims forward. Who the actual heir turns out to be will, of course, be decided by history; in fact there's no reason to limit the choices to those who were part of the SCLC inner circle at the time.

Perhaps the leader will be a ghetto youth who wept at the news coming over an aging radio in a bare tenement apartment or across a television screen. Maybe the leader is a woman. Or not yet born.

But after April of 1968, while the ghettos smoldered in rebellion, a battle did indeed rage at the top.

In the three years between 1968 and 1971 — the years when Rev was at Breadbasket — the Black Panther Party arose on the streets of America's desperate Black communities. By 1971 J. Edgar Hoover's COINTELPRO, the murderous FBI plot against Black nationalist and left wing organizations, had effectively destroyed the Panthers. While COINTELPRO (which stood for Counter-Intelligence Program) targeted groups like the Communist Party and the Socialist Workers Party, the Panthers were singled out for a murderous assault that left dozens of young Black militants dead, thousands jailed, and countless more disorganized and demoralized.

The carnage was in retaliation for this brave young organization's "conspiracy" to feed hungry ghetto youth and resist police brutality.

Time will tell how much the COINTELPRO-ers were involved in the intrigues that went on in the SCLC wing of the movement. But regardless of what outside manipulation was present, there was no shortage of tension within the post-King organization.

It all hit the fan in 1971, when a financial scandal broke out; Black Expo monies from the previous two years, it was charged, had been siphoned off to a private corporation under Jackson's control.

Jackson had come under increasing attack for his relationships with a number of Chicago businesspeople, which grew out of his role as first the local and then the national director of Breadbasket.

The word "extortion" was kicked around practically from the time he took over the leadership of Operation Breadbasket. And as the movement took on the tactic of economic warfare (as Rev eventually did) it was used against other leaders as well.

Extort: "to obtain by force or threats," to "coerce," "exact," "gouge," "shake down," "squeeze," "wrench," "wrest," "wring."

Some might argue that the nature of Breadbasket's activity, even as King envisioned it, *was* extortion. All sorts of warfare (and the battle for racial justice in America was and is no exception) involve obtaining victory "by force or threats."

But extortion is also illegal, so those who have the legal machinery in their corner have the advantage.

The Black Expo scandal brought the battle between Jackson and Abernathy (characterized by his opponents in Jackson's corner as an out of touch old fogey who had opportunized off King's legacy) to a head. Jackson handed in his resignation, which Abernathy initially refused to accept; he demanded accountability from his younger rival for the Black Expo charges.

But by the late fall of 1971 Jackson was gone from SCLC and Breadbasket dissolved — to be instantly reborn when he formed People United to Save Humanity (PUSH) in December.

Everyone in the movement chose sides. Reverend William Jones went with Abernathy; he became the interim national director of Breadbasket, but with most of the street troops going into PUSH with Jesse it soon died out.

Rev — just turned 16 — was faced with a very adult decision. He was under the wings of both Reverend Jackson and Reverend Jones, who had parted ways.

Rev ultimately decided to side with Jesse in the dispute. But rather than follow him into PUSH (as did most Jackson supporters, including Percy Sutton) he formed his own organization.

Thus the National Youth Movement was born.

•

Shortly after Jackson's departure Rev approached the late Bayard Rustin, a movement veteran who was more moderate than many of his colleagues. Rev explained that with Jesse gone, he was leaving also to form a new group with his own crew made up of Tilden students and kids drawn from the church. He was going to call it the National Youth Movement.

Bayard Rustin gave Rev $500 for seed money.

Rev then went to some Black businessmen he had met during his years at Breadbasket who would help the young activist (legally a minor) with the intricacies of incorporation. They included Freeman Boyland (currently the head of personnel at the *New York Times*); Lawrence Bland, the head of the National Bankers Association, an umbrella group of Black banks; the Reverend Mel Wimberly; and L. Bruce Hopewell.

They needed a lawyer. Someone knew of a Harlem attorney who could handle the delicate matter of incorporating a civil rights organization led by a precocious 16-year-old with the goal of organizing inner city youth across the country.

The lawyer was David M. Dinkins, who charged Rev $3,000 for his services; the young activist raised and paid the fee that went to the law firm of Dinkins and his partner Ivan Michaels.

Fundraising to cover the cost of the incorporation took the form of a business luncheon at the New York Hilton in 1972, whose speakers included Rep. Shirley Chisholm and Brooklyn politico Howard Samuels. Freeman Boyland brought out newspaper guild people, who bought a few tables.

Rev jumped right into action after the formation of the youth movement. He ran its operations while serving an internship at the Human Resources Administration, where he worked for Lindsay appointee Jules Sugarman, the new head of the department.

Rev organized a Minority Youth Day in Brooklyn, with the help of Chisholm and Sutton (and received a congratulatory letter from Mayor Abe Beame, who noted he was "impressed with your constructive record of obtaining 4,000 jobs and two large training programs for young people"). He held a press conference with Sutton and Basil Paterson (then with the *New York Law Journal*); they called on Governor Nelson Rockefeller — who had ordered the massacre of 43 inmates at Attica

State Prison — to meet with Rev to discuss the problems of Black youth.

In March 1972 Rev attended the National Black Political Convention in Gary, Indiana which brought together thousands of Black political activists and leaders to plot out the future direction of African American politics and to lay the groundwork for a "Black Agenda."

The Reverend Jesse Jackson and Gary Mayor Richard Hatcher were among those calling for independent Black politics (although the convention would ultimately decide to give the Democratic Party one more shot). Rev attended as the convention's youngest delegate (appointed by Chisholm) and a member of the platform committee.

Rev also organized a Kwanzaa ceremony, which got him his first press coverage in the *New York Times* (this may explain why the "newspaper of record" always starts his career at age 16); the piece profiled the 16-year-old boy preacher celebrating Kwanzaa in Harlem. The *Sunday Daily News* followed with a sizable profile of its own, marveling "at the admiration other youth seem to have for the teenage preacher-leader."

Into politics

The bigwigs in the Black political establishment didn't need the *New York Times* to tell them about the young Rev's considerable oratorical skills. There were few people who weren't taking note of Rev's talent in firing up crowds, an essential element of politics.

Long-time Brooklyn politico Wesley "Mac" Holder, the manager of Shirley Chisholm's 1972 Presidential campaign, got in touch with the Rev on her behalf and pressed him into service as youth director for the campaign. Rev traveled with the candidate once again, this time graduating from holding her pocketbook on street corners to organizing college students.

One day, they were sitting in the Bedford Avenue Democratic Club in Brooklyn with two other young men.

"Alfred," she said, "I want you to help these young men. They're running for office."

Rev looked over at them as the candidate continued speaking.

"I want you to do all the speaking, because neither of them are great public speakers. But they're on the Chisholm team." Shirley was in the habit of speaking of herself in the third person.

Rev agreed to take the job; he would speak on behalf of the candidates, do the sound in the streets, and whatever else was required to get the message to the people.

One of the young men was the late Vander Beatty, then a state legislator who was going up against fellow Brooklynite Waldaba Stewart for the State Senate.

The other was Edolphus Towns, who ran unsuccessfully that year for State Assembly against the incumbent Ed Griffith. Towns came back in 1973 to win a district leadership, going on to become a deputy borough president and eventually a congressman.

But in 1972 their spokesperson, appointed by their mentor Shirley Chisholm, was the Reverend Al Sharpton, at 17 still a year shy of being eligible to vote himself.

The year 1972 was a turning point in African American politics. The repercussions of the fateful decision taken at the Gary convention to concentrate Black political energies on electing more Blacks to office through the two party system rather than on taking the African American electorate independent are still being felt. In one sense the strategy has been a success; the number of Black elected officials has increased by 365% since then.

But the poverty level of the African American community has grown even more, as has police brutality. Two decades and two Jesse Jackson Presidential campaigns later, the political direction of the African American community — in particular, how to use the Black vote to empower the community (and not just its official leadership) — is still a matter of intense debate.

In 1972 the Reverend Al Sharpton was already, at the age of 17, an established figure in the mainstream Black political movement.

Rev was aware that his involvement had much to do with his ongoing search for someone to fill the void left by the traumatic departure of his father years earlier. Rev's actions up until this point were guided largely by his emulation of men he had chosen to fill that void — Adam

Clayton Powell, Jr. and then the Reverend Jesse Jackson. He wasn't just among their supporters. He wanted, badly, to *be* Adam, to *be* Jesse.

His activities at the newly formed National Youth Movement were guided by the same principle. Rev wanted to build a movement which would fight for Black people in the same manner that Breadbasket had under Jackson's leadership, but under *his* leadership.

He saw himself as becoming a nationally known civil rights leader in the charismatic, flamboyant, civil disobedience tradition of Powell and Jackson. It was the Jesse with the Afro, the sideburns, the medallion and vest; the Jesse who had led the Poor People's March of 1968; who had taken people up to the Department of Agriculture that year, run up a bill in the dining room and told the government to pay — *that* Jesse. The Jesse who unseated Chicago Mayor Richard Daley at the 1972 Democratic Party National Convention, charging that his delegation was in violation of the newly won, more inclusive delegate rules that the civil rights movement had been fighting for at each of the past two conventions.

It wasn't the later, "Presidential" Jesse Rev was following, because that Jesse didn't exist yet; it was the Jesse who had seized the hearts of thousands of young Black people like Reverend Al Sharpton.

Rev sized up all the fratricidal infighting within the movement at the time (almost all of which seemed to center around his new hero) and concluded that much of the criticism leveled against Jesse was born of envy.

"Sure, lots of these guys have philosophical differences with Jesse," Rev thought. "But how about giving him credit for what he's done?"

Wasn't Jesse competing in Chicago with Elijah Muhammad at his peak, and with the Black Panther Party, and with the whole established, old guard leadership of the mainstream civil rights movement — Whitney Young, Roy Wilkins and company? Hadn't he built a national base? That wasn't easy to do, operating in such a crowded field and coming out on top!

Rev had nothing but admiration for his suede-vested hero.

The fight for new leadership was on. It had been foreshadowed when

New York City police launched a bloody raid on the Nation of Islam's Mosque #7 on 116th Street in Harlem. Rev went up there as head of the National Youth Movement. Jesse, who was now heading up PUSH, was there. And so was a young minister of the NOI named Louis Farrakhan. It was the first time their paths had all crossed.

Rev had already begun to take stock of where he had been and where he was going. He sat down one day for a heart to heart with another of his mentors, Shirley Chisholm.

"I got friends out there in the Panthers getting killed and going to jail, other friends on drugs dying, other kids in Viet Nam." Rev's whole crowd had become draft age, prompting him to head to the local draft board and file for a deferment as a minister.

It was a very frightening thing, he said, to be graduating from high school in 1972 in America, with practically everyone he had known from junior high school either dead or in jail. He began feeling, despite his highly extroverted lifestyle, lonely and frightened; every day he wrestled against the odds of his own death. Despite all he had accomplished, despite all his friends in the movement, he was young and Black and living in the haunted house of America, which meant that destruction was close upon his heels. Was he to be next?

There was a conspiracy afoot, a conspiracy to destroy Black youth. And that gave a definite direction to an organization called the National Youth Movement headed up by the Reverend Al Sharpton.

Rev agreed with the Black Panther Party that a war had been declared by white America against the Black population. Rev's hero Jackson was in agreement with what the Panthers were saying, tempered by a church view, which stressed the necessity of taking individual responsibility for one's life.

Rev traveled to Chicago, where he met Bill Hampton, the brother of Fred Hampton. The Panther leader had been murdered as he slept by an army of Chicago police officers, which also killed Hampton's plans to forge a Rainbow Coalition (he coined the term) that would bring the Panthers together with Latino, Native American, Asian and white organizations — the beginnings of a Black-led, broad-based movement for social justice.

Bill Hampton told Rev first hand how they had killed his brother in cold blood, further evidence that America had genocidal plans for Black youth.

Many of the kids who came into the National Youth Movement to participate in the employment and other programs that Rev — emulating the work of Jackson's Breadbasket — was struggling to put in place talked with him of yet another menace they faced on the streets.

Police brutality.

It was clear that the National Youth Movement would have to go beyond the framework established by Operation Breadbasket if it was to have a real impact on the lives of young Black people.

EIGHT

A Godfather and a Youth Movement

One of the first cases Rev and the National Youth Movement took on involved the opposition of white residents of Canarsie to the busing in of Black children to the local high school. Rev joined Reverend Wilbur Miller in leading that battle, which expanded when Sonny Carson and others in the Black nationalist movement joined in.

They won — the kids were sent to the school. And Rev leaned on his friend Bayard Rustin, who traveled in the same circles as Albert Shanker of the United Federation of Teachers, to get the union to pay for the buses.

Then, on the night of September 15, 1974, a group of eight Black teenagers were in a basement on Powell Street in Brownsville, cleaning up the dingy cellar for a friend's surprise birthday party. Two police officers cruising nearby responded to a radio report of a "10-31" — burglary in progress — at the Powell Street address. Startled by the police bursting into the basement (where they were setting up for the party without permission from the superintendent), the teens ran; one of them tossed a pipe that struck Officer Frank Bosco in the leg.

Bosco took off after young Claude Reese, who ran up a flight of stairs from the cellar. The 14-year-old, holding a keyhole saw in his hands, turned back as Bosco reached the bottom of the stairs. Bosco fired one shot, killing the youngster.

For Rev, it was one more casualty in the deadly war against Black youth. Every case was another outrage, like the murder the year before of 11-year-old Clifford Glover, shot in the back by Police Officer Thomas Shea because he and his stepfather looked like two "perps" the cops had received a call about. Typically, the cases involved young people given the death penalty on the spot simply for being kids — for such crimes as being in a basement where, yes, they shouldn't have been...

Rev took on the Reese case right away, preaching at Claude's funeral and leading a march outside Mayor Abraham Beame's City Hall office. Brooklyn politico Sam Wright was in the City Council at the time; Rev stood up during one rally to challenge the *man* part of his councilman title.

In no time, Rev was learning about the inner workings of another wing of the movement that were as revealing as his first encounter with the rowdy goings-on of the "non-violent" SCLC.

At that time the writer Amiri Baraka, formerly known as LeRoi Jones, was the dominant Black nationalist in the country. Rev remembered him from the '72 Gary conference. Baraka — based in Newark, New Jersey — was embroiled in some sort of conflict with Sonny Carson and Jitu Weusi; like Baraka, both had involved themselves in the Claude Reese case.

Rev called a meeting one night at his home in East Flatbush, where he still lived with Ada. Much to the surprise of both Sharptons, Carson and Weusi showed up with about ten bodyguards apiece, while Baraka was accompanied by 20. The four men sat down in the room which Ada had made into a dining room, their massed bodyguards all standing around them waiting for the one wrong look that would start a war, right there in the little room!

That was perhaps the only time Rev ever received a chewing out from his mother about what he was doing in the movement.

As far as the Reese case was concerned, a complaint filed with the Civilian Complaint Review Board was deemed "unsubstantiated," while the Firearms Discharge Review Board found the shooting to be in accordance with the guidelines of the Police Department. No indictments against Officer Bosco came from the grand jury, and a federal investigation found no wrongdoing by the police.

The Godfather

I thought I had seen God when I met Adam Clayton Powell. I knew I had seen God when I met James Brown.

— Rev

In 1973 Rev's search for a father figure to fill the void finally ended. That year (and under tragic circumstances) he met the perfect mentor.

Rev made the acquaintance of James Brown's son Teddy not long before the young man's tragic death in a car accident in upstate New York. Rev had occasionally chatted with Brown when they both lived in St. Albans. The Godfather made it a habit to give pep talks to the neighborhood kids.

Brown, an undisputed genius who is largely responsible for the development of modern popular music, was devastated by the loss of his son.

The bereaved father had risen from the direst Southern poverty to become the world's most influential performing artist of the latter half of the 20th century. The Godfather of Soul had had plenty of ups and downs throughout his long and illustrious career, being regularly victimized in the course of refining his art by vulturous record companies and concert promoters. He dealt with his personal tragedy the only way he knew — performing with all his heart and soul; he was trying to stifle the pain that seized hold of him whenever he stood still long enough to think about what had happened.

James needed someone to fill the void left by the sudden loss of his son, someone to whom he could pass on the wealth of knowledge he had accumulated during his amazing career, and who in turn would care for him and help him to carry on.

For Rev, the Godfather was not only the most commanding stage presence of the day, but someone who was putting out a vital message across the jagged edges of that funky beat:

"Say it Loud! I'm Black and I'm Proud!"

The fateful day came in 1973, when Rev journeyed across the Hudson River to Newark Symphony Hall, where the Godfather was performing and was introduced to the legend by a disc jockey who was a mutual friend.

Practically on the spot, the Godfather pledged his support for the fledgling youth movement. And he had some advice as well.

"Reverend, you gotta go for the hog," he drawled. Enraptured by his first meeting with the legend, Rev didn't bother to ask just what he meant; only later did he learn that the Godfather was referring to big money. Rev and Ellis Fleming, an African American businessman and board member of the National Youth Movement, continued chatting backstage.

James came back to make the final preparations for his appearance — and the three men kept talking, the two visitors so lost in the conversation that they were oblivious to their surroundings.

Then James walked out onto the stage to start the show, and it was only the sound of a screaming crowd roaring a collective YAAAH! which made Rev realize that they had all walked out onto the stage together!

James grabbed the mike and launched right into his act, becoming a gyrating blur in front of them as he began singing his opening number. Rev looked at Fleming, Fleming looked at Rev, and they broke into a dance, slowly shimmying their way off the stage; their very brief career as background dancers for James Brown ended as quickly as it had started.

For the first 18 years of his life, nothing Rev did was ordinary, so it was not to be expected that his first meeting with James Brown would be any different.

Soon enough, Rev was hanging with James the way he had with Adam and Jesse before him. James promised to do some benefit shows for the youth movement at the Albee Theater (now the Albee Mall) in Brooklyn. They sold out two shows before an audience of 8,000 kids.

Rev invited all of the Black nationalist establishment (Rev called Sonny Carson, whose documentary "The Education of Sonny Carson" was being filmed, onto the stage), and presented James with a huge painting as a gift.

James looked out at the packed crowd the Rev had brought in and said, "Rev, you do what I say and I'm going to take you around the country with me."

Rev was not aware that this larger-than-life American hero who had launched the careers of so many other artists was having trouble selling out his own shows. James' refusal to be ripped off by the big money men of the entertainment world had earned him a bad reputation among promoters and producers. For James, the organizing skill that he saw in this young preacher/activist was like a breath of fresh air.

The night of the benefit, James Brown and Reverend Al Sharpton became father and son. It had been love at first sight, combined with a deep mutual respect and mutual need. As James promised, he took Rev around the country with him; they started that very next week with a trip to California for a taping of "Soul Train."

Everywhere they went, Rev tried to launch a chapter of the youth movement using the contacts — primarily local disk jockeys and organizers — supplied to him by James.

They spent the better part of the year traveling together. It was during that tour that James asked the young preacher to promise that he would wear his hair in the famous Brown fashion for as long as the singer was alive.

Back in New York, James posed a harder challenge. The message in Brown's artistic work, from "Say it Loud" through to the 1974 hit "Funky President", was the same one that Adam Clayton Powell had put out 40 years earlier when he marched on City Hall and other bastions of authority with "the people of the streets, the failures, the misfits, the despised, the maimed, the beaten, the sightless and the voiceless."

"We gotta do it for ourselves," James would say. Madison Square Garden had been less than eager to book the Godfather — they were worried about "rowdy" crowds. Brown knew the boy preacher's reputation as a master of the time-honored civil rights tactic of the boycott, learned from Reverend Jesse Jackson. And he knew Breadbasket's reputation for applying pressure on the corporate world where it could hurt — their pocketbooks.

"Go rent the Garden and don't tell them who you got," the Godfather instructed his "son."

"$60,000," the Garden's management told Rev.

"I know," Rev replied.

"Have $20,000 here in 30 days."

Rev was back in 20 days, with the $20,000. Back home, Brown was ecstatic. "The kid did it!"

Well, not quite yet. Forty thousand dollars more was due in 30 days, and then would come the real test. When Rev arrived at the Garden offices with a check for the balance in hand, the inevitable question came. "Who's your act?"

"James Brown," he said.

"Sorry, no deal," was the retort. Rowdy crowds, and all that.

The young Rev took a deep breath, his boyish face stern as he stared at the seasoned pros. "You took my $20,000, and my $40,000, and I got a contract. You got to let him play, or I'm going to boycott and disrupt every New York Knicks game!"

The James Brown July 4, 1974 date at Madison Square Garden was a sellout.

For the rest of the decade, wherever James went, Rev went. It was a hectic time on and off the road.

Like Jesse Jackson, Rev continued to expand his base of business contacts in the worlds of entertainment, sports and other enterprises where the African American community supplied the profit margin and often got little or nothing in return for their ticket money except a show and rough handling by security guards. He lived the same apparently dual life he had led since his teenage years, rubbing elbows with some of the biggest movers and shakers in the country (as either their friend or foe) while maintaining his contact with the folks on the street whom he had vowed never to leave.

And he became immersed in the world of politics, making his share of allies and enemies.

In 1978 Rev's old friend Shirley Chisholm leaned on him to go up against Brooklyn State Senator Major Owens, now a member of the US House of Representatives.

Chisholm at the time was in a coalition with longtime Brooklyn political operative Sam Wright. To his enemies, Councilman Wright was a "poverty pimp" who controlled a patronage machine and a multi-million dollar anti-poverty program empire. To his friends, he was, well, probably the same thing.

Political machines stay in place by supplying goods to their constituents (that is, the fraction of them who vote). Some machine operators are called "reformers," which means that they are not attached to the corrupt machine currently in place. Until they get in, that is, and become the "regulars."

This is not to deny that there are maverick politicians who are actually committed to serving the community and not the powers-that-be. Or that there are Adam Clayton Powells seated in Washington (although they only seem to come along every 50 years or so). We are speaking here of the normal machinery of American electoral politics.

Rev remembered Adam's advice: you have to deal with whoever is there.

But almost as soon as Rev was asked to run against Owens, he received a call from his potential opponent. Owens the reformer denies having asked Rev to abandon the challenge, and having offered him a job in return for the favor.

Regular Sam Wright supplied Rev with a tape recorder hidden in a briefcase to have any such offers preserved for posterity (not to mention publicity). But technical difficulties denied him the opportunity he hoped for.

As it turned out, Owens had other ways of blocking the challenge; in the course of the campaign, Rev hadn't managed to get his voting address straight (the consequence of complications stemming from a very brief marriage, which had been annulled back in 1972). The reformer promptly took Rev to court and had him tossed from the ballot, a time-honored technique of regulars and reformers alike.

•

By this time, control of New York City's political machinery had passed into the hands of an ex-reformer, former East Side Congressman Edward I. Koch.

In 1977 Koch was appointed manager of a city which had been taken over two years earlier by New York's financial elite in a political sleight of hand under cover of the city's "fiscal crisis."

Like the international "oil crisis" of the same period, the Big Apple's fiscal crisis was an immense conspiracy contrived by Big Money to seize direct control of New York, eliminating whatever semblance of democracy existed. Like the rest of the planet's finances, New York's had been operated at a deficit, borrowing what was needed to make it through the week and paying off debt service to a consortium of banks.

No doubt inspired by the success of the 1973 oil shortage hoax, in 1975 the banks pulled New York City's credit out from under it, refusing to lend it any more money. The city was thrown into near default, paving the way for the banks to take direct control in the form of the so-called "Emergency Financial Control Board," i.e., the banks themselves.

The blame, of course, was laid upon Adam Clayton Powell's "people of the streets, the failures, the misfits, the despised, the maimed, the beaten, the sightless and the voiceless." In 1975, that meant the millions who lived in New York's impoverished Black and Latino communities, accused by the powers-that-be of mooching all the city's resources and driving out the white middle class "tax base." It was nonsense, of course; the city's failure (rooted in systemic, institutionalized, official corruption) to provide opportunities for "the people of the streets" to lead a decent life was what prevented the tax base from expanding.

Ed Koch promised them he would fix all that, and immediately began — two years before the advent of "Reaganomics" — to dismantle New York's already inadequate support systems for the masses of the poor, as well as institutionalizing a racialistic attitude in city government that effectively declared an open season on poor people of color.

In the coming decade, Ed Koch established himself as the spokesperson for New York's version of the new world order to come. Meanwhile, out on the streets, the voiceless millions watched helplessly as vital services were cut, police shot to kill without fear of retribution, and the city's white enclaves put up barricades around their turf.

It was a stark enactment of class warfare, except that in New York City circa 1977 the war was one-sided, with Koch and the bankers reigning supreme. Over 10 devastating years would pass before an uprising on the streets, with Reverend Al Sharpton among those leading it, defeated Koch. For now, the city lay barren and lifeless.

Rev was no longer a kid. After graduating from Tilden in 1972 he had attended Brooklyn College as a political science major for two years, but his outside activities drew him from the classroom. Splitting his time between his youth movement work and his increasing responsibilities with the Godfather, Rev surveyed the New York scene. He remembered that Jesse had expanded beyond Breadbasket's economic program and immersed himself in the brutal world of Chicago politics, doing battle head to head with the hitherto unchallenged "Boss," Richard Daley.

Rev went into action. Soon after Koch assumed office, the National Youth Movement took over the city's Department of Manpower, then headed by reformer Stanley Breznoff, a longtime administrator of the city's welfare bureaucracy. Demanding more summer jobs for Black youth, Rev and the kids and a group of ministers sat in at Breznoff's office demanding a meeting with the mayor.

Koch refused the group's request that he push the feds for more money for the kids. Rev countered that the mayor had apparently had no problem challenging Jimmy Carter around his support for Israel (Koch had just embarrassed the Georgia Democrat by handing him a letter on the subject in the course of a Presidential visit).

"What about a letter asking for more jobs for the youth of the city?" Rev urged.

"No," said the mayor.

"Then we're not leaving the room."

Reverend Al Sharpton's first arrest as an activist came after Ed Koch called the cops on him. The battle lines of the coming decade had been drawn.

•

Soon after the arrest Minister Louis Farrakhan, who had just begun his mission of rebuilding the Nation of Islam which had fractured after the death of Elijah Muhammad, came into town for a speaking engagement at the Baruch College campus of the City University of New York.

Farrakhan came to Brooklyn the night of Rev's arrest to speak on his behalf and on behalf of the three other ministers who were briefly jailed. Staying with a niece in the Madison Square Garden area, Farrakhan was escorted around town by Rev for a few days.

Stripped by Elijah's son Wallace Muhammad of any authority, in these difficult times Farrakhan spent the week with Rev accompanied only by a solitary bodyguard. As he prepared to leave, he turned to Rev with gratitude in his eyes.

"Brother, I want to thank you for driving me around," he said solemnly. "These are dangerous times — some of Wallace Muhummad's followers want to kill me. You were risking your life driving around with me. I didn't want to tell you, but I felt I had to."

Rev, equally serious, turned to the minister. "Well, I got something I have to tell *you* that I didn't want to tell you."

"What's that, Brother Sharpton?"

"I've been driving you around and I don't have a driver's license!" Both ministers broke out laughing, and headed off on their separate ways.

●

Through it all was life on the road with James, seeing the country and the world. James' trip out to Zaire in Central Africa for a show the night before the "Rumble in the Jungle" between Muhammad Ali and George Foreman introduced him to Black fight promoter Don King, thereby extending Rev's contacts to one of the few professions that might be even shadier than the entertainment business: professional boxing.

A complex and unpredictable figure, Don King became another of Rev's supporters in the early years of the Youth Movement. As a Black ex-con, King already had two strikes against him when he entered the white-run world of boxing promotion in the 1960s.

Rev had first come to King's aid in 1975, when Muhammad Ali changed promoters to fight Ken Norton at Yankee Stadium. When Ali signed with Bob Arum, King's white nemesis, it was a devastating blow to the Black promoters who were finally beginning to wrest control of Black boxers from a white corporate world which would put nothing back into the Black community except the battered bodies of fighters once they were no longer usable.

To Rev, the Ali-Arum contract was an opportunity to make a point to Black celebrities and entrepreneurs: they needed to be reminded, they needed to be *pressured*, to "remember" their communities, which were after all the ultimate source of their earnings. Reverend Al Sharpton, known to all in the Black business community for his organizing skills, could be helpful in their struggles in a hostile white business world. And they could help him build the National Youth Movement.

Rev struck back at the corporate sports establishment and blasted Ali for leaving King. He led a sit-in at the Garden, and took over Madison Square Garden president Michael Burke's office. Rev negotiated a deal for closed circuit TV contracts for Black promoters, and Ali soon returned to King.

Alfred Sharpton, Jr., 1955.

With sister Cheryl, c. 1957 (top left).

Wonder Boy Preacher, age 7 (bottom left).

With nephew Kenny at home in East Flatbush, Thanksgiving, 1969 (top right).

The National Youth Movement president, 1975. At left is Adam Clayton Powelll III; at right is Chicago youth organizer Dwight McKee (bottom right).

101

Preaching at Washington
Temple Baptist Church,
age 22.

At the White House with the
Godfather, 1981
(opposite page).

With Adrienne and James Brown and Muhammad Ali (top left).

With Ali and Donald Trump (bottom left).

Clowning with Donald Trump and Don King (top right).

Giving out Christmas turkeys with Don King, Charles Rangel and David Dinkins (bottom right).

Brooklyn Courthouse, December 22, 1987, the morning after
the Day of Outrage (above).

Preparing to lead thousands through Howard Beach after murder
of Michael Griffith, December 27, 1986 (top right).

The beginnings of a coalition, with Reverend Saul Williams of
Newburgh, New York and Minister Louis Farrakhan, December
1987 (bottom right).

At the Democratic National Convention with Tawana Brawley
and Alton Maddox, Jr., 1988 (top left).

Marching in Albany, New York with singer Pete Seeger,
Alton Maddox, Jr. and C. Vernon Mason on the anniversary of
Dr. King's death, April 4, 1988 (bottom left).

Facing the press with Moses Stewart and Diane Hawkins (above).

Into Bensonhurst with C. Vernon Mason, Kathy Jordan Sharpton, Alton Maddox, Jr., Diane Hawkins and Moses Stewart, May 13, 1990 (top left).

Teaneck, New Jersey, April 1990 (bottom left).

Dr. King's birthday in Bensonhurst, with Moses Stewart, Alton Maddox, Jr. and Dr. Fred Newman, January 1990 (top right).

Bensonhurst, January 12, 1991 (bottom right).

Celebrating acquittal with Alton Maddox, Jr. and
Reverend William C. Jones, July 2, 1990 (top left).

With Forgotten Youth of Atlantic City, July 1990 (bottom left).

At the African American Day Parade, 1990, with
Dr. Lenora Fulani and Moses Stewart (above).

With Betty Shabazz, Kathy, Reverend Jesse Jackson, Ashley and Dominique (above).

Kathy Jordan Sharpton (top right).

Backstage in Hollywood for the Godfather's triumphal return, with MC Hammer and Adrienne Brown, June 1991 (bottom right).

The seizure of Liberty Island, New York, August 28, 1990.

PART II

We told y'all we were coming! We told you we were going to tell the nation about the way you were treating us! Your tourists are now going to ask you, what is going on? City of New York, here we are! Tell the world! No Justice! No Peace!

— **Rev at LaGuardia Airport, January 27, 1988, before his arrest for blocking an entrance ramp**

NINE

"The new Black leader of the '80s"

In 1980 Rev got a call from James suggesting that they do a gospel/rap record. Rap was yet another of the genres invented by the Godfather, even though the credit goes to such pioneers as Harlem's Sugar Hill Gang, whose 1980 "Rappers' Delight" was the first mass hit for the music born on the streets of the ghetto. But James had been rapping for years on and off the stage, his 1970s "Brother Rap" and "King Heroin" being just a part of the documentary evidence.

Rev flew south to attend the annual disc jockeys' convention sponsored by Jack the Rapper; while he was there, he and James went into the studio and laid down "God Has Smiled On Me," with James on vocals and Rev preaching.

As they were cutting the record, misfortune struck. James' manager Hal Garner, with whom Rev was staying at the Holiday Inn, suffered a heart attack. After he left the hospital, Garner headed to Atlanta and never returned.

As he almost always did when things got tough, James turned to Rev for help.

"Reverend, I need you to stay on the road with me now," the Godfather told his young friend. "I don't trust no one else but you counting my money."

119

And as he almost always did when James came to him, Rev agreed. Thus began a two-year, full time sojourn with James that would take Rev on the road to both the White House and marriage.

•

You can be up to your boobies in white satin, with gardenias in your hair and no sugar cane for miles, but you can still be working on a plantation.

— **Billie Holiday, in her autobiography**
Lady Sings the Blues

Rev was working overtime getting club bookings for the Godfather, whose career had taken a downcurve after yet another bad experience with yet another record company. James was at the height of his creative powers, blazing new paths in the music that would become known as funk and launching dozens of talented young musicians on often lucrative careers.

But the music business cared little for such things as artistic genius; James had the inconvenient habit of demanding what was his, and the industry responded by making his career as difficult as possible. Rev worked heartbroken at times, seeing what James had to go through; he did everything possible to make things go smoothly for his and the world's Godfather. The band often traveled by bus while Rev and James went alone by plane, carrying all their luggage with them. Rev leaned on every contact he could think of, from Don King to Black record company execs, to come up with the cash for airline tickets for the two of them so the traveling expenses wouldn't have to come out of James' pocket.

But even if they were dog days, it didn't keep the James Brown crew from stopping at the White House.

Soon after the 1980 election of Ronald Reagan, Rev came to James with an idea.

James had known a Republican honcho, the late Lee Atwater (much to Rev's chagrin, James marked himself down for the "party of Lincoln" on his voter registration card), who had worked for another of James' political acquaintances, South Carolina Senator Strom Thurmond.

"Mr. Brown, you remember Lee Atwater? He's working in the White

House now on Vice President George Bush's staff." James was happy for his old friend; Rev continued with his plan.

"Mr. Brown, we ought to try to get you an appointment with President Reagan and Vice President Bush, to explain to them the importance of a Martin Luther King holiday."

"Try to set it up, Reverend," James said.

Rev sent off a telegram to the White House, and within a week they got a call back saying that on January 15 — Dr. King's birthday — the White House would receive Mr. Brown and Reverend Sharpton.

Off they flew to Washington, airline tickets paid for courtesy of Don King, and checked into a hotel. The next morning at 8 AM they met with Atwater at the White House over breakfast. Atwater took them over to meet with Vice President Bush for an hour and a photo opportunity. Then James met privately, sans Rev, with the new President for a bit, after which Rev and James held a joint press conference. They told the White House press corps what they had said to the President and Vice President about the importance of Dr. King's birthday.

Despite the constant pressures and the grueling schedule, by 1981 things were looking up for Rev. Working out of James' Augusta office, the 25-year-old former boy preacher was practically running James' business while preaching locally in Georgia and South Carolina. One crusade in Waynesboro, Georgia had drawn thousands.

•

But Rev was also getting homesick. It was partially a longing to settle down with Kathy Jordan, the stunning back-up vocalist for James with whom Rev had spent much of his time since they first met.

Near the end of the '70s James, who had fired one of his back-up singers, was searching for a replacement. In New York for a gig, he enlisted Rev's help.

"Reverend, the guitar player [Ronald Laston] has a friend, grew up in Niagara Falls with him, a church girl. Maybe we should hire her. You interview her and see if she's any good."

"Interview her and see if she's any good?! I don't know nothing about singers!"

"Just see if she's a decent girl — *I'll* judge her singing."

James was playing a gig at My Father's Place, a trendy club in Roslyn, Long Island. Rev interviewed Jordan before the show and reported back to JB. "She seems nice, don't seem wild." James ran a disciplined ship, and these were essential qualities.

"OK, tell her to sing background offstage tonight at My Father's Place."

The show opened as usual with the band warming up the crowd; one background singer was onstage, and Kathy sang offstage. James hit; after two or three songs he danced to the back, where Kathy was behind the curtain.

"You're hired."

Rev didn't see Kathy for a while after that — she was off to Europe with JB on tour. Their next meeting was in Augusta, when the band came through. Kathy and Rev struck up a conversation; soon he was calling her "Church Girl." Then dating her. They've been together ever since.

•

But settling down wasn't the only reason that Rev wanted to go back north. There was trouble at home in New York, in Bed-Stuy and other communities. And it was escalating. Eleanor Bumpurs, a 67-year-old Bronx grandmother, had not yet been murdered by police who came to enforce an eviction notice; Michael Griffith had not yet been beaten to death by a dozen white cops; and Bernhard Goetz hadn't yet shot down four Black teenagers in a subway car. But these things would happen soon, and many similar atrocities were already occurring daily although without the front-page headlines that would accompany such cases later on. There was work to do. The Adam Clayton Powell portion of Al Sharpton's soul was tugging away at the part that had been shaped by James Brown.

Rev's chance to leave came — like most things that came to him — as a result of his successful organizing. Rev and Kathy and the rest of the JB crew were in California; the call of the streets echoed in Rev's ears during his weekly conversations with the Reverend Lawrence Harvey, who was running the day-to-day operations of the Youth Movement back in Brooklyn.

Out in California, James noticed a makeup artist who was doing makeup for Kathy and Martha High, another back-up singer. "That woman's kinda cute," said James in his scratchy South Carolina drawl. "See if you can get her phone number," Rev was instructed.

"I don't mind giving you my answering service number, but you should know that I am no groupie," the makeup artist, whose show business name was Alfie Rodriguez, told Rev.

James called and spoke to her, and was only able to secure a date by agreeing that Kathy and Rev would come along. A double dinner date, with a respectable clergyman present, would be just fine.

Which started the ball rolling for James and the future Mrs. Brown. Dates became courtship, and eventually marriage. Adrienne ("Alfie") was not only a skilled makeup artist, but knew the production and management ropes as well. As soon as she moved into James' South Carolina home, Rev saw his opportunity. James had stood by him from the time when he was an unknown teenager, and Rev would not leave him until he knew that James had someone who could look out for him. Adrienne was that person.

"I'm going to New York. I want to build the Youth Movement," Rev told Kathy, explaining that they would see each other on the road and be married eventually. He quickly packed his bags and went to sleep, not waiting for a response. He awoke the next morning to find Kathy's bags packed. "What time are we leaving?" she asked.

They called "Mr. Brown" from New York to explain, knowing that to announce their intentions in person would have been fruitless. James was certainly not going to let them leave. But Rev would keep his promise — never to change his hairstyle as long as James was on this earth.

Rev had been all around the world with James, even to the White House. And on Tom Snyder's NBC evening show, James and Muhammad Ali had introduced Rev as "the new Black leader for the '80s." To many, these were just more crazy words from two of America's most "far out" African American celebrities. But like much of what these two have said, the words turned out to be prophetic.

The Reverend Al Sharpton was never one to ignore prophecy.

•

Back in New York, Rev threw himself full force into the National Youth Movement. He was a whirlwind, sitting on subway tracks to protest racism at the Metropolitan Transit Authority, jumping up on the desk of the schools chancellor during the battle for a minority appointee to that post, marching on City Hall, going everywhere and anywhere noise had to be made.

Rev didn't just make noise. He brought out the people. Like Adam and Martin and Jesse before him, Rev knew that he must bring out the "despised, the voiceless, the people of the streets" to press their case, defiantly and non-violently. In America circa 1981, the despised and voiceless were, more and more, the Black youth who were the first generation to grow up without a dream — the dream that also died when the assassin's bullet cut down America's last great hope, the Reverend Dr. Martin Luther King.

Rev and Kathy stayed with some friends for a while, and then with Ada for a while more. They finally found an apartment on Vanderbilt Avenue in the Flatbush section of Brooklyn, where they eventually married and had their children.

Rev and Kathy still spoke to James nearly every day, doing their best to dodge the Godfather's attempts to convince them to come back. Rev geared the Youth Movement back up, moving it into St. Mary's Hospital in Brooklyn, where they had a room that served as an administrative office with access to a conference area which could seat 300.

Rev initiated the organization's Saturday morning rallies, hired a staff and then dived into the first issue that the National Youth Movement would take on after his return: the battle for a Black schools chancellor to preside over New York City's overwhelmingly Black and Latino education system.

Arthur Bramwell, a Republican district leader in Brooklyn who was a member of the board of the Youth Movement, joined Rev in the battle alongside Dr. Lenora Fulani, later to become the chairperson of the independent New Alliance Party (which in 1980 had initiated, along with the Black United Front, the eventually successful "Dump Koch" movement).

Rev dived into the fight with what was, even for him, uncharacteristic flamboyance. It was a new stage in the development of his mature organizing.

Their efforts paid off; Rev's unique brand of showmanship-activism made the issue hot enough so that the city's Black political establishment was able to push through the nomination of an African American candidate, Thomas Minter.

Rev himself never spoke about Minter as a candidate; his role was to get enough attention focused on the basic fact that 75% of the schoolchildren in the city were kids of color, and so should the chancellor be.

Things reached a head one night as the nomination of Robert F. Wagner, a Koch buddy, approached. Rev made the evening news and the morning headlines when he leapt up on the desk of the president of the board of education to prevent Wagner's nomination. Negotiations ensued for a compromise candidate, Latino educator Anthony Alvarado, who eventually won. It was Rev's first major victory of the '80s, which the *New York Times* only grudgingly acknowledged in a profile following his 1991 near-assassination.

TEN

Trials and Tribulations: The Funding of a Movement

Fast forward: June 1990: It's weeks into the trial at the cavernous, windowless courtroom at 111 Centre Street in lower Manhattan. Weeks without daylight. New York State Attorney General Robert Abrams' multi-million dollar paper chase had resulted in a massive 67-count indictment against the Reverend Alfred C. Sharpton. As the city begins to warm itself, Rev is reluctantly accepting the fact that he will spend this spring — at least the daylight hours — locked away from the streets that he loves.

Across the East River the Bensonhurst trials are underway, and the Rev is sorely needed; from the start, Brooklyn District Attorney Charles "Joe" Hynes' case against the dozens of killers of Yusuf Hawkins has been badly botched. Only seven of the killers have even been indicted, and the street heat that had been so effectively applied around the clock in the Howard Beach case, the heat that kept then-special prosecutor Hynes on the case two years earlier, is now generated only on the weekends, when the fraud trial is adjourned. "Innocent until proven guilty" notwithstanding, Rev may be free on bail but he's a nine-to-five prisoner of this case, as is his attorney and friend Alton Maddox, Jr., who like Rev has traded in his protest outfit for a dark business suit.

In the courtroom lead prosecutor Victor Genecin is trying to make the case that Rev is little more than a common street thief. He constantly refers to the

126

mountains of paper, neatly numbered, ordered and bound, lined up side by side on the prosecution side of the well.

The paperwork is supposed to be the documentary evidence for the charges that Rev engineered the theft of money and other "instruments" from some of America's biggest corporate powerhouses, including Donald Trump. According to Genecin, the greedy, seedy Reverend didn't stop there; Rev's alleged victims included even Don King, who has been accused of many things — but never of being a sucker.

How does the state plan to prove such a case?

Genecin has charged that Rev received, on behalf of the National Youth Movement, $250,000 in donations he had solicited from dozens of individuals and corporations. That was no secret — many of the contributions were given at gala affairs. The state argues that the National Youth Movement was merely a paper organization created by Rev as a vehicle to feed an insatiable wallet and ego. Therefore, according to the State of New York, any money received by Rev through the Youth Movement amounted to theft.

Bobby Abrams assembled dozens of counts charging grand larceny, schemes to defraud, and falsifying business records without a single complaint ever being lodged by any of the alleged victims; in fact, none of the contributors claimed they were robbed even after the indictments had been handed down! Only Robert Abrams saw a crime.

•

Somewhere into the second week of the trial, a revelation begins to sweep through the courtroom.

It's a simple discovery, but one that is lost through the first week of accusations and counter-accusations. From the first hints of an investigation Rev and his supporters have charged that Abrams' case is a massive conspiracy, a vendetta against a civil rights leader who challenged the state's political and law enforcement establishment. But there is more.

The angry whispers started almost simultaneously in different parts of the courtroom. "They just can't stand to see a Black man make money!" As the prosecution's case drones on, and the political oratory fades, another aspect of the case becomes clearer. It predates Al Sharpton and his nemesis Robert

Abrams. Its impact begins to be felt as soon as the preliminary yelling quiets down. The stench of racism — raw, ugly and deep-rooted — fills the room. The participants in the spectacle at 111 Centre Street settle uncomfortably onto their benches for the long haul.

Funding a movement

What disappeared along with the promise of a better life for the despised and the voiceless that the Great Society was supposed to bring was a cornerstone of the movement of the '60s — the support of the white, liberal establishment, i.e., money. Traditional liberal dollars were not available to a National Youth Movement.

In one odd respect Robert Abrams and his assistant prosecutor Genecin were right. The National Youth Movement was *not* traditional, *not* legitimate. It was a movement of Black youth, desperately poor, often hungry, often in "trouble," beautiful and ugly, joyously creative and painfully hardened, cynical, brutal and brutalized. It cost money for them to be heard.

The key was the network of contacts that Rev had made in his years with James, the Black business figures around the country who formed a tight-knit grouping that, despite occasional internal quarrels, always maintained the cohesion necessary to survive in a hostile white corporate world.

Aware of Rev's successes in cases like Ali's defection to Arum, Black promoters came to Rev for help when a number of Black artists who were becoming super-rich superstars by "crossing over" into the white pop market were, at the same time, dropping local Black promoters from their tours.

It was right up Rev's alley, what with his training from the Breadbasket days.

"This is nothing but business apartheid," Rev said, springing into action. He held a press conference in Philadelphia to demand that Black entertainers work with Black concert promoters, and soon Tina Turner and Lionel Richie were hiring Black again. When Whitney Houston did a Carnegie Hall date for white promoter Ron Delsener, Rev led a picket outside; he christened the crossover superstar "Whitey Houston."

But while business was picking up for the promoters, the National Youth Movement — more and more immersed in struggles in the Black community — was having trouble meeting payroll and staying afloat.

Then along came the biggest crossover of them all: Michael Jackson, and the Jackson Victory Tour.

Don King was originally set to handle the tour, and Rev gave him the rap about looking out for the Black promoters. But soon King found himself muscled out by promoter Chuck Sullivan, who bought the tour from the Jacksons and didn't want King in.

King and Rev teamed up, using a press conference to advise the Jacksons that they needed to hire local promoters and that King needed to return to the tour. If not, they could expect to see Reverend Al Sharpton jumping up on stage at every show.

Sullivan contacted Rev to work out a solution. While still in negotiations, Rev called a press conference to *defend* the Jacksons against media accusations that they had been overcharging for tickets. It was one thing to be in negotiations, but Rev was not going to allow the Jacksons to be held up to a racist double standard. "You would not be saying this about Bruce Springsteen," Rev told the media.

This statement in the midst of the heated negotiations impressed Michael, and he kept it in mind at the big meeting in Kansas City right before "Victory" was scheduled to start. The hours before the first date of the monster tour, which promised to net millions, were ticking away as Michael, Marlon, Tito — *all* the Jacksons (who were not just an act but a corporation) — gathered in the lush Kansas City hotel suite. It was time for final negotiations, final offers, final concessions, and prayers.

"If we bring in the local promoters, what will it do to enhance the tour? Why do we need them? We're hot." This from a Jackson attorney, arrogant, dismissive.

Rev explained. "You're hot, alright, but this is a 'victory' tour. Whose victory is it? It's really the Black kids in the ghetto who bought the Jacksons' records since they were little kids in Gary, Indiana. They are the ones who made the victory because they're the ones who invested in the

Jacksons and believed. White kids never heard of the Jacksons until the last couple of years with the *Off the Wall* album. How could you turn your back on the people who made you when no one else believed in you?"

A slight crack in the granite. What should the Jacksons do?

"Each city should have the Black promoters form a 'pride patrol,' " replied Rev without missing a beat. "That way kids who believe in the Jacksons can tour the perimeters of the stadiums, telling people not to mug anybody. There's a problem with vandalism and muggings at concerts. Tell them don't vandalize the cars, that we're proud and let's show our best conduct. And the Jacksons can visit people in the hospitals, and go into the community and encourage kids to get a scholarship."

The seconds seem like days to Rev and the others in the room. Then, slowly, Michael Jackson raises himself up from the floor.

"I like that. I like what he's saying. We'll do it, but on one condition, Reverend," Michael said to Rev. "You've got to go with the tour because otherwise I don't believe the promoters will do it."

Rev found himself at the head of a four-person Jacksons Community Relations Team, with a half million dollar budget for a 43-city tour. It wasn't a lot of money for a tour that size; still, it was $10,000 per city slated — minus expenses for the team — to make its way back into the community, a community badly in need of whatever it could get. It was a small "victory."

Rev's operation actually ended up in debt, but he was satisfied. It was the first time the community had input into a major tour.

But the work was exhausting, tapping even the limits of the inexhaustible Rev. "Pride patrols" were formed in every city they visited; Rev received commendations back home in New York. In Chicago, local gang members were hired for the "pride patrols" (in an interesting twist, they were hired after applying a little Rev-style pressure of their own), and free tickets were given out to poor kids.

In Atlanta Rev defused a potential boycott of the tour by none other than Hosea Williams and the SCLC; Williams charged that tickets to hear the Jacksons were too high and the mega stars were too unappreciative of Black kids. Rev, who already had been through it all with the Jackson team, straightened *that* out quick.

Similar happenings occurred in Miami, where the Black community was battling a mayor who had just fired the Black city manager. Since the mayor was sponsoring the Jacksons' show, a boycott of the show was called there in retaliation against the mayor. Rev negotiated a solution: the city manager came to the show, thereby ending the boycott and paving the way for the Community Relations Team to do its thing there.

Few people, including the Jacksons' attorney Joel Katz, would dispute that every bit of the $500,000 was well spent. But just a few years later, Robert Abrams would look through the prism of white law enforcement and see half a million dollars under the control of Reverend Al Sharpton and charge theft. He turned a blind eye to the fact that Rev's business relationships helped finance a movement that otherwise would go unfunded.

Goetz

Rev arrived back home from the tour exhausted. Even while on the road with the Jacksons Community Relations Team, Rev — relying on his contacts from his James Brown days — was continuing to build a national framework for the Youth Movement.

Then one morning in December, the daily papers are splattered with the story of an anonymous subway gunman — white — who had shot four young kids — Black — on a train the night before.

Already, even before anyone knew the identity of the self-styled vigilante who had immediately fled the state, Bernhard Goetz was being hailed as a hero by the press and a frightening array of political forces. It was automatically assumed that the bloody shooting, which left one of the youths who was shot in the back permanently paralyzed, had been justified because the gunman was, no doubt, about to be mugged.

Sitting in the National Youth Movement offices that morning, Rev turned to one of his young staff members, Renato McCrae, who later went on to a singing career.

"I think this is wrong. How come everyone is going to convict these boys? At best they have a hard case to prove intent. It's racist to say because they're young Black kids he assumed they were muggers and he had a right to execute them."

Rev got hold of the family of Darryl Cabey, the paralyzed youth, and went as soon as he could to St. Vincent's Hospital in Greenwich Village to hold a press conference and prayer vigil for Darryl. It was the start of the media's peculiar romance with the Reverend Al Sharpton.

The press insisted that Rev's actions were nothing short of scandalous — the prayer vigils in front of St. Vincent's Hospital for Darryl; the marches in front of Goetz' apartment building on 14th Street on the edge of Greenwich Village; the repeated demands that America's new hero be indicted.

Goetz got off on the first grand jury probe; Rev demanded a new one. He started marching on the Manhattan district attorney's office, and he met with the then-United States Attorney, Rudolph Giuliani, to demand that Goetz be brought up on charges of violating the civil rights of the four young men.

The case began to get national and international coverage, enough to expose that the public's perception of Goetz was extremely polarized. A second grand jury subsequently indicted the man who, far from being a simple all-American hero, was according to his acquaintances an unrepentant racist and quite, quite nuts. By the following year the pressure Rev put on the authorities sent Goetz, much to his surprise, off to trial.

The media flurry soon turned into an all-out blitz. In the wake of it Rev's relationship to the New Alliance Party's Fulani grew tighter as she began fielding troops alongside those of the National Youth Movement.

Through it all was the historic Presidential run of Rev's last mentor, Reverend Jesse Jackson; Rev did his part the best way he knew how, encouraging the other famous Jacksons to help the man who was leading an insurrection within the Democratic Party which he called (summoning forth the memory of Fred Hampton's murdered dream) the Rainbow Coalition.

Although Rev was thrilled by Jesse's groundbreaking Presidential run in 1984, he found the New York City mayoral candidacy of Black State

Assemblyman Herman "Denny" Farrell the following year nothing to write home about.

Farrell, a long-time Harlem-based cog in the Democratic Party machine, was widely regarded as a "front" for Governor Mario Cuomo, who was eager to let the national party people know that he had the burgeoning "Dump Koch" movement simmering on the streets of the city under control. Earlier that year, an anti-Koch coalition had formed to unite against the evil mayor. The grouping was all but ready to select Puerto Rican politico Herman Badillo, a former deputy mayor, as its unity candidate when Farrell barged in at the 11th hour to announce his candidacy. The cagey governor had hoped to take the wind out of the Dump Koch movement's sails by throwing Farrell — a well-behaved and congenial hack, who on his best days managed to be mediocre — into the ring. The ploy succeeded.

Rev went after Farrell repeatedly, slamming him in the media for his failure to take a stand against Goetz.

Also on the ballot that year was a transportation bond issue — Proposition One — which Rev said was racist because once again the Black community was left out of the plans to rebuild the subways.

"We need to demand Blacks on the MTA board, just like we fought for a Black schools chancellor," Rev told his troops. He took out ads in the Black press opposing Proposition One, a move which turned out to be his first direct clash with darling-of-the-liberal-establishment Mario Cuomo.

"If Cuomo doesn't put a Black on the MTA board, I'm going to sit on the subway tracks," Rev warned. The governor dodged Rev's requests for a meeting until Rev showed up early one morning at Grand Central Station with 100 kids from the Youth Movement and hopped onto the tracks.

Rev rallied Black City Council members Mary Pinkett, Enoch Williams, Archie Spigner and Wendell Foster to back his call for more Black representation on the transit board at a City Hall press conference. Cuomo agreed to meet.

Rev arrived at the meeting with Foster, Spigner and Williams, Sylvester Leaks from the Youth Movement, Casper Yasper, an associate of Congressman Charles Rangel, and State Senator Vander Beatty.

Before Rev could speak Foster, an ordained minister, piped up. "Governor," said the Bronx legislator. "I want you to understand that my role here is to get you and Reverend Sharpton together. I had nothing to do with his sitting on the subway tracks!"

Rev was flabbergasted! He had been double-crossed, right there at the bargaining table!

But Rev, remaining cool, went after Cuomo like gangbusters; he charged the board with practicing apartheid and argued for hours. As the meeting wound down, Cuomo gave Rev instructions. "There's a room full of press out there. You can tell them you met with me and that I've agreed to increase Black representation on the board. You got your meeting."

"Oh, no," Rev responded, calling the governor's bluff. "*You* go out there with me and tell them." Shortly afterwards, Mario Cuomo was standing by the governor's seal, next to Al Sharpton and a crew of councilmembers jockeying for a photo opportunity.

Cuomo made the announcement, and soon afterward formed a committee charged with finding Black reps for the board; the committee included Laura Blackburne of the NAACP and one Reverend Al Sharpton.

Something called crack

But as Rev continued the seemingly endless battle against racial violence and institutionalized segregation — what he called "apartheid," wherever he found it — he was discovering a new and vicious enemy that had mysteriously infiltrated an already devastated and desperate community.

Crack.

Rev was among the millions of Americans stunned by the death of a young basketball star, Len Bias, the victim of something new and deadly called "crack." Rev attended the funeral with Bishop Washington, and also brought along a record promoter named Bob Currington who had worked with Rev on the Jacksons' tour.

As they sat in a hotel room that night, an unnerved Rev turned to Currington.

"You know, Bob, we need to deal with this; we need to stop this crack epidemic if it's gonna kill people like Len Bias." Rev decided that night to channel his outrage into an all-out anti-crack drive.

Rev met the next morning with Jesse Jackson, who had spoken at Bias' funeral, and members of the Rainbow Coalition. Then he flew back to New York, and immediately called a meeting of the Youth Movement's staff.

"Starting this Saturday," Rev announced solemnly, "we're going to deal with the crack issue. We'll continue our voter registration work and agitation against Goetz and racism, but we must do something about the drug epidemic."

They began to wrestle in the staff meeting with ways to dramatize the problem. A shocked Rev listened as kids from the Youth Movement told him that the police in their communities were themselves involved in the drug trade.

Rev listened in amazement.

"The police ain't busting a lot of people even though they know where the crack houses are," they told him.

"Yeah, they get payoffs from the guys dealin' and some of them are even partners with the pushers!"

At the time Rev's office was still at the St. Mary's Hospital complex on Rochester and St. Marks Avenue in the 77th precinct, the heart of Bed-Stuy. Within a year, things would get so out of hand at the 77th (local drug dealers were coming down to the precinct to complain about cops ripping them off!) that the entire force of 200 plus was transferred, and a number of cops went to jail.

But the scandal of the 77th was yet to come. For now, Rev patiently began compiling the information on police involvement in the drug trade that the young folks were feeding him. He meticulously followed up all the information, checking every drug "spot" address the kids gave him.

Rev called his staff together again.

"OK, the way to bust this up is two-part. One, we need to get entertainers to go public and start popularizing the anti-crack message. Second, we need to go right to the point of confrontation like we did with Goetz, and like I did with the Black artists who wouldn't work for Black promoters."

"How are we going to do that?"

"We're going to the crack houses and I'm going to paint them with red paint to symbolize the bloodshed they're causing."

Everybody in the room thought not only that Rev had lost his mind, but that he stood to lose his behind in two days of painting crack houses.

Rev went on, unperturbed. "At next Saturday's rally we will march out and do it." The first week they did Brooklyn, the second week, Harlem — accompanied by Congressman Rangel, who headed up the House subcommittee on narcotics. Rev's friend Melba Moore joined as well. The third week they hit spots in Queens.

Needless to say, the crack house paintings brought national attention to the epidemic; by July, Rev was holding press conferences calling on stars to join the effort. An exhausted Rev was satisfied, for the moment, by having shown that crack was something more than the killer of a well-liked basketball star named Len Bias. One, it was the scourge of a whole community. Two, there were some people in high places and precincts who were looking the other way — and worse.

As he took kids out into the streets to paint the crack houses red, Rev discovered some disconcerting relationships between the supply of crack in the community and the local precinct.

Now Reverend Al Sharpton had a new enemy. As word of the investigation into the funny business at the 77th began to get around the precinct, death threats started coming in over the phone. Some held Rev and his little band of "crackbusters" responsible.

To the shock even of his staffers, Rev had taken the first list of crack houses he compiled and, with the cameras rolling, laid it on the doorstep of US Attorney Giuliani.

Meanwhile, the bills were piling up again. Renting buses. Carfare and expenses for the kids (Abrams' prosecutors would claim that Rev was "paying kids to come to rallies," a charge that many in the community and the jury found more laudable than criminal). Paint and paint cans. Salaries. Even limousines. Don King sent Mike Tyson to make anti-crack appearances but the champ needed limos. Melba Moore would do some spots, but Rev had to come up with transportation suitable for a star. Rev was forcing crack into the spotlight, but it was costing money.

So he came up with yet another brainstorm — a "War on Crack Celebrity Dinner." Bring out the stars for a benefit. For good measure, share some of the proceeds with an anti-drug program. Daytop Village was chosen, and received $6,000; Melba Moore headed up the star-studded guest list. At 111 Centre Street one day, jurors and spectators were treated to a toe-tapping videotape of the event, courtesy of the New York State Attorney General's office.

The funding for the dinner came in part from the earnings of Hit Bound, the brainchild of Black promoter William G. Garrison. In mid-1985 "WG" had proposed to Rev that the Youth Movement form a promotion company. Rev, using his contacts and organizing skills, would get the acts and record promotion deals. Kids would learn record promotion and marketing; they could get paid for going to their local record stores to set up promotional layouts and the like. Hit Bound's profits would be split 50-50 between Garrison and the Youth Movement.

But now, going over the piles of paper his investigators have gathered, Robert Abrams can only see more money going through Rev's hands. A Black man — one who had challenged his authority — making money. Forget why, forget on whose behalf. Robert Abrams sees a Black man making money and he sees a crime. But it will be left to the jury to decide Rev's guilt or innocence.

The "War on Crack Celebrity Dinner" was a stunning success. It was a scintillating affair, with Don King, Melba Moore, Freddie Jackson, Michael Spinks and more boxers than a pugilists' convention. Even Borough President Howard Golden was moved enough to proclaim the 23rd of September, 1986 "National Youth Movement Day in Brooklyn."

In addition to the $6,000 netted by Daytop Village, the Youth Movement took in another 10 G's or so. Rev would have been happy just to break even with all the risk involved in such a venture.

More importantly, the issue was now in the national consciousness. And Rev watched with a mixture of sadness and delight as hardened and innocent young folks, their futures uncertain, mingled with the greats at a place called the Waldorf-Astoria Hotel.

"Most of these kids ain't never even been to Manhattan," Rev thought to himself. "Now I got them at the Waldorf with the stars that *they* made into stars!"

Rev turned to some of the kids, and did his best to get a message across, something to build the self-confidence of children who every day were told in a thousand ways that they were worthless. "If Don King can do something positive after what he went through, so can you," Rev said.

As Rev left the dinner, he was approached by Randall Pinkston from Channel 2 News.

"Reverend, they just busted the police from the 77th precinct."

Rev hit the airwaves that night to tell the world that the Youth Movement knew it all along, but he was ecstatic anyway. Despite the irony of the bust coming the same night as the dinner, and the precinct being just a stone's throw from his office.

Rev went to his room to rest up a bit. The phone rang, and he reached over drowsily to grab it.

The voice at the other end killed any hope of putting aside the deadly seriousness of the issue at hand to catch a few winks.

"You will one day pay," said the voice. After doing a mental double take, a furious Rev made preparations for an early morning press conference in front of the 77th precinct house.

"They didn't get all of them," he announced angrily, and demanded a meeting with the head of the precinct. Rev went into the police station accompanied by Sylvester Leaks, the Reverend Jerry West, State Senator Marty Markowitz and several other community leaders, demanding that the whole hierarchy who had ignored his warnings be replaced.

"The community is under siege," he declared. "You can't trust the cops or the robbers."

Years later, after his honeymoon with the powers-that-be during his drug fighting days was over, Rev reflected on the police threat, and wrestled with the connections between his confrontation with a gang of dirty cops and the leaks to the press about his dealings with the FBI.

●

As the weeks ground on during Rev's 1990 trial, Melba Moore and Don King were among those who came out to the courtroom on Centre Street to support their friend and conscience. Melba remembered the dangerous treks through the crack-infested streets, with Rev never too busy to see to it that the kids ate and got home safely after the marches.

King remembered how Rev had stood by him after he was indicted on — and subsequently acquitted of — similar charges in an equally massive case.

King's trial got underway in 1985. The world-famous promoter, whose wild shock of hair and bizarre (and brilliant) personality were familiar on several continents, might have felt like a very lonely man had it not been for Rev and the National Youth Movement.

Every day for a solid seven weeks, Rev was in the lower Manhattan federal courtroom at Foley Square, backed up by a contingent of Youth Movement members. Those who had been the recipients, at one time or another, of King's support and largesse — folks like Benjamin Hooks, Coretta Scott King, and even Jesse Jackson — were conspicuously absent. The TV cameras caught Rev and Kathy walking out with a stoic King after he was arraigned.

Seven long weeks later, a triumphant King was acquitted on all 23 counts.

Between their two cases, these two mavericks had their share of escapades.

In 1987 Rev convinced King that he had made a mistake by letting a fight go down in Sun City. South Africa had lured a number of white and African American performers to lend de facto support to apartheid by their appearance. Not only should King apologize, Rev advised, but he should do something to help the anti-apartheid movement. Two groups that needed help were Randall Robinson's TransAfrica here in the US, and Oliver Tambo's African National Congress in South Africa.

King pledged $100,000 to TransAfrica, and early in 1987 King and Rev flew to Washington, DC for an announcement press conference with Congressman Bill Gray, Randall Robinson and tennis player Arthur Ashe.

Not long afterwards Tambo, leader of the ANC, came to the US. King and Rev went to Riverside Church in Harlem to hear him speak. The next morning Tambo was scheduled to address a record industry luncheon arranged and hosted by Rev and the National Youth Movement at the Parker Meridien Hotel, where he and King would call on the record industry to join them in producing a mega-concert against apartheid, with all the proceeds to go to the ANC. Tambo and Jesse Jackson were to be among the luncheon speakers.

Rev and King headed to the Berkshire Place Hotel that morning to pick Tambo up, while all the record industry big shots and media waited at the Parker Meridien for the announcement. Tambo's representative, the late Johnny Makatini, came down to the lobby with bad news. "He can't appear with Don King," Makatini said. "We've been told by the State Department to stay away from Don King."

"Oh, my God!" Rev exclaimed.

A compromise was proposed. Maybe Tambo should just appear with Rev, who was then the height of respectability. "That," thought Rev, "is crazy." But in the middle of it all, King let Makatini have it.

"You African Uncle Tom! How you gonna let the State Department of the United States tell you who to be with when you're here because you're fighting your own 'State Department' in South Africa!"

Makatini went upstairs, and returned shortly after with a disheveled, harried Oliver Tambo in tow, press conference-bound.

ELEVEN

Interlude:
Rev and the Feds

Rev's association with the FBI has been the subject of hundreds of thousands of words and countless miles of video footage. Although the relationship dates back to the early 1980s, it only mysteriously became an "issue" in 1988, at the time when Rev was recognized as the leader of an independent, grassroots upsurge that had grown in the wake of Howard Beach and, most significantly, when Rev had entered into a coalition with leaders of the "militant" nationalist movement — which, by their own admission, had been riddled with police infiltration.

Rev's relationship to the feds was a complicated one; part entrapment (a forced cooperation growing out of Rev's longtime relationship with the entertainment industry, which could accurately be described as mob-infested) and part the Reverend's own initiative in taking information on dirty doings — picked up in the course of his work — to the proper authorities.

In 1983, while Rev was home in Brooklyn and in the midst of the battle for a Black schools chancellor, he was working out of an office on West 54th Street in Manhattan that had been donated by the Spring Record Company.

At the time the company was owned in part by the brothers Roy and Julie Rifkin, acquaintances of James who had brought the Godfather to

Polygram Records and negotiated a major record contract for him.

Spring's vice president was a guy named Joe Medlin, an associate of Rev's National Youth Movement and one of the top record promoters in the country. It was Medlin who got Spring to donate the offices. Medlin noted that the company, which was practically 100% white right down to the secretaries, had an all-Black roster of artists; as such, he argued, it ought to do something for the community. Rev's credentials as an activist — including the backing of James himself — were solid in the industry, so the offices were given over to the Youth Movement for Rev's work in promoting Black artists.

Then one day one of the Rifkin brothers, told Rev that he had a friend who would like to meet Don King.

"He's a film producer."

"No problem," said Rev. Why not bring some mutual friends together? They agreed to have lunch.

The get-together took place at a fancy private joint on 57th Street called the Atrium Club. Rifkin's friend turned out to be flamboyant mobster-turned-snitch Michael Franzese, a film producer and (unknown to Rev at the time) the extremely wealthy son of alleged Colombo family crime boss John "Sonny" Franzese.

Franzese introduced Rev to his friend (Rev was not told he would be there), a fellow named Victor Quintana.

Also unbeknownst to Rev, Quintana was an undercover FBI agent.

The four men chatted about Franzese's friend's desire to get into the promotions business. Quintana, Rev discovered, had formed a promotion company called TKO Productions, with offices adjacent to Madison Square Garden. Quintana's partner was a fellow named Reggie Barrett, also unfamiliar to Rev, who had worked for Muhammad Ali and done some jail time. Barrett had at one time fallen out with Don King, and was now having problems "getting to" the splashy promoter. Quintana wanted to know if Rev could help him contact King. He had "millions of dollars" made in South America at his disposal, Quintana told Rev, and wanted to get in on some fights.

"No problem," said Rev.

Rev telephoned King and set up a meeting for the following week with Franzese, Quintana, Rifkin, King, and King's attorney Charles Lomax. At the meeting, which Rev attended, King let it be known that he wasn't interested in getting into anything crooked (this being an industry in which corruption is discussed as easily as the weather) but that he would definitely keep them in mind as fights came up and he needed investment or co-promotion.

End of meeting.

From that point on, Quintana began wining and dining King, who wanted nothing to do with Reggie Barrett, who had a rep as a "paper hanger."

A paper hanger was someone who passed bad checks, not popular in any business. From then on, Barrett disappeared from the scene as suddenly as he had arrived.

Then Quintana started wining and dining Rev, and taking him around town. Quintana confided in Rev that he made his bucks in drugs in South America. Even though Quintana the fed was lying, he wouldn't have been the first person made rich from dope with whom Rev, the kid off the streets of Brownsville, had sat down.

"But I'm not into that anymore," he told Rev.

Later on, Quintana seemed to change his mind. He let Rev know that he had a big drug deal in the works, and would like to meet some people Rev might know in Brownsville to cement the deal.

"I'm not into that," Rev told him. "No thanks."

"You wouldn't have to get involved; you'd just introduce me to somebody."

"I'll think about it," said Rev, ending the conversation.

Kathy and Rev started talking about this Quintana fellow.

"He's real suspicious," Rev told her. "He got a Rolls-Royce and don't know how to drive it. He got a penthouse in Lincoln Center, but doesn't look like nobody lives in it. His office doesn't look like he really does business. Why is he just waiting to do business with Don?"

Then Rev discovered that the younger Franzese was Sonny Franzese's kid.

"Well, that doesn't make him a gangster," Rev thought to himself.

"He's dealing with Universal Pictures and everybody else, so why should I think any different?"

Then there was the obligation to help Rifkin, because Rifkin was helping Rev.

One day Quintana telephoned to invite Rev to his little-used apartment.

"I'm getting ready to leave," the mystery man told Rev, adding that he was eager to leave a couple hundred thousand in a National Youth Movement account.

"I'll call you back," said Rev. "I don't know if we can do that." Rev never called and never made it to Quintana's fancy, fed-subsidized pad.

Soon thereafter, Rev was paid a visit by two FBI agents at Youth Movement headquarters. One was an agent named Joe Spinelli.

Born in Astoria, Queens in 1949, the mustachioed Spinelli joined the Bureau in 1975 after graduating from John Marshall Law School. He served as a special agent with the FBI until 1985, including nine years of work assigned to the New York City office. Spinelli handled the part of the notorious "Abscam" sting operation against members of Congress that focused on Staten Island Congressman John Murphy. In July of 1985 Spinelli left the Bureau to join Cuomo's Criminal Justice Program, and in January of the following year became New York State's first Inspector General.

Spinelli told Rev that they were getting ready to subpoena him to appear before a grand jury; that Victor Quintana was an undercover FBI agent; that they had tapes of Quintana and Rev talking to a drug dealer; that he had better come clean with them because they knew he and Don King were fixing fights.

"Indict me," challenged Rev.

"What do you mean, Reverend?"

Rev explained what he meant to one of the FBI's top sting artists.

"First of all he proposed a drug deal to *me*, which I never followed up, never agreed to. If you got a video tape of that you got absolutely nothing but your man trying to entrap me, and entrap me unsuccessfully.

"Secondly, Don King and I never fixed a fight. In fact, I don't even deal with fights with Don King. My relationship with Don King is totally about what he is doing with the community, so go ahead and indict me!"

That was the last Rev heard from the two agents; he never was subpoenaed for a grand jury.

Don King — it turns out he was the target of a four-year investigation — was subsequently indicted. The indictment contained no mention of fixing fights. Eventually he was acquitted of all charges.

Four years of careful work by the feds down the drain.

Then when Rev went after the crack trade, he came up with an idea.

"Let me call these guys back."

Rev got the feds on the phone. "Listen, you said if I ever knew anything wrong to call you. I'm calling."

They met, and Rev told them he had some drug situations he was eager to bust in Brooklyn. And he knew some people in the record industry who were trying to intimidate him because of the pressure the Youth Movement was putting on Black artists to go with Black promoters.

"We were threatened by gangsters," Rev said.

Rev was told an agent had been assigned to handle the drug situation, and someone to handle the threats. Nothing seems to have come out of the drug information Rev passed on, while the gangster types never threatened Rev in front of an agent.

Apparently, the main target of the feds throughout Rev's association with the FBI was Don King. Rev, they thought, was close enough to the promoter to answer questions that came up in the course of their investigation. Like, was he in the room when King supposedly coerced Bone-crusher Smith into a contract?

That's what Spinelli wanted to know after he joined Cuomo's staff, and was investigating King on behalf of the State of New York.

Rev told Spinelli that he knew nothing about any coercion, and then moved on to another topic.

"Man, all that drug information I gave you, and it looks like all you wanted was Don King or me."

"Oh, well, you know…"

"I'm still painting crack houses."

"Yeah, I saw it in the paper."

"Why don't you all help me? I've dropped stuff to Giuliani and Maloney and they don't even call us back."

Spinelli promised to introduce Rev to someone in the Eastern District federal court who would help. Rev started giving information to this new fellow.

But the tape-happy feds weren't satisfied with the names and addresses on pieces of paper that Rev gave them.

One day Rev's contact came up with a proposal. "Look, give us something concrete to go on."

"I don't know how to get anything concrete," Rev replied. "Kids give me names."

"Well, see if you can set up like you're doing a drug deal."

"Yeah," said Rev. "But you bring in strangers, they get scared. That's messed up before."

The agent proposed putting a special, tapped phone into Rev's house so they could get some tapes.

Nothing came out of the home phone routine. Soon, Rev's new agent began talking about getting into some boxing things with him again. In other words, King.

"How come you all never go after Bob Arum?" Rev asked angrily. And that was that for boxing.

•

In January of 1988 Rev got a call from his contact, asking if he had ever messed with anybody in the police department.

"Why?"

"Because the police department is getting ready to come out and say you've been an FBI informer for five years."

Then came the reporters from *Newsday*, including then-columnist Mike McAlary, now with the New York *Daily News*. The *Newsday* team claimed that their sources had a videotape with Rev talking about getting into a drug deal.

"Let me see it," said Rev.

He never did.

To date no one has ever produced one.

But on January 20, *Newsday* kicked off a series of front page articles detailing Rev's relationships to a host of law enforcement agencies dating back to 1983. The first one, called "The Minister and the Feds," charged that Rev had been "secretly supplying federal law enforcement agencies with information on boxing promoter Don King, reputed organized crime figures and Black elected officials, according to sources." The sources were, and remain, unnamed.

Among the Black figures Rev was reputed to have informed on were Wendell Foster, Sonny Carson, Al Vann and Major Owens. Of these four, Foster was an occasional coalition partner, Carson a current coalition partner and Owens a long time political opponent, while Rev's contact with Assemblyman Vann was practically zilch.

When a longtime Rev ally, the late State Senator Vander Beatty, was busted in a blatantly political sting operation for election fraud in the midst of his bitterly fought race against Owens for Congress in 1982, Rev, Sylvester Leaks and Arthur Bramwell — all longtime political opponents of Owens — signed a counterclaim charging there was corruption on Owens' side.

Beatty's prosecution was blatantly political; many believed that there was funny business going down on both sides, so anything short of prosecuting both candidates was a clear case of political bias.

Newsday followed up its first story two days later with "The Minister and the Mob," detailing the Franzese episode and Rev's attempts to buy into a garbage company that was reputedly controlled by the mob.

Rev had toyed around with the investment idea while he was pushing for contracts to be awarded to Black-owned companies; something called Consolidated Carting was on the market at the time, but all evidence points to Rev having backed off from an attempt to put together a consortium of Black investors at the first indication that mobsters might be involved.

A week after the *Newsday* series the *Village Voice* chimed in with more of the same in a political hatchet job called "The Hustler." The *Voice* was (and is) a longtime opponent of Rev and a supporter of the Owens political camp in Brooklyn; its rehash of the stories can only be chalked up to thinly disguised political motives.

•

The public revelations of Rev's interlude with law enforcement officials raised countless questions, although none of them have been asked or answered in any of the journals that have published the information.

Number one, of course, was the timing. The information passed on to *Newsday* (the series was clearly based on information *supplied* to the team of reporters, not the product of a journalistic investigation) came precisely when the coalition was seriously shaking up New York's political scene, from the Howard Beach case through the first Day of Outrage.

Anyone remotely interested in the development of the coalition knew there were tensions, particularly between Rev and the "militants," who have been known on more than one occasion to charge political opponents with being "cops."

Furthermore, it is a felony for anyone to pass on confidential information obtained in the course of a federal investigation — to a newspaper or to anyone. Why hasn't the leak been investigated?

This question arose again when the final report of the findings of the grand jury investigating the Tawana Brawley case was leaked to the press, this time to the newspaper of record itself, the *New York Times*.

Did the feds use Rev for their own purposes, leaving him high and dry when they were finished? The investigations they pursued seem to indicate that — based on the amount of attention devoted to going after Don King and the ostentatious lack of interest in Rev's leads on Brooklyn drug dealers.

And who *did* leak the stories?

Joseph Spinelli seems an obvious starting point, although things are not always as obvious as they seem. In any case, Spinelli's graduation from the FBI to a job as Cuomo's top spook at a time when the governor had declared war on the movement raises some interesting ethical questions.

As the *Newsday* stories were about to hit the stands, federal "sources," fully aware of the mob's penchant for retaliation, told the paper that Sharpton could get federal protection if he asked for it.

One of Rev's contacts in law enforcement even called to check up on him to make sure he was "alright" after the stories hit, and apologized that he couldn't repudiate what he knew to be lies because company regulations barred him from speaking publicly about cases.

"Tell my wife that at my funeral," said Rev, hanging up the phone.

What really bugged Rev was that no one seemed to give him credit for the dangerous mission he and his colleagues were on. Mobsters who were being wiretapped were talking about blowing his brains out during one of the marches in Bensonhurst. When Rev got a little concerned about that, he was accused of posturing. There might be every reason to believe that one reason for painting Rev as an "informer" was to get him killed.

And in this business people do get killed.

•

Newsday took one more shot after Robert Abrams' grand jury issued its long-awaited report on the Tawana Brawley case. Officially entitled *Report of the Grand Jury of the Supreme Court, State of New York, County of Dutchess, Issued Pursuant to Criminal Procedure Law Section 190.85 Subdivision (1)(b)*, in 170-odd pages it claimed that Tawana herself was responsible for the too-often-described brutalized state in which she was found (including cutting her own hair off, burning her clothes and using the charcoal to scrawl racist slurs on her body and smearing herself with dog feces). Why did she do all this? Because she was afraid to go home.

Soon after the report came out, *Newsday* ran the final (and certainly the most dangerous) of its "The Minister and the This and That" series. This time it was a frontpager penned by occasional *Newsday* writer Ron Howell (whom the white-owned and -run liberal tabloid often assigned to write its "Black" feature stories) and called "The Minister and the Fugitive." In this installment Howell has Ahmed Obafemi, a leader of the New Afrikan People's Organization (NAPO), charging that Rev had attempted to squeeze him for info on the whereabouts of Black Liberation Army leader Assata Shakur (JoAnne Chesimard) in 1983.

Spreading stories that Rev was snitching on members of the underground (and police-infested) Black liberation movement was tantamount to calling for Rev's own assassination. But in fact it was Howell who had busted Shakur a year before, when *Newsday* revealed that the fugitive was residing in Cuba! What would make a self-proclaimed "revolutionary" like Obafemi (a marginal figure in the African American community) take his story to Howell and *Newsday*, when it was Howell who snitched on Shakur in the first place?

As for Obafemi's charge, *Newsday* quoted the FBI agent who headed the hunt for Shakur. "Bullshit," he said. And like *Newsday*'s entire "The Minister and..." series, corroboration was provided only by a mysterious unnamed "law enforcement" source, which none of the many authors of the series, including Howell, were willing to give up despite the gravity and danger to Rev involved in turning the "charges" into "news."

•

Rev had reacquainted himself with State Senator Vander Beatty in 1982, a decade after he first went out stumping for the up-and-coming member of the Shirley Chisholm machine in Brooklyn. In '82, Beatty had set his sights on a congressional seat; after first weighing a race against the soon to be disgraced millionaire Fred Richmond, Beatty wound up running head to head against fellow legislator Major Owens; Rev supported his old colleague.

Beatty was unique among politicians. Number one, he was intelligent, which right away makes an elected official unusual, whatever her or his leanings. And although politically erratic, Beatty showed another rare quality — guts. In 1979 he initiated a Recall drive against Koch, just as most politicians were beginning to make their peace with the new order that Koch's election represented. It was something Koch and many others never forgot.

After coming out on the short end of the fight-to-the-finish feud that the 1982 race against Owens turned out to be, Beatty "went away" — politician talk for going to jail. But by 1990 he was quietly planning his political comeback, hoping to work his way up the rungs from the district leadership level.

The veteran politico sought Rev out after coming home, and the two would regularly sit down to dinner and a chat. Beatty told Rev about his plans to go for the district leadership, and they continued talking. One summer night in 1990, Beatty paid a visit to the Slave Theater, which Rev was packing every Wednesday and Saturday with meetings of the United African Movement.

Beatty came up on the stage and whispered to Rev, "I need to see you."

"I can meet you at 11 o'clock tonight at Junior's, Vander," said Rev, referring to the popular downtown Brooklyn eatery with the world famous cheesecake.

When Rev arrived at 11:15, Beatty was already there. A few members of the opposing political camp were on hand as well, but at the moment it was a friendly rivalry, with both sides laughing congenially.

It was the first time in a long time that Beatty, almost always in a hurry, seemed relaxed and comfortable. Rev nearly forgot about Beatty's anxious request to see him as they amiably chatted the hours away. Around 1 AM, Beatty got up to leave. Almost as an afterthought, he leaned over to Rev.

"Oh, the thing I called on you about is could you call Bill Tatum and ask him not to hurt me too bad," Beatty said, referring to Wilbert Tatum, the editor of the *Amsterdam News*, the country's leading Black newspaper. "I know he's coming out with an editorial on who to support, and I know he won't support me, but tell him don't kill me too bad!" They all laughed, and Beatty went on his way.

The next day Rev was in Atlantic City, New Jersey working with the Forgotten Youth organization, based in the resort town's impoverished Black community. It was his first meeting with Forgotten Youth, made up of young people who had grown up in abject poverty while millions of dollars changed hands every day just a short walk away on the boardwalk. When greedy developers were let into Atlantic City to get in on the newly legalized gambling business, they were supposed to invest in the community but they never did. Hence, the Forgotten Youth.

Coming over the Verrazano Narrows Bridge into Staten Island that night after the meeting, Rev had his driver stop at a phone. "Let me call in to Kathy and see if we need anything in the house."

"Kath, we made it back," he said, which was always reassuring knowledge in this business. "I'm at the Verrazano. Do you need anything?"

"No," said Kathy. "You know, it's a shame about Vander."

"What do you mean? What happened to Vander?"

"You haven't seen the news?"

"No, I've been in meetings all day. *What* news? I just left Vander at one o'clock this morning."

"Rev, he was killed today."

Rev couldn't believe his ears. He drove straight to Beatty's house. As soon as he saw the face of his old colleague's wife, he knew it was true.

That was why Rev made so much noise. If they were going to make him pay the ultimate price, it would have to be on national TV. He has, after all, not stopped hollerin' since the doctor slapped him.

TWELVE

No Justice, No Peace

Rev kept painting the crack houses into the autumn of 1986, expanding out of the ghetto and taking the paint cans right smack into the finance capital of the world.

Wall Street, like the poor communities of America, was reputed to be snowed under by the white powder too, and Rev wanted to make sure that the wealthy were brought before the law as well.

Needless to say, Rev made few friends in high places with *that* move.

As the year wound down, Rev headed into Philadelphia for another Hit Bound, star-studded anti-crack concert with his old friend Melba Moore and Freddie Jackson, one of the hottest performers in the country at that time.

Rain put a damper on the ticket sales that night, even though 10,000 kids came out. Hit Bound lost a bit of money, but Rev was happy that the alarm about crack continued to be sounded.

"We're closing the year with a bang," Rev told his staffers back at the Youth Movement. "We did our unity dinner, we put crack in the spotlight as a national issue, we got the stars involved in painting the crack houses. It's been a great year as far as I'm concerned."

•

It was the second Christmas in a row that the holiday season brought bad news. As he was making his Yuletide preparations, Rev got a call from one of his young "crackbusters," a fiercely loyal Youth Movement member named Derrick Jeter who was known to all as "Sunshine."

"Rev, my cousin Michael was killed out on the Belt Parkway."

"What happened?" Rev asked with concern.

Sunshine recounted the facts as best he knew them at the time; 21-year-old Michael Griffith, Michael's cousin Curtis Sylvester, Michael's soon-to-be stepfather Cedric Sandiford and their friend Timmy Grimes had gotten stuck out on a deserted stretch of highway in a place called Howard Beach as they were trying to find the home of Michael's employer to pick up his wages. Michael, Cedric and Timmy had walked a ways down the highway in the frigid winter night before stopping at a pizza joint to use a pay phone to summon help. Within minutes a white mob emerged from the pizza shop and swarmed upon the three men, chasing them for blocks. As he ran in terror, Michael was struck by a car on the darkened Belt Parkway.

"I'm really sorry to hear that," said Rev. "Where do his parents live? Maybe I can go by and offer condolences." Derrick gave Rev the address where Cedric Sandiford lived with Michael's mother Jean Griffith.

The next morning, two of Rev's aides from the Youth Movement went by the Griffith home to bring condolences from Rev. Jean Griffith told them that she wanted to speak to Reverend Sharpton himself.

At 10AM, Rev went by with Arthur Bramwell, the Brooklyn district leader and a Youth Movement board member, to offer his condolences.

Rev felt a stab in the pit of his stomach when he spotted Cedric Sandiford. The tall, dignified native of Guyana was terribly beaten, his face cut and swollen. But mostly, Rev was anguished by the look in Cedric's eyes, the pained look of a man suffering the double hurt of losing his son and his dignity.

Rev heard again the ugly story of what had happened that night, and the further ugliness of the indignities Cedric had suffered at the hands of the police, who treated him like a captured criminal, roughing him up, throwing him against the car (driven by court officer Dominic Blum) that had killed Michael, and giving him the third degree while his stepson's shattered body lay lifeless on the pavement.

For now, the family was waiting on Jean's oldest son, Christopher, a talented young photographer, who was looking for a lawyer.

The night before, New York Mayor Ed Koch had announced that he was posting a $10,000 reward for the apprehension of Michael's killers.

"That's a miniscule amount for the life of a Black kid," Rev thought angrily, convinced the mayor was doing his usual grandstanding. Rev went downstairs, and consulted with Bramwell. Between the two of them they put together a thousand dollars, and Rev returned to the house, telling the family the Youth Movement would match Hizzoner's bounty.

As New York City approached the end of the Koch decade, its government had become openly racialist. At the end of 1986, people of color still could not walk in certain neighborhoods without fearing for their lives. Rev knew that, and so did most of the people whose lives were so circumscribed.

But Rev also knew that he faced a formidable enemy in Ed Koch and the city's powers-that-be. Koch had survived that decade in office not simply by being a willing tool of the establishment (there were plenty of candidates for *that* job) but also by his consummate political skills, playing ethnic and racial blocs off against each other — "plantation politics," northern-style, at its finest.

Rev saw how Koch was already attempting to score political points by condemning the attack and offering a reward. That sort of grandstanding, Rev knew, would take the focus off the real issue, which was that Michael Griffith's killing was a symptom of a deeper problem — the entrenched racism of New York, racism that stretched into City Hall and lots of other places.

This was no ordinary criminal case. But some people were already at work who, for their own political purposes, wanted to portray it that way. Rev had to do something else that would keep the issue of racism at center stage, knowing full well how much that would upset a lot of people.

After informing the family that he was matching Koch's reward, Rev told them the plan.

"I'm going to Howard Beach in two days, and I'm going to let them know that we can walk anywhere we want in this country."

As Rev laid out his plans to turn up the heat in Howard Beach, Christopher returned to the house, telling the family that he was waiting to get in touch with attorney Alton Maddox, Jr., who had agreed to represent them.

"Great!" said Rev.

Since the early '60s Maddox, a fiery advocate who fought his way out of the poverty and segregation of tiny Newnan, Georgia to become one of New York City's most respected civil rights lawyers, had been at the center of countless police brutality and racial cases, including the 1983 killing of graffiti artist Michael Stewart by a mob of transit police officers, who choked him to death in the Union Square subway station for the crime of writing on walls with a marker.

Rev had first crossed paths with Maddox the year before, during Don King's ordeal down at federal court. At that time Maddox was defending himself against charges that he had assaulted court officers during the trial of confessed killer Willie Bosket, Jr., who had outraged authorities at every level of the criminal justice system by defiantly charging *them* with having created his sociopathic personality and vowing to resist any and every institution that took charge of him. One day court officers attacked Bosket, whom Maddox was representing; in the aftermath of the courtroom melee that followed, Maddox was charged with obstruction of government.

Rev ran into Maddox during the lunch breaks, and the two activists — who knew each other well from the city's Black media — got acquainted in person for the first time. Maddox was eventually cleared of the charges.

Pleased by the family's choice of counsel, Rev and Bramwell headed back to National Youth Movement headquarters to begin organizing a motorcade to go to Howard Beach. It was a good choice; within hours after the murder, the Queens district attorney's office under the leadership of now retired DA John Santucci set in motion an investigation which gave every appearance of willful incompetence. Maddox, no stranger to a legal system that by 1991 was itself acknowledging that it was rife with racism and practiced a double standard of justice, publicly expressed his reservations about the city's capacity to obtain justice for Michael Griffith.

As promised, Rev began a motorcade the following day from in front of the Griffith family home, leading scores of vehicles for the slow drive across the Queens County line and into Howard Beach.

"We're off to confront the white supremacists," Rev told his companions as they headed out.

As the motorcade arrived in Howard Beach, a car broke into the line right behind Rev's. He looked in the rearview mirror to see the familiar face of the Reverend Herbert Daughtry, pastor of the House of the Lord Church in Brooklyn and another fixture in the decade's endless series of police brutality cases. Rev got out of his car to chat with his fellow minister.

"Where you going?" Daughtry asked Rev.

"I'm going to stand right in front of the pizzeria that they ran Michael Griffith out of."

Daughtry was shocked. "I thought you were just going to drive by. You'll get *killed* out there!"

"We got to let these people know we're Americans, and we can go where we want," Rev responded, unbending. Rev instructed everyone around to get out of their cars. He and Daughtry and Reverend Jerry West walked out towards a *shocked* white crowd, and held a rally in front of a little place called New Park Pizza on a lonely stretch of highway called Cross Bay Boulevard in Howard Beach. They would be seen on television sets around the world that night. The battle lines were drawn.

"We'll be back Saturday," Rev promised, and began to lay plans for a massive march into the all-white enclave for December 27. In the course of the preparations the NAACP's Laura Blackburne joined the call for a march, and later told Rev that NAACP executive director Benjamin Hooks would be coming as well.

Saturday came quickly, capping off a week which saw attorney Maddox issue the first call for a special prosecutor in the case and charge the police with a cover-up. On the cold winter morning of the 27th, Rev soon realized that he and Hooks and the other activists at the head of the march would be leading *thousands* through the isolated stretch of roadway that led to the site of the attack.

Rev's strategy worked. Despite the attempts by Koch and the establishment to co-opt the case and lull those who were concerned into believing that justice would take its course, the announcement of the march had tapped into the outrage of the community. A multi-racial crowd converged on Cross Bay Boulevard in practically the middle of nowhere, in the dead of winter, to express that outrage.

Michael Stewart. Eleanor Bumpurs. Clifford Glover. Willie Turks, beaten to death by a white mob in Brooklyn in 1982, with no convictions ever forthcoming. The list went on and on through the '80s of Black and Latino youth — and grandmothers — killed by whites, in and out of uniform, and with never a single murder conviction. Three years earlier, Maddox, attorney C. Vernon Mason, Daughtry and other advocates had stood for two days before a congressional criminal justice subcommittee documenting the cases in meticulous detail, yet the outrages continued.

Now, on a highway echoing with the chants of thousands poised to embark on a non-violent protest against injustice, a new era dawned. The spirit of Dr. King was alive on the streets of Howard Beach! Now, perhaps, the victories that movement had won in the South could happen here, in the North.

On the boulevard, the NAACP's Benjamin Hooks grabbed Rev's arm, and the two generations of civil rights leaders looked back to make sure the crowd of thousands was lined up in formation behind them before stepping off arm-in-arm for the two-mile march into Howard Beach, where a rally was planned. All along the route, local residents came out and jeered from either side of the wide boulevard. Many recognized Sharpton as the one who had brought the protesters out to disrupt the ordinary routine at New Park Pizza earlier in the week, and singled him out for special abuse.

Hooks turned to his younger marching partner. "Boy, do they hate *you*," he told Rev.

Alongside the marchers, Police Commissioner Benjamin Ward — the first African American to hold that position in New York City —

lectured a group of white kids leading the jeering section.

"Alright, alright, that's enough!" barked Ward in his best policemanly tone.

The white kids were unfazed, if not amused. One of the children of Howard Beach, who couldn't have been more than ten years old, stared at Ward indignantly.

"Who are you talking to?" the kid squeaked. "You're nothing but a nigger yourself!"

Rev looked back over at Hooks. "Looks like they got more jeers than just for me." They both laughed.

After they arrived at a local schoolyard for the rally, the NAACP's Laura Blackburne attempted to start things off with the national anthem, prompting opposition from the mostly young crowd. Rev took over. Presiding over the rest of the rally, he introduced all the leadership present, including Hooks, and led the march back into Howard Beach to the cars that stood waiting to take them home.

•

By now, both Maddox and C. Vernon Mason were serving as counsel to Cedric Sandiford, the key witness in any case the district attorney's office was going to put together. Taking a page out of Dr. King's tactics book, the attorneys concluded that the only way to ensure justice was to withhold cooperation from the local authorities and bring in higher powers.

In the South, the model involved non-cooperation with local sheriffs and courts and bringing in the feds (the lesser evil) to force through desegregation. In New York City in 1986, the tactic was to call in a special prosecutor to try cases the locals hadn't the nerve or desire to take on. At Michael's funeral at Our Lady of Charity Catholic Church, Maddox laid out the non-cooperation tactic.

Within days of Michael's murder a groundswell of outrage had been rising from the grassroots. As well, a leadership coalition based in the African American community began to coalesce. It was the beginnings of a mass movement, the first to emerge in a very long time. There had been the Dump Koch campaign of 1981, a grassroots upsurge that was masterfully co-opted by Cuomo the following year in his successful gubernatorial race against Ed Koch (helped by the flaking out of almost all the coalition forces the day after the 1981 mayoral election). A coalition of Black and Latino leadership had come together during the agitation for a Black schools chancellor which eventually became the Coalition for a Just New York — but that grouping went to pieces after its plans to put up a united mayoral candidate were shattered by Denny Farrell's last minute entry into the race. And there had been periodic, localized rebellions each time Koch closed a hospital or cut back this or that program.

This time, both the community and the leadership were coming together and growing. The leadership forces included many familiar faces: Sonny Carson, who had recently started something called the Black Men's Movement Against Crack; Daughtry; the Reverend Calvin Butts, who had inherited the pastorship of Abyssinian Baptist Church from the late Adam Clayton Powell, Jr.; and Elombe Brath of the Patrice Lumumba Coalition.

●

By December 27, no one could possibly deny that this case had been botched from Jump Street. That was the day that Queens Supreme Court Judge Ernest Bianchi, at a preliminary hearing, threw out murder, manslaughter and assault charges against Jon Lester, Scott Kern and Jason Ladone, three of the mob members who had been arrested. Bianchi charged them instead with reckless endangerment, and laid the blame on the prosecution for failing to produce Sandiford as a witness.

Everyone walked out of the courtroom simmering with anger over the indictment. Young Michael Griffith had been *murdered*.

"They just declared war on Black kids," said Rev to Mason, Maddox and Black trade unionist Jim Bell, who were standing behind him.

They walked out of the courthouse and back to the car. "Man, we ain't gonna let them go, are we?" Rev asked.

"What do you want to do? We're calling for a special prosecutor; that's the only way we can get it." Thus spoke the lawyers.

Rev wanted to do more. "Let's go by Jim Bell's office and organize." Rev, Mason, Maddox and Bell began holding daily meetings for the next two weeks at the Greenwich Village offices of District Council 65 of the United Auto Workers.

Right after the march in Howard Beach, and after Sandiford's cooperation was withdrawn, Rev and the coalition called for a march on the Greenwich Village home of Mayor Ed Koch. Things were heating up. Maddox's tactic of non-cooperation became the focal point (Cuomo and Koch hoped they could use Maddox' intransigence to break up the coalition).

But the mayor was having a hard time; he was roundly booed at Our Lady of Grace Church in Howard Beach; that was followed by a noisy anti-Koch demo outside a St. Albans church, where the cry "No Justice, No Peace!" made its way into the church from the street.

On December 30 Police Commissioner Ward charged that the legal team, and Maddox in particular, were taking on the case solely for financial gain from a possible civil suit on behalf of the Griffith family. Fissures began to appear in the coalition; most of the activists supported Maddox but Congressman Charles Rangel and Judge Bruce Wright criticized his tactics.

Then Koch tried to get the Black leadership to meet with him, but Maddox convinced Rev that the mayor's purpose was to line up support against Maddox's tactics.

Rev was initially not on Koch's invitation list. But the night before, the Reverend Jesse Jackson had appeared with Koch on the "McNeil/ Lehrer Report"; while there, the Rainbow Coalition leader explained to the mayor that there was no way he could call a meeting with Black leaders and not invite Al Sharpton, the person who had been leading the marches. Jesse vouched for Rev, telling the mayor he'd known him since he was "a kid."

"You've got to have him," Jesse told Koch.

Koch, of course, was quite familiar with the Reverend Al Sharpton, and he didn't like what he knew — from the time the mayor slapped the Rev with his first arrest during the schools chancellor protests, all the way through to the Goetz case.

But the mayor agreed to include him, and had one of his aides call Rev to issue the invite.

At a press conference before the meeting, with practically the entire Black leadership present, as well as the Griffith family, Rev lashed out at the attacks on Maddox and the failure of anyone thus far to come to the embattled attorney's defense.

"I think that it is wrong that we are not dealing with the attacks on Alton Maddox," Rev announced. "I think that Ben Ward is outrageous in his statements, and I would like you to know that I'm not going to any coon meeting with Ed Koch to rubber stamp this statement against Alton Maddox."

From that day on, the Reverend Al Sharpton and attorney Alton Maddox, Jr. would be *very, very* tight.

Of course, it was plastered all over the news the next day: "Sharpton calls Koch meeting 'coon meeting,' " and all that. But Rev had once again raised the stakes; while some leaders were unhappy with how things were being handled, Rev had sabotaged Koch's meeting for the very purpose of keeping the coalition unified. Some of the more faint-hearted might protest, but that would only help weed them out early on in the battle.

For two weeks they strategized and debated tactics at Bell's District Council 65 offices, beginning plans for the next big happening — a march on Koch's home. They toyed with and rejected an idea for a school boycott, but did hold demonstrations at police headquarters calling for Ward's resignation.

Right about then, Rev got called away on the road for some business with Don King. By January 13 Cuomo, after having David Dinkins — then the Manhattan borough president — sound out the Black leadership, agreed to appoint Charles "Joe" Hynes as special prosecutor in the case. Butts represented the coalition at the meeting at Cuomo's New York City offices; Rev, still on the road, was piped in by phone.

It was the first time in the history of New York State that a special prosecutor had been appointed in such a case, and Mario Cuomo, an aspirant to the Presidency of the United States of America, was not at all happy.

He would not forget, or forgive.

It was also the first time that Rev had met Joe Hynes, a former chief of the Brooklyn DA's rackets bureau, appointed special prosecutor during the city's highly politicized nursing home scandals, a former fire commissioner and later the Brooklyn district attorney.

Mason and Maddox did not want Hynes. They said he was a racist and cited, among other things, the fact that his summer home was in an all-white enclave in Queens.

But the coalition was making history and that was good enough for Rev; he was not terribly concerned with who was appointed, because he was going to keep up the heat in the street no matter what.

"I'm going to stay on him like his overcoat," Rev promised.

•

On January 21 the coalition launched the first "Day of Outrage"; over 10,000 people, many of them Black youth, assembled in midtown Manhattan and charged down Fifth Avenue for the planned demonstration at Koch's rent-controlled Greenwich Village apartment. Among those who endorsed the march was Jesse Jackson.

With Rev and the attorneys on Hynes every minute, the case proceeded. On February 9 the first indictments were handed up by a grand jury against a dozen members of the mob. Four of them — Jon Lester, Scott Kern, Michael Pirone and Jason Ladone — were slapped with murder charges. Pirone retained Stephen Murphy, a wild, street tough fireplug of a lawyer, whose confrontational and abusive tactics have invited accusations of racism against him — and have been successful.

On February 28 Rev's old colleague Hosea Williams flew into New York for a triple threat rally at Washington Temple; at issue were Howard Beach, Hosea's battles to desegregate Forsyth County in Georgia (where a rally led by the civil rights veteran had provoked the same violent response by the locals as had Rev's treks through Howard Beach), and the acquittal of the police officer who shotgunned 67-year-old Eleanor Bumpurs to death for not paying her rent on time.

"We've marched, we've demonstrated and we've done what we can do politically," said Rev. "We must do more. So we come to the church, to ask for its support and blessings."

While he was in town, Hosea awarded Rev the Martin Luther King, Jr. medallion for his work in the struggle, a reward whose previous recipients included Mao Tse-Tung, Muammar Qaddafi and Kwame Nkrumah.

Rev hasn't taken the medallion off since.

●

In the meantime Rev kept up his other activities, continuing to advocate on behalf of the ever growing roster of victims of racial violence. On a hot Sunday afternoon in May Rev returned for an angry demonstration, co-led by NAP's Fulani, at the 77th precinct in Bed-Stuy. Despite the scandal and shake-up at the crooked precinct, it was still business as usual in the 77th, where police had killed 21-year-old Darren Mark Culler in a raid on a suspected crack house on May 19, the birthday of Malcolm X.

Officer Kevin Ahearn claimed he shot the young man after he came at him with a knife.

Except Darren Mark Culler didn't have any fingers.

"We're not begging, we are demanding," Rev told 250 members of the community. "We are summoning our moral power today."

After a hot summer passed, jury selection got underway for the trial of Lester, Pirone, Kern and Ladone. The large Queens County courtroom was packed every day. Rev and the attorneys, as promised, stayed right on top of Hynes and the prosecution team.

Rev conferred again with Maddox and Mason.

"The only way this trial is going to work is, number one, we got to keep constant vigilance. Second, we got to keep the issue in front of the public, on the front burner."

Hynes came in every day with the family, and stopped to consult with Rev and Daughtry and the attorneys. Every single day, the coalition kept the heat on, working virtually as Hynes' partner in the case. Anytime

Rev saw or heard or sensed something he didn't like, he'd pass a note. Then there would be a delay, a recess, or whatever else was necessary to get the matter straightened out. They talked. They argued.

Every day.

Meanwhile, defense attorney Murphy was at his wretched best, tearing into Timothy Grimes and other witnesses with an evil vengeance. At one point Timothy — who to this date has not been able to put his shattered young life back together — threw up his hands in disgust and stormed off the stand, nearly cracking under Murphy's questioning.

Maddox told Rev to sit down with all of the groups involved in the case. Rev called a meeting at DC 65, and concluded it with a press conference at which he served as spokesperson for the group. He announced that they would vigilantly monitor the upcoming trial, and that on December 21 they would stage a day of civil disobedience — another "Day of Outrage" — to protest racism in New York.

"We are fed up with a lot of the foolishness in this city," said Rev.

•

On December 9, 1987 — nearly a year since the murder — the defense rested and the case went to the jury.

Rev decided that now was the time to put pressure on the jury to have the courage to do the right thing.

"We don't need to interfere with the jury," said Rev. "What we are gonna do is raise our *moral* indignation. Every hour the jury is out, we are going out in the hall and get on our knees and pray for justice."

The Reverend Timothy Mitchell, pastor of Ebenezer Baptist Church in Flushing, Queens and a former marching partner of Dr. King, came and joined them for the prayers. Every night on the evening news, Rev and his ad hoc congregation were shown keeping vigil in the courtroom hallways. If the jury was still out come sundown, they lit candles, joined by Jean Griffith and other family members.

The days passed without a verdict, and the vigils continued. Rev announced that the Day of Outrage would proceed as planned. That night, Rev joined with hundreds of others packed into Our Lady of Charity for a memorial service marking the first anniversary of Michael's death. He spoke of the youth.

"Every child in these United States will be told a story, as Michael's mother was told, about 'bringing me your tired, your huddled masses yearning to be free,'" Rev preached. "And when she came, and when her son came down to get a paycheck, the Statue of Liberty wasn't holding no light for Michael.

"But we're gonna raise that light up if it takes all the strength in our arms; we're gonna make justice reign even if it costs us our very life. We will not let you down, Michael, because some of us would rather die on our feet than keep standing on our knees..."

That night Rev came home to an unpleasant surprise.

Stuck on his door was an injunction barring the Day of Outrage from happening. He called around to find that *everyone* had been served with an injunction.

"What do we do?" his coalition partners asked. "If we disobey, we go to jail!"

"The whole idea is civil disobedience anyway!" Rev responded.

"Well, we don't believe in civil disobedience, because we don't believe in non-violent submission," some of the more militant members of the coalition said. But Rev knew that the majority of those in that camp were on parole and couldn't engage in acts of civil disobedience because to do so risked arrest!

"Look, y'all do what y'all do, y'all do security, we're gonna do it our way," Rev told them.

With that, the coalition — defying the court-ordered (in all likelihood unconstitutional) injunction against conducting any acts of civil disobedience, laid out elaborate plans to block bridges and subways on December 21. It was what Rev had done in earlier times, except on a grander scale.

The next day at the courthouse, Rev announced that an injunction had been served against the Day of Outrage, but it would go forward. Right there in front of the rolling cameras he tore up the piece of paper.

"They can flush this down the toilet," Rev said angrily. "I am going."

Tim Mitchell decided he was down too, and told Daughtry so.

"If you go, I'll go," Daughtry responded.

The Fire *This* Time: The Day of Outrage

The jury went into its twelfth day of deliberations. Then, at 8 PM on December 21, a damp and chilly night, the city's heartbeat stopped for a moment as the verdict was announced. The jury had found the center point between the two racial poles that had divided New York for a year. The charges of murder against two of the defendants and attempted murder against a third were rejected; the three were found guilty on the second-degree manslaughter charges. All charges against Murphy's client Pirone were dropped.

Michael Griffith had indeed been killed by the white mob, the jury concluded. But murder — the taking of a life from a motive such as racism — had not occurred.

After spending the better part of a year on top of this case, Rev knew nothing of the verdict when it finally came down. While the Queens courthouse swarmed with reporters frantically filing the official story, Rev and the coalition and thousands of Black youth delivered their own verdict on the streets and subways of downtown Brooklyn: MURDER.

The Day of Outrage, banned by the authorities, had begun.

The *New York Times* was amazed, and it wasn't alone. The newspaper of record reported that several hundred protesters, "most of them Black," had shut down a major section of the New York City subway system "with surgical precision." While the tired jury agonized over the political considerations that needed to be weighed into their deliberations, the African American youth of Brooklyn and points beyond launched their own session in the courtroom of the streets.

For them, on trial this night was the festering system of oppression that has weighed on these post-Great Society young people — Rev's people — since birth.

As the evening rush hour approached, the youth systematically descended into the catacombs of the sprawling Borough Hall subway station in downtown Brooklyn. Within minutes, normal operations were brought to a standstill.

The seizure was more military than "surgical"; an army, not a medical team, had sprung into action here. The first trains that came in were seized by the youth, who pulled the little wooden handles on a rope that said "emergency brake."

This was an emergency.

At the IRT station, the trains were suddenly zipping past the station like terrified iron creatures desperately avoiding capture by the youthful soldiers.

"I know how to stop them," Rev told his colleagues. "We're getting on this track." Rev led a collective leap onto the tracks, his overcoat flapping in the damp and dank subterranean battlefield. He was joined by Reverends Benjamin Chavis, Timothy Mitchell and Herbert Daughtry and Brooklyn Assemblyman Roger Green; they planted themselves on the tracks of the outbound Number 4 train. Later they were arrested, and charged with obstructing justice, criminal trespass and disorderly conduct. On the other side of the platform, hundreds of youth laid siege to an inbound train. The entire station, a hub of the system, was soon shut down. Three blocks away, another group was moving in on the IND station at Jay Street. Back up on the street, the entrance to the Brooklyn Bridge, the main overland route in and out of the borough, was captured. Seventy-three mostly young protesters were arrested and held overnight.

Rev and his colleagues were released that morning on their own recognizance, while a team of lawyers headed by Maddox and including Alvaader Frazier and Harry Kresky of the Harlem-based International Peoples' Law Institution battled to have the remaining prisoners released.

Following Rev's arrest, the battle shifted to the youth, 100 of whom had taken up positions on the platform of the Number 4. Arms locked, proud, dignified, outraged and peaceful, they stood there defiantly. Facing them on the crowded platform were the same number of mostly white riot-gear-equipped cops, one fully armed officer for each unarmed, non-violent demonstrator.

C. Vernon Mason mounted a bench and announced, "Just so we are clear about our intentions, we shall not be moved." The line of youth held firm; a powerful chant of "Too Black, Too *Strong!*" reached the ears of the helmeted cops, who readied themselves to move in as the attorney instructed the youth in how to respond.

Police Chief Gallagher attempted to interrupt, announcing that the demonstrators were violating a court-ordered injunction which demanded that they show cause as to why the protest should not be stopped. Gallagher was shouted down.

"Mr. Mason is *speaking*," he was told. Mason eloquently established the moral authority of the demonstrators in the face of the display of police power. He demanded that Ed Koch show cause for the murder of Michael Griffith; of Eleanor Bumpurs; for the killing while in police custody of Yvonne Smallwood, a young woman who could have been any one of the demonstrators; for the killing of Michael Stewart, beaten to death by these same transit police; and countless others. Then the song "Oh Freedom" rose from the crowd, most of them born after Martin Luther King was killed. The song drowned out Gallagher's recital of charges and subsequent announcement: "You are all under arrest." Most of those held overnight were hauled off this IRT platform.

Rev heard about the verdicts from Maddox, who stood at the head of the thousands surrounding the Brooklyn courthouse the next day demanding the release of the demonstrators. Rev and Maddox hugged in the hallway as soon as they saw each other.

This was history-making time. Despite the acquittals on the murder charges, it was the first time that white assailants were going to jail for racist attacks. Rev was ecstatic.

And for the first time there was, in the community, a taste of power. The community had shown, under Rev's leadership, that the only way a case like this could be won was if the people were plunged right into the middle of it. Which is what Rev accomplished; never before had a case had the kind of direct community input as the prosecution of the Howard Beach defendants had seen.

Like his hero Adam Clayton Powell had done generations before, Rev had mustered the power of "the people of the streets, the failures, the misfits, the despised, the maimed, the beaten, the sightless and the voiceless." And they had challenged a system which had said to go slow, be patient, let the system handle it forever.

The system had been exposed as thoroughly corrupt, and a failure, and the people of the streets had begun to reshape it themselves. For the powers-that-be, particularly the liberal establishment centered on the governor, things were spinning out of control. Mario Cuomo brooded over how the power brokers of America could take him seriously as a candidate for chief executive of America, Inc. if he couldn't even keep his own home borough of Queens under control.

THIRTEEN

Robert Abrams, Tawana Brawley and the Entrapment of Reverend Al Sharpton

The FBI can feed information to the press to make your neighbor think you're something subversive. The FBI — they do it very skilfully, they maneuver the press on a national scale; and the CIA maneuvers the press on an international scale...the press is so powerful in its image-making role, it can make a criminal look like he's the victim and make the victim look like he's the criminal. If you aren't careful, the newspapers will have you hating the people who are being oppressed and loving the people who are doing the oppressing.

—Malcolm X, December 13, 1964 at the Audubon Ballroom, where he was killed two months later

Maybe it was the Presidential fever that gripped Mario Cuomo as election year '88 approached, and maybe it was forces far more complex and devious. But the facts are that as the movement that had come to life in 1987 swelled into an independent force with the power to decide the course of a major legal case, a far-reaching conspiracy to destroy that movement was set in motion almost immediately.

COINTELPRO (Counter-Intelligence Program) was the name that the FBI gave to its multi-million dollar plot to seek out and destroy any and every person, group or community that in any way threatened the

171

status quo. It was begun under the late J. Edgar Hoover, a notorious racist (and indeed, madman) who ruled the Bureau for half a century.

Hoover served under every President during that time — from the reforming FDR to the reactionary Nixon, and all points in between. Which is helpful in understanding the nature of the spy book-sounding operation called COINTELPRO. Which was not simply a basement operation that employed a team of spooks to infiltrate and disrupt "subversive" organizations. At the risk of sounding mystical, COINTELPRO is more of a concept than any particular operation, and one that can only be understood in the context of the complex network of institutions that make up what some call the state apparatus.

It would be simplistic to call COINTELPRO a project of the FBI, simply because that in no way explains why both G-men and the Communist Party USA were out to destroy the Black Panthers. We can only get a glimpse of something like COINTELPRO by taking a look at the complex relationship between and among that whole network of institutions — newspapers, political parties, corporations, police departments, etc. — and forces at the grassroots that arise to challenge their dominance.

By 1987 such a grassroots force had emerged, and it was challenging a status quo that spanned the spectrum from the most reactionary racists to liberals to the most fiery radicals. A status quo, after all, is a complex thing, but all its elements share one characteristic: TO REMAIN THE STATUS QUO.

●

Mario Cuomo and the status quo quietly, if nervously, bided their time throughout the Rev-led revolt over Howard Beach. A seasoned political operator, the governor knew that it would be self-destructive to react precipitously to a situation that had gotten so out of control; Cuomo had enough resources at his disposal to choose precisely when, where and how to counterattack.

The time would be the winter of 1987; the place, a little upstate New York town called Wappingers Falls.

It became known as the Tawana Brawley case, and within a matter of months it shattered the new movement that had risen from the streets; by the middle of 1989, Rev was on trial for his life, facing a massive, multi-million dollar case brought against him by the attorney general of the State of New York.

But Mario Cuomo and the status quo and whoever/whatever else was involved in engineering the massive operation failed — fatally — to take one thing into account, and that was that the spark of rebellion, even when dimmed, can never be fully extinguished as long as there is still life in a community. Shortly after Rev was hauled into court to begin the trial that was supposed to eliminate him forever, that spark was ignited in a place called Bensonhurst, and it exploded into a Black revolution on the streets of New York, with Rev and a new generation of leaders out on the front lines again.

But all that seemed a lifetime away when the activists from the Howard Beach movement first heard about the case of a little girl in upstate New York named Tawana...

•

Lillian Howard, an actress and activist in her local NAACP in Newburgh, New York, was at the meeting at which Rev and the coalition announced the December 21 Day of Outrage. Howard's son Timothy was an inmate at the Orange County jail in upstate Goshen, where — as in most of the jails in the New York State penal system — white guards constantly ran amok.

Howard told the coalition that she sincerely wished it could do something about the correction officers' brutality in the Orange County jail, where the guards were reported to have donned white sheets and beaten a group of Black and Latino prisoners senseless.

Howard also told the coalition the story of a young African American girl named Tawana Brawley, who had been kidnapped and raped by a group of six white policemen over a four day period during Thanksgiving week.

There were some early overtures by the family, which was being represented at the time by the local NAACP, for Maddox, Mason and

Rev to get involved, but as of yet no one had made direct contact.

There were already strains in the coalition by the time the Brawley case came along; they first became evident in the planning for a march that was to take place on December 12, 1987 in Newburgh.

In a way, Rev's alliance with some of the more "militant" elements of the movement was a new development; Rev, throughout his career as an activist that stretched back to his teenage years, was a product of the mainstream civil rights movement, from Powell to Jackson. The militants comprised a whole other wing of the movement. They included Sonny Carson, Father Lawrence Lucas, a Roman Catholic priest from Harlem, and a grouping known as the New York 8; their name came from a federal case brought against eight self-described revolutionaries who had been brought to trial following a massive pre-dawn COIN-TELPRO raid on their homes by hundreds of feds in 1985.

The "8" had been betrayed by an informer within their ranks, but went on to beat that case and join forces with Carson's Black Men's Movement Against Crack and Lucas to form a loose coalition of their own.

At the time of the Howard Beach case, Rev was having success in bringing together practically the whole spectrum of mainstream civil rights activists and Black political figures on a variety of cases, including the "crackbusters" crusade and a campaign for more Black involvement in the front offices of professional baseball.

In 1986 police killed a Black man in the Bronx named Kilroy Burke; Rev, after putting up the money for the funeral, joined forces with Bronx Councilman Wendell Foster to call for a Black district attorney in that borough. While in the midst of that fight and the battle of Howard Beach, Maddox pressed Rev to expand the base of the movement.

"You got a lot of the mainstream leadership together around the sports issue. Now you need to get a lot of the militant leaders coalesced."

Rev knew Sonny Carson from the days when they fought to integrate the schools in Canarsie, and from the Claude Reese case in the '70s. Rev set up a meeting with Carson, attorneys Maddox and Mason, activists Elombe Brath and Jitu Weusi, and Viola Plummer of the New York 8 at Junior's Restaurant in Brooklyn one morning. Rev brought along Arthur

Bramwell and some of his Youth Movement staff. They decided there that they would work together on the Kilroy Burke case and began planning the Day of Outrage.

The new coalition was together again when Lillian Howard came along with the Tawana Brawley story, and outrage swept the room. There was unanimous agreement on one thing.

"We need to go up there and do something."

The coalition decided on December 12 for an action, and then kicked around ideas on what that action might be and where exactly they would carry it out. Although only an hour and a half car ride from New York City, the area was like another world for most of the activists.

"I used to preach at a church up that way in Newburgh," said Rev. "Maybe I can get it. It's a Baptist Temple, a big church."

"Yeah, I know the guy," said Reverend Tim Mitchell. "Saul Williams." Rev and Mitchell went to the phone and called Pastor Williams, a passionate Baptist preacher who, like Bethany's Reverend Jones, spoke in a deep and distinguished voice. Rev got on the line, and reminded the minister of how he used to stand on a box and give the sermon at his church as a boy preacher.

"OK, I have no problem," said Williams after hearing the request to use his facilities. "How's your mother?"

Reverend Williams had a few more questions, too. "Who's coming with you?" he enquired nervously, knowing something of Rev's reputation since his boy preacher days. "Don't have any of them crazies in my church!"

"Oh, no!" reassured Rev. "Tim Mitchell's here." Rev put Mitchell on the phone, who also had a pastor's voice which could reassure anyone of anything. There was no mention of the fact that any of the "militants" would be coming along as well, not to mention another surprise guest.

They put out the call for the December 12 rally, with Rev, Mitchell, Mason and Maddox putting up the money for the buses.

During the week Rev got a call from his old friend, Nation of Islam Minister Louis Farrakhan, who had risen to national prominence in the wake of the 1984 Jackson Presidential campaign. He too was coming.

They all arrived at the packed church, now surrounded by members of the Nation's Fruit of Islam; the Fruit searched everybody entering, as is their custom wherever Farrakhan is appearing (Rev, familiar to the NOI security people, was allowed to come through unchecked).

But the New York 8's Viola Plummer, known to have a volatile temper, took offense at the search and said so, charging that the Muslims were taking over the rally.

Once inside, she stormed into Pastor Williams' office and confronted the Muslim leader, requesting that he leave in language not generally acceptable to believers. The Fruit of Islam were readying themselves to send Plummer and Carson to the hereafter when the Minister intervened.

"Wait a minute, brothers," said Farrakhan, who also has the capacity to calm the most agitated of souls. "You must respect people and their rally."

A major argument ensued; Pastor Williams, who knew Farrakhan from Jackson's campaign but didn't know the militants from Adam, said, "This may be your rally, but this is our church and he's not going anywhere. If anyone's leaving it's *you*, whoever you are." A compromise was finally reached; Tim Mitchell would preside and everyone would speak at the church rally.

"We're in a state of emergency in the State of New York," Rev told the 1,000-strong rally before it took off for a march through the streets of Newburgh. Rev pointed out that Cuomo's Presidential aspirations were at variance with the fact that he presided over a state infested with racism.

Farrakhan brought his usual fire to the rally, proclaiming that "In Newburgh a new movement has been born," and warning that the Koran calls for "an eye for an eye, a tooth for a tooth — until you understand as you bury your sons and we bury ours that this must cease!"

The December 12 incident catalyzed the tensions which beset the coalition from that point on, which were exacerbated by disagreements about money that had been raised, first for the buses for December 12 and later to post bail for the Day of Outrage defendants.

After the December 12 rally Rev, Mason and Maddox began making contact with the Brawley family: her mother Glenda, stepfather Ralph King and aunt Juanita.

The case was still before the local authorities, and as in Howard Beach it was looking very much as if a cover-up was in process. Maddox, as he had done so successfully in Howard Beach, advised the family not to cooperate if they weren't assured that the assailants would be brought to justice.

By early January the grand jury that had been convened by Dutchess County prosecutor William Grady issued subpoenas for Tawana, Glenda, Juanita and Ralph. Maddox, along with Rev's aides Derrick (Sunshine) Jeter and Perry McKinnon, went up to see the Brawleys. Maddox returned to New York having won the Brawley family over to the tactic of non-cooperation. As they had done before, Rev, Mason and Maddox put out a call for a special prosecutor in the Brawley case.

•

But no sooner had Rev gotten himself involved than outrage struck again, this time in yet another all-white enclave.

It was still a year and half before the Brooklyn neighborhood of Bensonhurst became known around the world as the place where Yusuf Hawkins took his last steps, and which ignited a revolution on the streets. But for anyone who later tried to claim that the Yusuf Hawkins killing was an "isolated" incident, consider Christmas 1987 in Bensonhurst.

Having finished Christmas dinner at the Marlboro Houses project in Bensonhurst, Steven and Sylvester LaMont headed up Bath Avenue with a shopping cart to collect cans and bottles. In New York City thousands of people make their living collecting cans and bottles, each of which is worth a nickel. Like thousands of other New Yorkers, the LaMont brothers were working Christmas night.

Steven and Sylvester made their way to 24th Avenue, meticulously shaking dry the empty cans and bottles and placing them in their carts. Then, on 24th Avenue, just off Bath, the brothers came upon 10 or so white teenagers leaning on a double-parked car. As the brothers passed, they became unwilling actors in a scene that has played itself out thousands of times. First a verbal assault — "What's in the cart, niggers...you robbing houses?" Then the chase, and the beatings — the weapons this time included a marble table top, broken over the head of one of the brothers. And the war cry that had risen from the frenzied voices of residents of the shrinking white enclaves where racial violence and murder breed like cancer:

"Howard Beach!"

The bruised and battered LaMont brothers joined the ever growing list of victims of racial violence in New York. They survived that night, unlike dozens of other Black citizens who haven't in recent years; unlike Alfred Sanders, who was cut down in a hail of police bullets three days later in neighboring Queens County.

"Meet us in Bensonhurst"

Rev took the offensive when he heard about the case of the LaMont brothers.

"We are a people with integrity," Rev told the press. "We are a people that don't believe in racism. But you hold your press conferences against *us*! Why don't you hold them against those who perpetrate racial violence? You want us to work together? Well then, Mr. Koch, and Mr. Jewish Leader, and Mr. Catholic Leader — meet us in Bensonhurst!"

At a meeting in Reverend Daughtry's House of the Lord Church, Rev and the coalition announced that they would be heading out to Bensonhurst. Once there, the 500-strong march was met with the kind of vicious racism that characterized the 29 marches Rev led after the killing of Yusuf in 1989.

This was the last march that the coalition which had formed around Howard Beach did together. Even this one was tense, with the formerly-behind-closed-doors arguments now bursting out into the open. Death threats by white racists against Rev were phoned in, prompting a beefing up of the already edgy cops. The New York 8 wing had agreed to come only if the 8's Coltrane Chimurenga could head up security. The 8 had a fit about the extra cops who were called in because of the death threats against Rev; they argued about bail money that had been raised at a rally by the militants while the Day of Outrage defendants were waiting to be released. The militants had pulled their people from in front of the precinct to hold a bail rally at Boys and Girls High, and now there were fights about what had happened to the money. The seeds of dissension had been sown; barely a month after the Day of Outrage, they bore their full fruit.

Even without the intervention of whichever outside forces manipulated the dissension into an open split, the coalition had been tense from the beginning. With a movement bubbling on the streets (and even under them, as had happened during the Day of Outrage), every variety of leader and would-be leader in the greater New York area began jockeying for position, some to lead the movement, some to influence it in one direction or another, some to cool it out.

There were Rev and Maddox and Mason, a triumvirate that had come together in the course of the Howard Beach battles. Their tactic was to fight the authorities in the courts, backed up by the masses in the streets, to wrest victories from a racist power structure that otherwise would not bend.

Mason was prone to challenge the system from within, piling up case after case of racial violence victims and running an insurgent challenge to Manhattan District Attorney Robert Morganthau in 1985, when he pulled a respectable third of the vote.

Maddox had no love for the establishment — Black or white — whatsoever. His sneering accusation of "Ni-gro" leveled at any Black establishment figure he suspected didn't have the people's interests at heart was withering. The fiery rhetoric went with a talented legal mind. Maddox was also one of the hardest working attorneys in the business. Less politically calculating than Mason, who was always wary of burning his bridges, Maddox often seemed as if he were on a suicide mission, willing to risk all for a client or a cause.

There were the militants, who saw the marches in a whole different light. As self-proclaimed revolutionaries, their agenda was to build the marches up to larger and larger numbers, which would culminate at a given time into a "general strike" that would bring the city to a standstill.

And there was the world of Black elected officialdom, who wondered anxiously what to do with this movement of their constituents that was operating independently of them.

Before the final split in the movement, Rev got a call from Herb Daughtry saying they all needed to sit down with Manhattan Borough President David Dinkins and the rest of the Black politicians to cool everyone's tempers off a bit. Daughtry often sought to serve as a bridge between the Black establishment and Democratic Party reformers on the one hand and the more radical elements on the other.

The "peace meeting" took place at Dinkins' offices downtown. Among the participants were Bill Lynch (later...a Dinkins deputy mayor), Daughtry, Brooklyn Assemblyman Roger Green, Father Lawrence Lucas, Jitu Weusi, Maddox and Rev. Dinkins walked into the room and had everybody seated before he spoke up.

"I wanted to meet with you, because I think you're making a lot of moves, and I'm the top Black elected official in this city and you all *never talk to me*. How do you think I feel?" Dinkins directed his gaze at Rev. "Every time I go into a TV studio, the first question they ask me is, 'What do you think of Al Sharpton?' *You're* not an elected official, *I* am."

"If you did your fucking job, they'd be asking you about *you!*" Rev shot back. Of course all hell broke loose, but after hours of arguing it ended peacefully, with everyone agreeing to work together and coordinate activities.

Peace lasted for a whole three weeks.

In mid-January, Rev spoke at a memorial for Dr. King; seated beside him on the rally stage, Herb Daughtry leaned over. His eyes were solemn.

"I understand that everybody's coming out with something against you. Be careful."

The withdrawal of Dutchess County District Attorney William Grady from the grand jury investigation of the Tawana Brawley case was overshadowed by *Newsday*'s publication of the first installment of its feature pieces on Rev and the feds. Two days later, the second *Newsday* story hit, this time eclipsing the news that Grady's replacement, Poughkeepsie attorney David Sall, had stepped down too. Sall claimed that no local attorney could investigate the case; although he (like Grady) refused to give details, it became clear that the prime suspects were local law enforcement types.

At least the living suspects. A part-time police officer, Harry Crist, had already been found with a bullet through his head in December, not long after he'd been hanging out with Assistant District Attorney Steven Pagones and State Trooper Scott Patterson.

Add Tawana's scrawled note insisting that she wanted Frederick Scoralick, the local sheriff who headed up an all-white force, "dead," and you have the makings of a case of good old boys with good connections having their way with a young Black girl and expecting not to have to answer to anybody for it.

The initial response of the coalition forces was to reject the *Newsday* pieces as an attempt to split up the movement.

"I have no proof about Al Sharpton," said Sonny Carson. "This whole thing probably comes out of the governor's office. The government comes up with all kinds of things to throw us off course."

Jitu Weusi explicitly likened the articles to the COINTELPRO operation and demanded to know the names of the unnamed *Newsday* "sources." State Senator David Paterson termed the articles "an attempt to discredit a movement bigger than Reverend Sharpton or *Newsday*."

New York's tabloid press was unsure how to gauge the response to the "revelations," since no one — including those who were cited as having been spied on and snitched on by Rev — was coming out swinging against him. *Newsday* headlined one January 21 sidebar "Black Support for Sharpton," while the *New York Post* of the same day ran a headline that read: "Not Many Leaders in Radical Rev's Corner."

The morning the story broke, Rev got a call from Maddox.

"Don't say anything. I'm with you. I think this is ludicrous and I'm calling around to everyone else. Meet me at WLIB [New York's Black talk radio station] in an hour."

Rev headed upstairs to the station. He walked past most of the militant leaders who had gathered in the lobby, looking sheepish. Mason and Maddox were already there.

"I'm going on the air to defend Sharpton," Maddox said. "The whole thing was obviously a set-up for someone to kill Reverend Sharpton and make it look like gangsters, or even Don King, had him killed."

By now most of the press in the world was represented. The three men took three or four dozen phone calls during the morning and afternoon. There was near-unanimous support.

But the two wings of the coalition now headed on their separate paths, with the Carson/New York 8 grouping (joined by Elombe Brath of the Patrice Lumumba Coalition) calling itself the December 12 Coalition.

They did separate demonstrations, too. On January 27 Rev led hundreds in the bitter cold out to LaGuardia Airport, where he and Mitchell were among 11 arrested after they blocked off an entrance ramp to the airport. The sounds of "No Justice, No Peace!" reverberated through the late afternoon chill.

"No justice, no peace!" repeated a young African American baggage handler as she emerged from a terminal amidst startled throngs of hurrying tourists. "That's *right*."

Rev was keeping the heat on.

"They said I gave information on drug dealers and mobsters," Rev said at a rally the night before at Mitchell's Ebenezer Baptist Church. "Wednesday I'm a snitch. Friday I'm a mobster. But I'll meet with a mobster or a saint or a sinner if it's to save Black children!"

It was after that protest that Rev's aide Perry McKinnon mysteriously told this writer he had a story "that will make you famous."

•

Soon after, Rev got a call telling him to get on over to 'LIB because Cuomo was coming to announce a special prosecutor in the Brawley case.

Cuomo made up his mind that he would have his attorney general, Robert Abrams, take the job.

The governor never actually made it to the station, but he and Maddox, Mason and Rev argued back and forth for half an hour on the

"Gary Byrd Show."

Abrams immediately announced that John Ryan, head of the criminal prosecutions bureau, would handle the details of the investigation.

"Abrams is already passing the buck," Rev charged. "He's not willing to use the weight of the attorney general's office to support Tawana."

They went up to consult with the Brawleys; two months after the rape, Tawana was still physically out of it, barely able to walk and not talking. Ralph King was a very angry person; Glenda a little calmer. They were relieved to know that Rev was going to be more directly involved.

Tawana recognized the chubby Rev from the "Morton Downey Show."

Within a few weeks, things got dangerously intense within the movement, following an almost textbook COINTELPRO script.

On the night of March 3, the newly renamed December 12 Coalition held a "forum" at Harlem's Harriet Tubman School; in actuality it was a five-hour trial of Al Sharpton.

The December 12 Coalition claimed to have conducted a three-month "investigation" of Rev's activities, and branded him an "enemy of the people" in a report read by Coltrane Chimurenga.

The "charges" were: Rev broke discipline and went his own way on the Day of Outrage, causing mass arrests; he had offered $300 to Sonny Carson to sit on the dais during a planning meeting for the demo; he threatened to spread rumors that Carson's Black Men's Movement Against Crack was into coke; the demonstration led by Rev at LaGuardia Airport was "unauthorized"; the January march against racism in Bensonhurst was recklessly planned, with Rev supposedly telling the cops that there was a death threat against him before that march.

Chimurenga, with a long history of inflammatory language and activity (the year before he had been responsible for attempting to incite physical violence *against* NAP's Fulani at the march down Fifth Avenue to Koch's home), called the last charge "a ploy to get the cops to come into our ranks and destroy us." Chimurenga and the rest of the "8" had received considerable support from Fulani during their troubles in 1985, only to split with her following their legal victory.

The new independent Black movement was dividing. Political differences?

It happens all the time. Sectarianism? Maybe. And maybe not.

•

Early in February Bill Cosby got in touch through Mason: he and Reginald Lewis, the publisher of *Essence* magazine who had recently bought Beatrice Foods, wanted to put up a reward for anyone with information that would lead to the arrest and conviction of those who had done this to Tawana.

"Set up a press conference."

After Cosby's announcement came a call that Cuomo wanted to meet with the three activists that afternoon.

"No, let's do it tomorrow," said Rev, who now knew he was embroiled in a political war with a powerful governor that was going to be fought both on the streets and in the media. "If we meet today, the governor will try to upstage Bill Cosby's announcement by saying he's coming to the table. Why don't we let Cosby's announcement ride as the story, then meet with the governor in the morning and let whatever he does with us be *tomorrow's* news."

Everyone agreed on the move. Rev called Cuomo's office back to relay the plan, only to get a call ten minutes later from the governor himself saying he would send his plane for them.

"No, we'll get there on our own, Governor," Rev replied. "We'll be there in the morning."

The next morning their driver was late; they wound up flying "Air Cuomo" anyway — after Rev gave the driver a serious cussing out. They got off the plane and were escorted by state troopers to the governor's office. Next thing they knew, they were standing before Cuomo in front of his famous George Washington desk.

"Hello, gentlemen," said the governor.

Rev, Mason, Maddox and Tim Mitchell met with Cuomo for about four hours.

"This is nothing against you personally, Governor," said Maddox, a model of conciliation. "You are the only white man I've ever voted for in my life."

"You made history with Howard Beach, at our expense," said Rev.

"You can make history again, but you got to make Bob Abrams adopt a hands-on policy."

The Brawley support team was interested in having four things happen: Abrams must conduct the grand jury investigation himself; he must prep all witnesses himself; he must speak to Tawana himself; and he must conduct the trial himself if there were indictments.

In another room, Cuomo called Abrams, who said that he was not going to let these gentlemen dictate how he did business.

There were a number of back and forth calls like that, and then the governor decided to get tough.

"You know a lot of people in the white community don't believe this happened at all. I'm going against the grain here, and you guys can be made to look like the biggest frauds in the world if you don't play ball."

"We didn't come to play at all," Rev shot back.

They wound up agreeing on three out of four and held a press conference to tell the world.

On March 20 Fulani — who was now an independent candidate for President of the United States — and the Women of Color Caucus of the New Alliance Party led 300 women through Poughkeepsie chanting "Stop the Rape, Stop the Lies!" At a rally afterward, women from all over the state voiced their support for Tawana.

No Democratic Party officials or establishment leaders participated — just as they didn't in any of the subsequent marches that Rev would hold. The balance of forces was tipping, but the situation was becoming increasingly dangerous because this time, unlike at Howard Beach, the powers-that-be were determined to give *nothing* up.

But for the moment, things were looking up: the full intensity of Cuomo's ruthless plan to destroy Rev and the movement was not yet evident; the governor continued to act as if he was just engaging in the usual give and take such negotiations involve.

He wasn't. The plan was to give up nothing. And Tawana was the key. Any time Rev and Tawana's other advisors made a demand, Cuomo and Abrams wanted to talk to Tawana. Rev and the rest of the team, of course, weren't going to hand her over unless it was clear that the case would be tried with the intention of nabbing Tawana's assailants.

Cuomo had learned well from Howard Beach. This time, he and Abrams used every resource at their disposal (and those resources, from *Newsday* to the entire law enforcement establishment, were considerable) to make it seem that Tawana, her family and their advisors were the ones standing in the way of justice being served.

"This is a movement that no paid provocateurs, no Uncle Toms, can stop," Rev said at an Albany rally in April to mark Dr. King's birthday; he, folksinger Pete Seeger and 12 others were arrested for civil disobedience. "Elected officials have to answer to why they're not here. After Jesse starts the revolution in New York State on April 19 [the date of the New York State Democratic Party primary], we may have to finish it in local areas by retiring some of these people to the Uncle Tom sanitarium and let them rest for the rest of their lives there!"

A revolution had indeed begun, forging an independent movement of Black leadership and their supporters: Rev, Mason and Maddox, Fulani, Farrakhan.

But Mario Cuomo was out for blood, and the movement was to be formed and shaped by a series of defeats. Howard Beach would not be repeated.

•

Late spring saw a series of almost comical mishaps on the part of those who were out to nail Rev and the whole movement. The fact that Cuomo and Abrams still succeeded, despite such blundering, is only an indication of how mediocrity backed by brute force can prevail against righteousness.

The absurdities perpetrated by the attorney general and the press were endless.

Minutes of the grand jury hearings were stolen early in the probe by an Abrams employee. A Black investigator on the Abrams team was arrested in Brooklyn for selling two ounces of coke to an undercover agent. Then there were "Mad Mike" Taibbi's Channel 2 broadcasts. Taibbi was put on the Brawley story after Channel 2 inexplicably pulled veteran reporter Chris Borgen from the story he had been covering since the beginning. Taibbi dragged a tragi-comic parade of "witnesses" across the screen:

Kids who were paid ten bucks and a hamburger to say they saw Tawana partying in "Crack Alley" during her disappearance — only to have their own parents come forward to denounce such child abuse on Taibbi's part;

Samuel McClease, a Crazy Eddie's salesman who claimed he bugged homes and offices and taped Rev, Mason and Maddox saying Tawana was lying. McClease told his story to both Taibbi and Abrams, and had them going until his tapes turned out to be blank;

Perry McKinnon, Rev's one-time driver, who appeared on Taibbi's show claiming that the whole Tawana story was "a pack of lies" and he just had to tell somebody about it. McKinnon, a former cop, failed to mention that Taibbi wasn't his first stop; he was shopping the story around for a good few months (including his whispered "Hey, I got a story that's going to make you famous" line on the bus after the LaGuardia Airport Day of Outrage) before landing on "Mad Mike's" six o'clock spot. What was especially troubling about McKinnon (whose own relatives stepped forth to characterize him as a loon) was that he (and many others like him) was hauled before Abrams' grand jury, despite his own admission that he hadn't a shred of information about what had happened to Tawana.

Abrams clearly was only concerned with pulling in witnesses who could discredit Tawana and her advisors, rather than carrying out his legal obligation to investigate what actually happened to the young woman.

"It don't look like they're going to investigate this rape even if we give them videos of it and have Mother Teresa brought in on Tawana's behalf," Rev thought to himself.

After each battle, Rev and his soldiers came up victorious; ask any reporter who covered the countless press conferences where Rev skillfully demolished the latest outrage that came from Abrams' office, the press, or some other swamp.

But they were losing the war.

•

By summer, Abrams began taking criminal action — not against Tawana's assailants, but the person whom the attorney general had decided was the *real* criminal.

Abrams tried to throw Glenda Brawley in jail.

Unlike Cedric Sandiford, Glenda's refusal to participate in a bogus investigation was not to be tolerated.

There were a number of problems. First and foremost was the issue of protecting Glenda; Abrams was threatening to arrest her for defying the subpoena.

"Let's put her in a church, and let them try to defy church sanctuary," said Maddox defiantly.

Which was fine, except Rev had to find the church. Maddox didn't know any, and Mason's suggestion of Calvin Butts' Abyssinian Baptist was nixed by Butts himself.

For his part, Rev went on camera and ripped up Glenda's subpoena, announcing that she was headed for sanctuary.

"Seventy-two hours to reconsider," said Abrams, which is how much time he was going to allot before he would lock up the mother of a Black teenage rape victim.

That night, Maddox put Glenda into the back of his car and drove her to an undisclosed location for her to make up her mind about what she would do.

Rev talked long distance to the out-of-town Tim Mitchell.

"Y'all can *start* in my church," Mitchell said.

Rev went to fetch Glenda and brought her to the church, then called the wire services to inform them that they had taken sanctuary at Ebenezer Baptist; in no time, Rev saw more TV cameras then even *he* had ever seen surrounding the church!

But that night, the board of trustees at Ebenezer Baptist voted that they could not stay.

Rev called on Reverend William Jones.

"Come over to Bethany," said Rev's old mentor.

On a trip upstate soon after, Rev and Tawana were intercepted by TV reporter Tim Minton. She took the opportunity to say her first words on camera.

"All I want is justice and I'm not lying."

Meanwhile, the now maddened press was harassing the Brawley family to death. Tawana was staying with her Uncle Matthew in Monticello and being tormented there, with the press — led by "Mad Mike" Taibbi — following her from school. Rev decided to move in on the situation.

He drove all the way to Monticello alone, and talked with Tawana.

"I don't want to stay here with my uncle," she told him.

"Pack all your clothes in a bag." Which she did.

They walked out in front of the press. Rev and Tawana got into Rev's car, and they sped off. They drove to the ice cream parlor for some cones. Then Rev drove down the back street and told Tawana to slip through her uncle's basement window.

The next day, the press announced that "Reverend Al whisked Tawana away to a secret location."

Tawana was in the same place she always was, but she would now get a rest from the press.

•

It was going to be a long, hot summer, Rev thought. Something had to be done to break out of the impasse that Cuomo was manipulating from the governor's mansion.

"How are we going to bring this to a head?" Rev wondered.

Phil Donahue wanted badly to interview Glenda. Rev had done the show before during the Goetz and Howard Beach cases, and knew the talk show host well.

"The only way you can speak to her is to go live from Bethany, because we're not leaving sanctuary."

It was Donahue's first live show from a Black church.

Then Rev decided it was time to leave for a trip south. The Democratic

National Convention (one of Cuomo's favorite outings) was about to get underway in Atlanta.

"We need to go down and force the Democratic Party nationally, Jesse Jackson and all the others, to take a position," Rev said.

At the time, Abrams was hot on Glenda's trail (or at least acting like he was, since many of his activities by then were pure provocation). Maddox, who was also licensed in Georgia, had been spending time there already, working to keep up his license requirements, and Fulani was planning a week-long demonstration outside the convention to support Jesse's campaign and to kick off her independent run should he (as was expected) get snubbed by the Democrats.

Minister Farrakhan was planning a Black Agenda conference to challenge the Democrats to heed the demands of the Black community, or take a hike.

Maddox was back in Brooklyn for a rally of thousands at Bethany Baptist, where Tawana took in the love of the community.

"We're going to shut Atlanta down," he told the roaring crowd, many of them veterans of the Days of Outrage. They knew just what he meant, and they were ready.

But how to get Glenda out?

They were going to meet up with Farrakhan in Newark for dinner, assuming they could get out. The tension mounted the night before the planned departure; a man claiming to be from Abrams' office told them, cowboy style, that the place was surrounded.

The next day, July 16, was hot and steamy. Again the crowd roared its support as Rev, Tawana, Glenda and Juanita emerged into the hot Brooklyn sun handcuffed to each other to board the bus for the ride south to see the Democrats.

Little did they know that Abrams had the Verrazano Bridge — the likely route they would take if they were headed straight to Atlanta — staked out, ready to intercept the bus and put their own cuffs on Glenda. It was by sheer luck that they were heading instead to Newark for dinner with the Minister and took a different route, going straight out of Brooklyn into Manhattan, and on through the tunnel to Newark.

In all likelihood the change of plans averted a bloodbath that would have been on the hands of Governor Mario Cuomo as Attica had been on the hands of Rockefeller the decade before.

The bus was packed and everyone tried to keep their spirits up with songs and chants.

Then Rev saw the sign in the Lincoln Tunnel announcing that you are crossing the "New York/New Jersey" border.

"We're outta here." On to dinner, and then the exhausting but joy-filled 18-hour ride to Atlanta.

Tawana sat next to Rev the whole ride, sleeping practically the entire trip. "I never saw anybody sleep like that," Rev thought, thinking about what this 16-year-old had been through these last few months.

The crew received a raucous ovation at Atlanta's historic Wheat Street Baptist Church, where Fulani had warmed up the standing room only crowd of 5,000 for Farrakhan's three-hour Black Agenda speech.

It was a week packed with marches, rallies, press conferences and more rallies at hotels and at Fulani's protest grounds opposite the convention.

The week further solidified the establishment of a new, independent Black political leadership. It had taken a young African American woman to begin the process.

The attack on Tawana was not in itself the catalyst; she had, after all, received wide support in the aftermath of her abduction. The cutting edge was who would join Rev in standing up to an all-out effort by the powers-that-be to *use* the case to destroy a movement. That new leadership took center stage at the Wheat Street Baptist Church while the Democrats gathered together to dis Jesse in favor of a Texas Dixiecrat named Lloyd Bentsen.

After stopping off for a visit with James Brown on the way back, they all returned home to the now familiar story of the "Final Report" of the grand jury convened in Dutchess County by Abrams. The report said Tawana had lied, her attorneys had lied, Rev had lied, Tawana had done it to herself, and the trio of supporters knew it all along.

The crowning felony in the whole sordid affair was the leak — weeks before the grand jury report appeared in October, 1988 — of major portions to the *New York Times*. America's newspaper of record was given the first opportunity to test the waters of public opinion regarding the report's bizarre claim that, whatever happened to Tawana, she did it to herself.

If anything was ripe for investigating, though, it was the massive leak of piles of secret grand jury materials to the press. Cuomo (who early in the Brawley affair had solemnly proclaimed "Tawana is my daughter") was very concerned about the leak. He appointed a special investigator to find what should have been no harder to locate than Niagara Falls.

Two weeks later the special leak prober closed the investigation, insisting there was no way to discover who made the hole in the dike. Case closed.

The man the governor appointed to catch the felons was none other than Charles "Joe" Hynes, the hapless special prosecutor in the Howard Beach case. Joe Hynes, it seems, was to be allowed *his* revenge, too.

When Abrams ultimately issued the "secret" grand jury report himself, it came complete with recommendations for disciplinary action against Mason and Maddox (such recommendations are almost never made publicly), and an announcement that an investigation of Rev was underway as well.

That was only the latest in a series of moves Abrams made which were ethically and legally dubious. But *he* was the attorney general — who was going to prosecute the prosecutor? In choosing Abrams (otherwise not one of his favorite political associates) as special prosecutor, Cuomo had made sure he had every base covered.

Rev seemed to sense the dangers and probable defeat that were in store while they were still in Atlanta. But although the powers-that-be looked like they had the upper hand, he knew the moral victory lay ahead.

In the middle of the hectic week, Rev brought the travelers from New York on a pilgrimage to the final resting place of Dr. Martin Luther King, Jr. on historic Auburn Avenue.

In a solemn and passionate ceremony Tawana laid a wreath of carnations at the tomb of Dr. King, which rests amidst the glistening waters of a fountain where millions of ordinary people (along with all too many vote-hungry politicians) have come to pay their respects. Rev delivered a prayer of simple eloquence which silenced even the usually belligerent press corps that dogged them everywhere.

"Since you've been gone, there's been a lot of tears shed. In the North now, we face what you fought in the South, but we have tried not to sell out. We have tried not to back up, just like when you stood against the war in Viet Nam.

"Many other Black leaders have been bought out, but we still try to hold up your name and your movement. We come to bring Dr. King a young lady who is innocent, who never did nothing to nobody, who was raped and sodomized. They have gone after her mother rather than deal with the racists who marked 'KKK' and 'nigger' on her torso. We promised her, like you promised Rosa Parks, that we would not let her down, no matter what they do to us.

"You taught us to stand for what was right. We didn't want to leave Atlanta without coming to tell you we were going to stand. If they indict us like they did you, we will still stand. If they castigate us like they did you, we will still stand. If they write editorials and cartoons, we will still stand. You promised us we would make it to the promised land. I know you would not lie to us, Dr. King. We will see you in the promised land.

"So now, in the name of Yvonne Smallwood, a mother just trying to cash her check to buy Christmas gifts, who was beaten to death by New York City's Taxi and Limousine police; in the name of Eleanor Bumpurs, Dr. King, a 67-year-old grandmother who was killed in her own home by two shotgun blasts; in the name of Randy Evans and Clifford Glover, two young men shot down by New York City police; in the name of even you, Dr. King — we come to leave this wreath.

"We're not the big shots, we're not the ones who will be meeting with Dukakis — we're the ones you died for. We're the ones who appreciated you shedding your blood. We will never forget you. We will never make a disgrace out of your name. We love you. We will see you on the other side."

Postscript: Spring 1990

It was ultimately left for a jury to prove that Robert Abrams willfully used his elected office and position as a public servant to engage in political warfare against his opponents, to wit, the Reverend Alfred Sharpton, Alton Maddox, Jr., C. Vernon Mason, and the movement they spearheaded in the latter part of the last decade.

It occurred around the third week of Rev's massive fraud trial the following spring.

The morning's and afternoon's testimony at the start of week three saw two more witnesses for the prosecution shot down from the stand by Rev's attorney Maddox, who had found his cross examinations of the state's witnesses to be little more than target practice. In the afternoon, a fellow from G Street Express (they produce rap artists Run DMC) testified that an altered receipt of a cash payment was his own doing, not that of Rev, as the AG had claimed.

Down went count number seven (falsifying business records in the first degree) of the 67-count indictment.

That was in the afternoon; the morning had been spent with Mitchell Lambert, the state's top investigator in the case against Rev, describing to Assistant Attorney General Paula Gellman dozens of items he swiped from the offices of the National Youth Movement when he and the boys, armed with a search warrant, raided the place in November, 1988:

"What's this, Mr. Lambert?" asked prosecutor Gellman, holding up a piece of vouchered evidence.

"That appears to be a check," the seasoned investigator responded dryly.

This went on for an hour and a half. Then Maddox, trying what may have been the last case of his career (having just been mugged for his law license by the very people he was defending Rev against) got up for the "cross."

Maddox was barely interested in describing items pilfered from Rev's Youth Movement offices; *he* wanted the witness to tell the jury who *he* was. This Lambert fellow, it was quickly established, worked for Robert Abrams.

"It would be fair to say that he is your boss?" asked Maddox, eliciting a "Yessir."

"And when were you assigned to this investigation?"

Investigator Lambert waffled a bit, then 'fessed up: around October, 1988. That's about all Maddox needed from this witness, because in his opening statement to the jury the Georgia-born civil rights attorney had already explained that Abrams pulled out all the stops in his vendetta against Rev *after* the AG closed his case on Tawana Brawley — which just happened to be in October of 1988.

•

Weeks later, as the June sun began warming the city, the jury hearing the case went out for its final deliberations following Maddox's startling courtroom announcement that he was resting his case without calling any witnesses for the defense.

They thought about the mountains of testimony from the attorney general's office purporting to establish that Rev was a crook. And they thought about Maddox's contention that the whole affair amounted to a political vendetta by Bob Abrams. Then they went through each of the counts and checked off "not guilty" 67 times.

It took the jury exactly six hours to agree with Maddox that the whole two-year, multi-million dollar affair was politically motivated.

Which happens to be a crime.

FOURTEEN

Black Revolution in New York

Nineteen hundred and eighty-nine opened with Rev launching an all-out war against Koch, police brutality and all the escalating ugliness of New York City. The list of police brutality cases had by now grown unwieldy. The case of Richard Luke, shot dead by police in a Queens housing project, ushered in the new year.

And a protest against Rev's old "friend" Donald Trump. Rev brought his troops out after the billionaire rich kid, in the midst of the Central Park rape case, took out full-page ads advocating the death penalty for Black youth. Rev remembered back to 1987, when Trump and his friend Don King were putting together a Tyson fight in Atlantic City. "Bring Al Sharpton along!" Trump told King before a press conference to announce the fight.

Next thing he knew, Rev was airborne in the Donald's private chopper with Trump and King, heading for Atlantic City. Trump gave Rev an aerial tour like they were flying over a giant monopoly game.

"I own that; I own that; there's the lot I own where I'm going to build the Taj Mahal..."

Rev's gaze was rivetted on the shoddy huts where *his* people live in the most abject poverty.

"You're lucky I don't live in this town, because I'd run your ass over into the water," said Rev.

King grabbed his chest like he was having a heart attack. "He didn't mean that! He didn't mean that, Donald!" The two Dons were splitting some big, big money for the fight at the time. "A complete opportunist," thought Rev about the rich kid Trump. "But he has balls!"

•

One day in June 1989 after yet another meeting on yet another brutality case Rev arrived home to a phone call from Jack Newfield, a former writer for the *Village Voice* who was then making his home at the *Daily News*.

"I understand you're going to be indicted within the next two weeks," Newfield told him.

Something in Albany was leaking again.

"Well, that's strange. I just wrote a letter asking if I could go before the grand jury and explain my finances," Rev replied.

"Well, we'll see what happens," said Newfield before hanging up and heading for his typewriter so he could get the story in the *News* the following day.

Newfield was half right. On the day his story came out Rev got a call from the attorney general's office to let him know that they were downstairs to arrest him. He'd been indicted. Could he come down to open the door?

Rev headed downstairs to find that the whole street had been blocked off; Abrams had not lost his flair for the dramatic. Rev, wearing one of his favorite jogging suits, got into a car and they drove off into Manhattan.

The phone rang as they headed over the Brooklyn Bridge; the agent driving changed expression slowly as he listened to the voice on the other end. Then he turned to his prisoner.

"Reverend, I'm sorry, but I have to put handcuffs on you," he apologized. "They're going to have cameras here for you." Abrams was playing his catch for all it was worth. Arriving at the jailhouse to a sea of cameras, Rev remembered some words of Malcolm's that he had read as a youngster: "Use the media to talk to your people."

So Rev started hollerin' his head off. "Don't worry. They did this to

King. They did this to Garvey. Don't worry." Rev still had no idea what he was being indicted for, even as he was tossed in a cell to await Maddox's arrival.

But the legal sharpshooter couldn't make heads or tails out of the indictment. "All I can tell is that it's a lot of counts of some kind of fraud," said the baffled attorney.

Rev took a deep bow as he was brought into court, refusing to be intimidated while the eyes of the community were on him.

"How do you plead?" Rev was asked.

"I plead that the attorney general is insane," Rev responded. Everyone in the courtroom burst out laughing.

"I plead my client is innocent," said Maddox.

Rev was subsequently re-arrested, brought into Albany and holed up in a cell all night to be arraigned on tax charges there.

A funny thing happened on the way to Albany. One of the chief investigators in the AG's office stopped the car.

"Do you want some food, Reverend?" The next thing Rev knew he was handed some Chinese goodies.

"Let me ask you something, Reverend."

"What's that?"

"What really happened to Tawana Brawley?"

"You don't know?" Rev asked, flabbergasted.

"What *really* happened?"

"Well," said Rev, "if you're the chief investigator for the attorney general's office, and you're telling me that you really don't believe it was a hoax, you just vindicated my position, because I know it wasn't."

And they rode on into Albany without saying another word.

Up in Albany, released on $20,000 bond, Rev had the same attitude that he did downstate on the first arraignment.

"No, I'm not worried. It ain't over until the fat man sings."

•

Then in late August Rev got a call at the house, picked up by his aide Anthony Charles.

"It's a Moses Stewart. His son was killed in Bensonhurst."

Virginia-born and Brooklyn-bred, Stewart was a truck driver by trade. He spent seven years in the army, only to discover as much racism inside as there was in civilian life. Because he couldn't take the thought of being expected to defend his country while being constantly humiliated by superior officers, he eventually gave up on the idea of being a career military man.

He chose instead to make it as best he could doing the things that he was taught would deliver the American dream, working, raising a family, paying bills and getting ahead. And teaching his children, according to his religious beliefs, to do the right thing.

"You have to work in harmony with people, even people who don't like you," he would tell his three sons growing up on the tough streets of East New York. "You try to work with them."

Stewart and Diane Hawkins had been together since they were teens, bringing into the world and rearing three boys, Yusuf, Amir and Freddie.

The youngest of three daughters, Diane was brought up in Brooklyn's Bedford-Stuyvesant neighborhood before moving at age 12 to East New York. After being graduated from Thomas Jefferson High School, she went on to the CBI Trade School and trained to be a computer programmer while working as a telephone operator. She was terribly proud of Yusuf, who had just graduated from junior high and was on his way to the High School for Transit Technology.

Moses Stewart: "The day after the shooting took place in Bensonhurst, we were in front of my home at 485 Hegemann Avenue, and there was a gob of reporters outside the house. Someone out of the crowd yelled, 'If there was someone that you could call to help you in your plight, you and your family, who would you call?'

"So I told them that if there was anyone that I would call, it would be the likes of the Reverend Al Sharpton or Minister Louis Farrakhan. That's how it got out, and then one of the reporters handed me Sharpton's phone number. And I ended up calling him — the same day, as a matter of fact."

Diane Hawkins: "I would always watch the news and see other people going through these tragic situations, and all of a sudden it's *me*. There's no way I was going to sit back and let my son's death be in vain, like everything was OK. *It just doesn't work that way.* You can't sit back. So we had to get this type of attention out there to the people. Because you never know, it could have been anyone else's child out there — still could be — and we had to get a message across to the public that we were going to stand up for our son.

"I had no contact with Reverend Sharpton before the incident happened. But I felt, here's a Black man out here standing up for the people. He sort of reminded me of a Martin Luther King, and I always admired him for that."

Stewart: "He showed up that very afternoon and he's been with the family and me ever since."

Ever since meant nothing more than a Black revolution in New York City. As it turned out, Moses Stewart's decision to transform the anguish over the loss of his son Yusuf Hawkins into something larger would catalyze a chain of events that had been waiting to happen.

•

Rev rode out to East New York to the address he had been given. As they turned the corner, mountains of TV trucks and news people appeared. Rev got out of the car, which sent all the press running over to him.

"What do you have to sell, Reverend?" they asked the activist who was on trial for his political life.

"Nothing."

Down came Moses Stewart, whom Rev had never seen before.

"It's really him. It's really him!"

Rev came into the house, not knowing that the grieving father had worried that the reporters might have given him a bogus phone number. Rev met Diane Hawkins, and the rest of the family. Needless to say, everyone was shaken up and distraught.

They related the story of what happened to Yusuf as best they knew it: how he and his friends were surrounded as they looked for the address they had gotten from the *Buy-Lines* of someone selling a used car, how someone pulled a gun and shot Yusuf through the heart, where he was left to die on the sidewalk.

"Look," said Rev. "You want me involved, you've got to be sure, because there's going to be a lot of controversy with me being involved. We just finished the Brawley case, and the media are shooting us down like crazy. But if you want me involved, I'll go all the way with you."

Yusuf's kin not only wanted Rev, they wanted Farrakhan too.

"OK," said Rev.

Moses told Rev he wanted the press to leave him alone. "I don't know what to say to the press," he said, overwhelmed. "You handle them."

"Moses, they're *not* going to leave you alone. The first thing we should do is go on WLIB and let you talk and explain what happened."

"OK."

Rev got 'LIB on the line, and the two of them talked live on the air for a half hour or so, which didn't win them any friends from the white media waiting outside.

Then they got a call that David Dinkins, mayoral candidate, was on the way.

"What does that Uncle Tom want?" asked someone in the Hawkins home.

"You've gotta receive everybody at this point," Rev instructed. "The issue is bigger than politics."

Dinkins arrived in the late afternoon with Herbert Daughtry, Bill Lynch and Jim Bell in tow. They went upstairs.

Dinkins offered his sympathy and promised that when he was elected mayor, this sort of thing would never happen again. At that point, one family member let some of the outrage out.

"What do you mean, when you're *elected*? What are you going to do *now*? What are you going to do to fight for justice *now*, you Uncle Tom motherfucker?"

Rev tried to calm everybody down, and they reached an agreement not to say anything negative about the candidate. "Let him go outside and say what he's got to say," Rev said.

Dinkins thanked Rev and the family, and departed, stopping for a press statement before the crews outside.

Rev thought to himself that he could have killed the borough president's mayoral campaign right there — he was angry enough after hearing the family tell their story to do it. Then Rev thought about Edward I. Koch, and the years of pain *that* had caused *everyone*, and was satisfied that he made the right decision.

The phone kept ringing; this time Koch and police chief Ben Ward wanted to pay their respects. Moses agreed. Then Cuomo, who chatted with Moses and Diane.

"If there's anything I can do..." Cuomo began. Diane cut him off.

"Well, I suppose there are some things you can do," she told the governor. "You can talk to our advisor."

Rev took the phone and listened.

"This is Mario Cuomo. Whom am I speaking to?"

"This is Al Sharpton. How are you doing, Governor?"

It was their first conversation since Brawley. There was a long pause.

"Al! How have you been?"

"All right."

"Is there anything we can do?"

"Yeah. We need you to watch the State Compensation for Victims crew. The family has no money, and one of the immediate things they have to deal with is raising money for a funeral."

The governor agreed, and hung up.

Next on the line was Jesse Jackson. He called to inquire about the funeral arrangements. Jesse promised to come in as soon as he could.

And then, one of the police department's top brass came by.

"The mayor is on the way in a helicopter," the officer said. "He would like Reverend Sharpton to leave before he arrives."

"If the mayor wants to come he's welcome, but he's got to come with Al Sharpton here. That's our advisor!" Moses hollered angrily, having taken just about enough for one day. "He don't want to see Sharpton, he don't want to see *us*. In fact, tell him to turn his motherfucking ass around. Fuck Koch."

They looked out the window just in time to see a helicopter make an aerial U-turn and head back toward Manhattan.

•

Soon it was time to start marching. At the Slave Theater, home base for Rev's United African Movement, the buses were readying for the trip to Bensonhurst.

Rev looked over at Moses, who had approved the march, and said, "Now, I'm going to do one thing you're not going to like."

"What's that?"

"You can't go on this march."

"What do you mean?"

"You don't know what you're going to face. You're never going to be able to control yourself. I definitely don't want Diane to go, and the only way she's not going is if you don't go."

Rev put them in the car and took them home. Then the buses left. Five hundred marched that day, and it was the ugliest march that any of them had *ever* been on.

For the first time in his life, Rev looked around him and had a notion that hadn't passed through his mind in 20 years of marching.

"I don't think I'm going to make it."

That's how much hate and venom Rev saw; even a wedding party, including the bride and groom, came out of their reception to give them the finger and call them "niggers." Not to mention the watermelons, the white kids flashing their asses. Rev looked over at Yusuf's two brothers, who were in total shock. Rev marched everybody out of there as quickly as he could.

Tim Mitchell led another march the following day, with lots of the mainstream leaders, Black and white. They were shunning Yusuf's family advisor. Just to show that racism wasn't something that only Al Sharpton attracted, the Bensonhurst community gave them the same treatment.

Rev, in the meantime, formed a hands-around-the-block prayer meeting to protect the family after threatening phone calls began coming into the Hawkins home.

•

Rev took Moses for a walk two days before the funeral, stopping at a diner to have a bite to eat and to talk. Rev walked over to the phone and dialed a number, came back and got Moses.

"Moses, somebody wants to speak to you."

Moses took the phone. "Hello?"

"As Salaam Aleikum, brother!"

It was Louis Farrakhan. Moses' face lit up. His dream of having Rev and Farrakhan at his side had been accomplished.

"Invite him to the funeral!" Rev whispered, and Moses did just that.

"I don't know," said the minister respectfully. "I'll get back to Reverend Sharpton."

When Farrakhan finally jumped out of a car caravan outside the house Moses fell into his arms, ecstatic. The NOI leader came upstairs and talked to the family. Then they all got into cars and headed to the funeral; turning the block, they discovered the street was mobbed.

It was the beginning of the Black revolution in New York — led by Rev, Moses Stewart, Diane Hawkins, Minister Louis Farrakhan, Dr. Lenora Fulani, thousands of the despised and voiceless and locked out were taking to the streets.

Black Revolution in New York City

If we don't do something real soon, I think you'll have to agree that we're going to be forced either to use the ballot or the bullet. It's one or the other in 1964. It isn't that time is running out — time has run out! 1964 threatens to be the most explosive year America has ever witnessed. Why? It's also a political year. It's the year when all of the white politicians will be back in the so-called Negro community jiving you and me for some votes. The year when all of the white political crooks will be right back in your community with their false promises, building up our hopes for a letdown, with their trickery and their treachery, with their false promises which they don't intend to keep. As they nourish these dissatisfactions, it can only lead to one thing, an explosion; and now we have the type of Black man on the scene in America to-day...who just doesn't intend to turn the other cheek any longer.

— from *Malcolm X Speaks*

Malcolm X specifically entitled his talk in Cleveland that night in 1964 "The Ballot or the Bullet" because, like Rev and the masses on the street, he was issuing the powers-that-be a warning. J. Edgar Hoover might brand everyone in the movement "Black hate groups" (as the media and hacks would brand the youth who took to the streets a generation later), but Malcolm knew that forces larger than him and Hoover and a bunch of cracker Dixiecrats were at work.

•

The year 1989 was the year New York City was going to elect its first Black mayor.

It had been done before in big cities. Philadelphia elected Wilson Goode, a hack machine politician all the way, in 1983. He expressed his appreciation by dropping a bomb on 11 African American children, women and men in the MOVE family. Chicago elected Harold Washington, also from the machine, but with his other foot firmly in the grassroots. Washington forged a broad-based grassroots coalition that temporarily swept the white machine from power.

David Dinkins faced a New York City with a character all its own. David's machine all the way. Playing it by the book. But there was one difference. The Black revolution in New York City. It was on the streets, wherever David showed up. And in the papers he read over his morning coffee. Even on the ballot, where Fulani had a slot as the independent New Alliance Party candidate for mayor. Black revolution in New York City!

"We can do this! We always knew this! Yeaahh, Boooyee!" On the Brooklyn Bridge two days after Yusuf's funeral — the Brooklyn side of course — outrage had turned into open revolt. And quickly.

"We can do this!" The beloved cry of Flavor Flav — second-in-command of Public Enemy, the embattled troubadours of the Black revolution — echoed from the brick walls at the foot of the bridge. "We always knew this!"

Power. It was everywhere on the bridge that night.

Revolution. A grassroots uprising, bubbling up from the cracked and bloodied pavements of Brooklyn, and flowing through the streets to the bridge.

Michael Griffith. Eleanor Bumpurs. Michael Stewart. Clifford Glover. Elderly grandmothers and little boys. Murdered daily in cold blood on the streets of New York. Why? "Just because they're dark and lovely," sang Stevie Wonder.

"Fight the Power — fight the powers-that-be!" instructed Public Enemy's Chuck D.

It took everyone by surprise — everyone. Makes you wonder. Didn't anyone feel the rumbling in the streets? Didn't they listen to Black radio?

And didn't they hear what the Reverend Al Sharpton was saying, over and over and over?

NO JUSTICE, NO PEACE. It's not complicated. Without one, there would not be the other. And there hadn't been justice for as long as anybody could remember.

They didn't listen to Rev, and they didn't listen to the streets. They didn't listen to the youth, masses of them, Black and proud, who were listening to Rev. Then one day Moses Stewart made a phone call, and nothing would ever be the same.

Did anyone really think the Black youth of Brooklyn, of New York, of the nation, were going to be shot down in the streets by white police, by racists guarding their white privileges and white territories and white property (including, as has been their obsession since the first African male was brought to these shores in chains, their women) and there would be no response?

"Not in this day and age, my brother!" Public Enemy's Professor Griff explained to those who were listening to the radios and tape players on the street. The lynching of Yusuf Hawkins, 16 years old, on the streets of Bensonhurst was going to be the last time, Brooklyn's youth decided.

No one expected the revolution on the bridge.

Chalk it up to the stupidity of the FBI and the white corporate media that dutifully echo them. Any time there is trouble in the ghettos, the undeniable cause is agitators, troublemakers. Get rid of the agitators, and no more trouble. In 1963, J. Edgar Hoover described Dr. King as "a 'tomcat' with degenerate sexual urges." Five years later, King was killed. The movement didn't die, it exploded. Leaders don't make revolutions, people do. In the ensuing years it took the genocidal war unleashed by the degenerate Hoover against the Black Panthers and the Black community to quiet — for the moment — the Black revolution.

The police weren't expecting it. "We thought we had adequate numbers for the history of the organization that organized the demonstration," said NYPD Chief of Patrol David Scott, who was one of two or three dozen cops injured on the bridge. The New York 8, the "organization that had organized the demonstration," a police spokesperson said, "historically has drawn 150-200 people" to previous demonstrations. There were 10,000 people, mostly Black youth, on the bridge.

Even the New York 8 were surprised.

As has been the case in these demonstrations over the past few years, the December 12 folks led the marchers to a target — often this very same bridge — where a wall of cops waited for the inevitable scuffle, arrests and dispersal. Such was the case that Wednesday night, when the marchers met a blue wall of white cops on the Manhattan-bound lane of the bridge. There was pushing, shoving and screams as arms and night-sticks flailed and the deadly chokehold re-enacted in Spike Lee's *Do the Right Thing* was applied.

But not for long. This wasn't a march. In the previous 24 hours, the call had gone out on Black radio and in the streets to assemble at 4 PM on Thursday in the heart of downtown Brooklyn, the hub of the largest Black community in the country. Brooklyn responded. Youth responded. A thousand or so marchers left Grand Army Plaza around 5 PM, but from then on it was no longer the march that the New York 8 had intended. Brooklyn's youth joined in. The standard slogans of marches like these — militant as they are — suddenly sounded a bit abstract; a new generation, born and raised in households where portraits of the martyred Martin and Malcolm decorated the walls, spoke its own mind in unison:

"Fuck the Cops!"

"Fuck Koch!"

"Fuck *all* the Politicians!"

"Yu-suf! Yu-SUF!"

On the Manhattan-bound lane, the nightsticks stopped flailing and the chokeholds were released; the police found themselves under attack from every direction, surrounded by the youth who had taken the walkway, the Brooklyn-bound lane, the service road and all the high ground in the vicinity around the spot where the predictable clash was supposed to happen. Most of the youth had never met the march leaders, who were taking a beating at that moment down on the roadway.

Didn't matter. The white police officers were vastly outnumbered by Black youth (as is, of course, the case citywide). Bottles, tree limbs and rocks fell from every direction as 50 riot cops danced helplessly under a rain of revolutionary outrage on the Manhattan-bound lane. One by one, the officers were carried off to safety by their fellows.

"Black is back! Black people are the majority again! We can do this!"

In the days following, the march leaders and the police traded accusations as to who started the violence. Everyone seemed to miss the point, which 10,000 of the community's best and brightest knew all too well. It started with Yusuf. And Michael. And Mrs. Bumpurs. And the police. No one mentioned that for the first time in memory the New York City police had gone down to defeat. But the youth knew. "And we didn't even have to break out the hardware," they warned.

•

No more evidence was needed for the contention that there was a major, independent Black movement alive in New York than the scene at the Glover Memorial Baptist Church the week before. Thousands jammed the church and the surrounding community in the heart of Black Brooklyn to bid farewell to Yusuf Hawkins. They had also come to say farewell to any more killings.

It was the kind of scene that happens when a new and revolutionary movement comes of age. Inside were the leaders.

Rev, Minister Louis Farrakhan, Dr. Lenora Fulani, Reverend Timothy Mitchell, and Spike Lee were all inside. So was Michael Griffith's mother Jean, and her husband Cedric Sandiford, who had narrowly escaped death that night in Howard Beach. Rev spoke, Farrakhan spoke — two men who have been attacked and assailed and vilified by the powers-that-be for years. Public enemies.

Outside, the politicians began arriving. Governor Mario Cuomo. Mayor Ed Koch. Then Brooklyn DA candidate Charles "Joe" Hynes, running on the Howard Beach victory that never would have happened without this army in the streets.

Rudy Giuliani, lawman and then-Republican mayoral candidate, the man who turned a deaf ear to Rev's request that he use his resources to stop crack dealers and cops from killing the community instead of going after boxing promoters.

They had to be there. They were booed.

"Go home," the crowd told the governor.

"Koch must go!" the mayor was greeted.

"Rudy must go, too!" came the chant, which put an end to Giuliani's hasty plotting on how to cash in on the anti-Koch sentiment. But they couldn't leave.

They had to sit there listening to Reverend Al Sharpton and Minister Louis Farrakhan.

"It's kind of mind boggling to see Minister Farrakhan and Reverend Sharpton up on the stage and all of these people who dogged them, and dogged me, and attacked our people, sitting in the audience and having to listen through this," said Fulani. "I think that's when I realized that there was something afoot, that these suckers had no control over it because they had to be there by virtue of the seriousness of this racial crime."

Fulani had been brought into the heavily guarded church and through the police barricades (even in mourning a community remains under siege) because the community demanded she be let in.

"What's happening here is historic," said Rev. "Mario Cuomo in his worst nightmare would have to listen to Louis Farrakhan and see a crowd respond more to Dr. Lenora Fulani than to him!"

Even David Dinkins, who received warm applause from the crowd — the revolutionary motion in the community had as its number one concern the elimination of the evil that was Koch, and Dinkins was the weapon of choice — even Dinkins waited outside. The same Dinkins who sided with Koch in 1985 to keep Minister Farrakhan out of the city, who wouldn't be caught dead with Al Sharpton, and whose advance men told Fulani they would "fuck her up" if she got in the way.

Three weeks earlier the *Village Voice* (described by Rev as "ex-hippies who grew up to be just as reactionary as their parents") wondered aloud for eight pages why it was that so many folks in the working class Black communities of America followed, supported, respected Minister Farrakhan. Why don't they listen to "intelligent" Black leaders? asked the *Voice*.

•

"The longer we waste time in frivolous division, this will happen again and again and again," Farrakhan warned at Yusuf's funeral the week before. "But we say, like the Jews said, 'Never again, never again, never again.' "

"I'm petitioning Black leaders, preachers and activists that it's time for us to put aside our egos and save our children," added Rev. "It's time for us to protect our own." Fulani demanded that the leaders of the independent Black movement lean on David Dinkins to stand up to the powers-that-be.

The call for unity subsequently went out on the radio, with all sides of the independent movement summoning the community out to Grand Army Plaza the next day. There was more than a little optimism at the prospect of unified leadership — a prospect which evaporated that afternoon when many of the key leaders, including Sharpton and Daughtry, didn't show up, leaving the December 12 folks nominally in charge.

But after Yusuf's murder, the community was coming out no matter who was leading.

Jesse was in Brooklyn, too. Reverend Jackson took the opportunity to endorse Dinkins' campaign, calling the Manhattan beep a "voice of healing, a voice of redemption, a voice of reconciliation."

Jesse visibly cringed when Dinkins launched into his canned "more cops on the street" stump speech in the emotionally charged church. In the wake of Yusuf's murder Jackson had laced into Koch, pointing out that the mayor "has played the same role in New York that George Wallace played in Alabama."

Over the weekend after the insurrection on the bridge David Dinkins, soon to be elected the first Black mayor in the history of New York City, told the press that the revolutionary violence on the Brooklyn Bridge shouldn't reflect on him.

"I suspect the voters of New York are very sophisticated and intelligent people who realize," he said, "that I did not cause it."

"No, you certainly didn't," Rev laughed to himself, thinking back on the lawyer who charged him three grand to incorporate his little youth movement during what seemed a lifetime ago. "You certainly didn't."

Marching into the '90s

In New York City the 1990s opened with police officers of the 69th Precinct in Canarsie, Brooklyn stomping the life out of 27-year-old Dane Kemp, Jr. right on the floor of the station house. The police then moved on to younger targets, shooting down Robbie Cole on the streets of East Harlem because, they said, he had a gun (neighbors say the 14-year-old lay the unloaded and broken weapon in the street and pleaded tearfully for his life before he was shot). That was a few days after police shot down 14-year-old Jose Luis Lebron in Bushwick, Brooklyn — because, they said, he was reaching for a gun that he didn't have. That was four days after police killed Luis Liranso, 17, the same way.

It was the counter-revolution on the streets of New York. Just hours after the tidal wave of revolution that swept David Dinkins into City Hall, New York's Finest were sending out their own, deadly message — their answer to the installation by an angry and defiant community of the first Black mayor in the history of the Big Apple.

Within the first two months of the new decade, two dozen mostly young Black and Latino New Yorkers would be gunned down.

David Dinkins took office early in January in style, replete with a gaudy and gala shindig at the Winter Garden, located in the pits of the World

Trade Center in lower Manhattan. While a howling wind roared through the towers of the desolate monstrosity (the party was on a Sunday), inside New York City's Black and white reform establishment — which had just taken over the reins of government of a diseased and lifeless metropolis — celebrated happily. Elsewhere there was little joy, as tens of thousands jammed the city's shelters and any and every warm nook or cranny they might find in the sub-freezing temperatures.

But on the warm floor of the Winter Garden there were smiles aplenty as New York's yuppie/buppie/lib/rad establishment sported fur coats and tuxes and sampled hors d'oeuvres. For reformers, at least, there would be full employment this winter.

In Bed-Stuy, which now seemed a million light years away, Rev was making plans. January 15 — the 61st birthday of Dr. King — was approaching. Both the new reform palace guard and the new movement on the streets that Rev had led — Yusuf's movement — were going to commemorate the anniversary. And it was going to be a case study of the new face of power as the world's most important city ground its way into the last decade of the 20th century.

•

They streamed by the hundreds out of the Slave Theater in Bed-Stuy into the cool winter drizzle on Fulton Street in the heart of Black Brooklyn. It was a multi-racial crowd, laughing and boarding buses, getting ready for a march through Bensonhurst to demand, yet again, justice for Yusuf. It was Dr. King's birthday, and Reverend Al Sharpton and the movement he led were going to pay tribute the only way they saw fit — on the streets.

In City Hall, the new regime had birthday plans too. Dinkins (who had spent his first week in office slashing the city's budget) spent the second week plotting how to lay claim to the legacy of Dr. King.

"Were he here today," the new mayor told a smallish crowd gathered on the rain-and-reporter-soaked steps of City Hall, "Dr. King would be happy at the progress we have made, and he would look down and be happy that I have succeeded, that Doug Wilder has succeeded, that Ron

Brown has succeeded, that Jesse Jackson has twice run for President..."

Now of course they weren't buying it for a second out at the Slave (as the numbers showed; the Bed-Stuy crowd outnumbered the City Hall gathering four to one); *they* knew *precisely* how it was that Dinkins wound up in office. Which is why Yusuf's parents, Diane Hawkins and Moses Stewart, made their way out to Bed-Stuy on their way to Bensonhurst, searching yet again for an elusive justice.

Back at City Hall Reverend Herbert Daughtry and others fantasized aloud about this being the last time a march would be necessary, what with David behind the desk in the mayor's office and all. That kind of talk was beginning to irk the former New York director of youth operations for Operation Breadbasket of Dr. King's Southern Christian Leadership Conference.

"We didn't vote for David Dinkins because he was a Negro and we wanted to see him get a job," Rev told the fired-up crowd at the Slave. "We voted for him because we're tired of cover-ups of police brutality and racist violence in this city. David, is it going to be business as usual, or are you going to do what we invested in you to do?"

In New York City in 1990, there were now two contending forces for the heart and soul of the community, both of which were laying claim to the mantle of Dr. Martin Luther King, Jr. One had just found itself ensconced in City Hall, courtesy of the votes of an outraged community, while the other huddled together on the pavement of Fulton Street, ready to march into the fires of Bensonhurst.

A peek into the Slave Theater before the marchers set off for Bensonhurst gives a clue to the question of where the legacy of Martin Luther King — the real Dr. King — has come.

In the heart of Bed-Stuy, at a proud bastion of Black nationalism, Rev was preparing to lead a multi-racial march for justice, an African American preacher leading Black and white and Latino people onto buses, for a freedom ride into a place called Bensonhurst. Like Montgomery and Selma and countless white enclaves north and south before it, Bensonhurst had declared itself a place where people of color were not welcome, and defied the world to tell it otherwise.

Emerging from the Slave was the kind of coalition that Dr. King was forging in his last days, a generation ago — the last time Black *and* white America set off to follow a Black leader. And lest anyone think that Dr. King won the love of the powers-that-be for such a noble effort, remember that he was gunned down soon after his attempt to reach out — with some success — to the conscience of white America.

Not surprisingly, the evening news on the night of the 15th made it appear that the only whites out in Bensonhurst that day were the hoodlums on the street calling for the Reverend's neck. But despite the media's color-blindness, Rev had taken another step in his development as America's foremost civil rights activist, leading out into the street a coalition which included not only his United African Movement, but a multi-racial contingent brought by Fulani's New Alliance Party.

Rev explained the new look of the march to the hundreds who had gathered at the Slave before the buses departed.

"Now I'm not going to apologize...I'm a Black nationalist," Rev said, taking note of the multi-racial crowd — a first at the Slave. "And based on my feelings of that, I'm willing to work with other people as long as they know who I am. I don't deal with white stuff. I don't even have white sheets on my bed at home! But I'm willing to respect those that respect me, because it takes us *all* respecting each other for there to be justice for *everybody!*"

And then a page from Dr. King's own spiritual legacy, arrived at after years of searching for the driving force of humanity. It was love, King concluded. For Rev, it was respect.

"I could not love my people and want anything against your people that was unjustified," Rev told the audience. "So we don't never have to love each other, but as long as we respect each other, and with that respect walk into the bastion of segregation and racism called Bensonhurst, then we can make a difference in this town."

That said, Rev led a prayer for Martin, for Yusuf, for all the martyrs. At the close of the prayer, Rev looked up and joked. "Now you *know* I'm good — I got Fred Newman praying!" Newman, a Bronx-born Jewish leftist who had strategized NAP's growth into the largest progressive political party in the US in half a century, was among those in the audience who headed out to Bensonhurst that day.

"If I am only for myself, what am I?"

The Jew has been taught — and, too often, accepts — the legend of Negro inferiority; and the Negro, on the other hand, has found nothing in his experience with Jews to counteract the legend of Semitic greed. Here the American white Gentile has two legends serving him at once: he has divided these minorities and he rules.

—James Baldwin, *The Harlem Ghetto*

Rev's coalition with the New Alliance Party has been in the making for a number of years, going back to Fulani's participation in the fight Rev led for a Black schools chancellor, and on to joint demonstrations after Bernhard Goetz's subway shooting spree. Their partnership tightened in the course of the Brawley battle and Fulani's 1988 Presidential run; she made the case one of the centerpieces of her campaign.

In January of 1990 Rev and Newman were the keynote speakers at a forum on "Blacks and Jews in New York City," moderated by Fulani, at Brooklyn Technical College.

Like Rev, Newman had earned a reputation for defying the status quo; in particular, Newman had incurred the wrath of the Anti-Defamation League of B'nai B'rith (ADL) for his fiery anti-Zionism. Newman was perhaps the Jewish leader most responsible for keeping alive the fires of Jewish progressivism, a tradition that stretches back through the ages and into the civil rights movement. History student Rev had likened Newman to Rabbi Abe Heschel, who stood by Dr. King during the dog days of the civil rights movement, when liberal (and in particular, liberal Jewish) support evaporated after King's denunciation of the Viet Nam war.

•

The Zionist establishment had often quoted the saying of the medieval Rabbi Hillel: "If I am not for myself, who will be for me? And if not now, when?" But they cleverly left out a key line —"If I am only for myself, what am I?"

Together those lines summed up much of the complex tensions between the Black and Jewish communities as America wended its way through the tragedy of the 20th century; by the onset of the '70s the two communities, seemingly natural allies in the battle for justice, found themselves locked in combat. From Democratic Party politics on the Upper West Side of Manhattan to the fires of the Middle East, Jews had been set up — in a complex and tragic series of historical developments — to turn against people of color.

Intent on not pulling any punches or sweeping any issues under the rug in the building of the new coalition, Fulani, Rev and Newman took the stage before a multi-racial crowd of 500 people at Brooklyn Tech. Black and white and Latino, gay and straight, Muslims, Christians and Jews — all expressing a common weariness with establishment manipulations of the ethnic and racial equations of New York — sat down to search for answers.

"I felt, and the New Alliance Party felt, that we could not allow the white corporate media to have the last word on the issue of Blacks and Jews," Fulani explained.

Newman began by noting that he had first met Rev in the pages of the *Village Voice*. He knew then, he said, that Rev was a significant leader — significant enough to arouse the wrath of the lib-rad establishment. The Stanford University-trained philosopher said he wanted to examine the "and" in the phrase Blacks and Jews. "When you talk about the relationships of different groups of people, the most important thing to look at is who's putting them together." Until then, Newman noted, it had been the establishment which had brought Blacks and Jews together, for its *own* purposes.

As for Rev, the forum was a welcome opportunity to discuss Blacks and Jews away from the media hysteria and the sound bites.

"It seems rather strange to me that people who spend most of their time creating the tensions are the ones that have the audacity to convene the meetings to discuss something, as if they would really try to put themselves out of business — which would really ease all of our tensions," Rev said, to laughter and applause.

Zionism, Israel, Black nationalism, Jewish racism, Black anti-Semitism, David Dinkins, the US left, liberalism, unity, disunity — it was a rich, two-hour-long, no-holds-barred get-together, historic in its openness and made possible by the shared commitment of all the diverse parties to find, respectfully, common solutions.

A week after the forum, the new coalition took to the streets with a vengeance; the first stop, of course, was Bensonhurst, where a thousand marched through the winter cold while a defiant Rev carried over his heart a street sign that read "Yusuf Hawkins Boulevard." The New York City Council, which does little more than name streets, ignored the requests of Rev and Yusuf's family to rename the street where he was killed in his memory. The sign stayed over Rev's heart — which remained, for at least some Bensonhursters watching from the sidelines, the real target of their wrath.

"The dream is still unfulfilled, but the dreamers are still on the streets," Rev said during a rare moment of quiet in Bensonhurst. "Happy birthday, Dr. King. We're celebrating the way you would have. We're still in the streets marching, but we still believe that we shall overcome some day…"

•

On February 13, 1990 (two days after Nelson Mandela was released from Robben Island) Rev and two co-defendants were sentenced to 45 days in jail for "obstruction of governmental administration," "criminal trespass," and "disorderly conduct": they were charged with committing these crimes on December 21, 1987 — the Day of Outrage. The jailing was just business-as-usual harassment — Rev, the Reverend Timothy Mitchell and activist Charles Barron were released from their Rikers Island jail cells within hours after they arrived.

•

In April Rev was agitating again, except now he only had evenings and weekends available. From nine to five, he was locked in the lower Manhattan courtroom, bored silly with the rest of the spectators as Robert Abrams' finest tried to make a case against him.

The month found Rev out on the streets of Teaneck, New Jersey — a quick ride due west from New York City across the George Washington Bridge — where, again, a young Black man had died; 16-year-old Phillip Pannell, Jr., already wounded from a shot in his leg, had his hands above his head and was pleading for his life when a white cop shot him in the back. A grand jury refused to indict Officer Gary Spath.

Rev had watched the Pannell story on the TV news. The night after the killing, the long-abused Black youth of Teaneck (the town's carefully cultivated image of a model, integrated community shattered by Spath's gunshots) took to the streets in rebellion.

On the night of the funeral Rev was with Illinois Congressman Gus Savage, who was being forced to defend himself against charges of anti-Semitism. Rev brought the embattled legislator to Brooklyn for a support rally.

When Savage discovered that Louis Farrakhan, their mutual friend, was visiting the Harlem mosque they persuaded the NOI leader to accompany them to Phillip's wake.

From the moment Rev made contact with the Pannell family and promised to help, all hell had broken loose in the tree-lined suburb. Teaneck's liberal establishment went nuts at the mere thought of Rev and NO JUSTICE, NO PEACE! echoing down sedate Teaneck Road.

Not because he was an "outside agitator" (he had in fact been invited in), but because his presence there meant that he was *needed*.

And in Teaneck, he wasn't supposed to be.

But the hard fact is that Teaneck is a racially stratified town. It is divided, southern style, right down the middle, with the poorer, Black community confined to the south side of Teaneck Road, and mostly white middle class folks living to the north.

Rev was coming no matter what.

Savage, Farrakhan and Rev headed across the river in separate cars (Rev was cruising in Don King's limo). The scene at the funeral home was as tense as it had been the night the town exploded.

As they got out of their cars a cheer went up from the youth.

"Sharpton! Sharpton!"

"Farrakhan! Farrakhan!"

They reached the steps of the funeral home, where some of the local leadership, Black and white, let the press know that they did not want *them* there, but would let them in.

"We'll take you over this way, Reverend Sharpton," said local Black leader George Powell. Rev told him firmly but politely to get the hell out of the way, which he did.

With Savage and Farrakhan he went inside to view the body of the murdered youth, while the local activists — among them Reverend Herbert Daughtry, a long-time Teaneck resident — rushed the family out. Minister Farrakhan was infuriated at the insult; the following day, the papers reported that the Pannell family didn't speak to Rev and his colleagues.

Which was true, as the grieving family had been all-but-kidnapped by the local leadership. But despite that move, several eyewitnesses to the killing had approached Rev and asked him to get involved. They held a press conference together to announce that Rev was their advisor.

The local Black bigwigs spent the week trying to derail plans for a march the following Saturday. They had hoped to get Reverend Jesse Jackson to join them in condemning it, but *that* plan backfired. Jesse got on the phone personally with Rev to let him know he would be on TV that night, where he would announce his support for the march.

The march went off as planned, with over 2,000 people storming down Teaneck Road through the little town of 40,000 people — 13 busloads brought in from New York City were joined by hundreds of local youth.

Afterwards, Rev sat down with the young folks at the home of one of the local youth leaders.

"*You* all need to keep this going," he told them. "That's the only way there will be an indictment."

The young people of Teaneck took Rev's advice, and formed the African Council to keep the momentum going. The Pannell family, which had been double-crossed by the local leadership (they were more concerned with preserving their image than with getting justice for a murdered child), embraced Rev. In all, they did 29 marches in Teaneck and Trenton (one time walking from Teaneck all the way to the state capital) — until State Attorney General Angelo Del Tufo was forced to make an unprecedented move; while police officers throughout the state shook with anger, he appointed a second grand jury to reconsider the evidence in the Pannell case and Spath was indicted — for the first time in the history of the Garden State, a white cop was being brought to trial for killing a Black youth.

No Justice, No Peace — Pip, Pip, Pip!

Fourteen minutes after eight o'clock in the morning on May 4, 1991 Delta Airlines — flying non-stop from Atlanta, Georgia — touched down at London's Gatwick Airport. As word of the landing appeared on the battery of "International Arrivals" video screens posted just outside the Customs and Immigration area, the flock of reporters, photographers and TV crews who had been hovering expectantly went into battle formation to storm the barricades set up in the corridor.

Standing elbow to elbow with the newshounds was an array of London-based activists: representatives of the Pan African Congress movement, a contingent of students from the London School of Economics, members of the Afro-Caribbean Center, a phalanx of followers of Minister Farrakhan and the Nation of Islam, the Reverend Hewie Andrew of the New Testament Assembly Pentecostal Church, and organizers of a march planned for that afternoon to protest the murder of a 15-year-old Black youth, Rolan Adams.

Just behind them, but in clear and deliberate view, were posted two Uzi-toting airport police officers made barrel-chested by their visible bullet-proof vests. Grimly they watched the crowd watching the entryway. Tourists on the perimeter quickly got caught up in the excitement: "Who's coming?" one French student whispered. The candy-stand lady motioned to a nearby luggage porter. "Is Lady Di back from Brazil?" she asked. But that wasn't it.

The minutes ticked by. The status report on the video screens shifted from "landed" to "in Customs." More waiting. The tabloid photographers jockied for position. The brothers from the NOI steeled themselves, unaccustomed to a media spectacle of this magnitude (Minister Farrakhan's banning from Britain in 1986 attracted only minor publicity). The LSE students checked and rechecked the placards which they held tightly rolled until the time came to raise them up. The guards with the Uzi's kept their icy gaze trained on the scene.

Then, just before 9AM, the traveler whose impending arrival had provoked a week of taunting headlines in the British tabloids, a threat from Members of Parliament and the Home Office to deny him permission to enter the country, and a wave of anticipation and curiosity in the Black community, suddenly appeared. He walked slowly, almost tentatively, toward the gathering which lined either side of the exit path. The photographers brandished their cameras and the area was brilliantly illuminated by an unending succession of flashes. A cry erupted from the LSE students: "No Justiiiice, No peace!" Their welcome signs framed the crowd as it pressed forward. The Fruit of Islam began to encircle him, just a hair's breadth ahead of the reporters, who shoved microphones and notepads in his face. He paused momentarily, squinting, tired from the long journey, anxious over the tumultuous reception, determined, amidst the frenzy, that his message get through to his people. He moved on, the sprawling, self-appointed entourage in tow.

Rev had arrived in Britain.

For a while there it was touch and go. Conservative MP's lobbied strenuously for Home Secretary Kenneth Baker to ban the people's preacher from British shores. London's *Daily Mail*, among the most notorious of the city's inglorious scandal sheets, screeched "Keep This Man Out of Britain" in a front-page headline and the rest of the papers dutifully followed suit in their reporting or editorials. Accusing Rev of coming to Britain to fan the flames of racism and calling him "the most odious man in America," the tabloids went to town with grandiose lies (e.g., Tawana admitted she hadn't been raped; Rev went to jail for fraud).

Fred Newman, who would be in London with Rev, immediately took command of the counteroffensive. He asked the Washington, DC-based Rainbow Lobby to mobilize a campaign on Capitol Hill to muster congressional protest against the threatened ban. The Lobby's executive director, Nancy Ross, reached several members of the Congressional Black Caucus — with mixed results. Congressman Kwesi Mfume of Maryland agreed to contact the Home Office directly. "Mfume? Mfume? What kind of name is that? *That's* a member of Congress?" sputtered a Home Office functionary in the best tradition of imperial arrogance. Yes, Mfume's assistant assured him. Congressman Mfume was indeed a member of the United States Congress and, furthermore, he was outraged at the exclusionary shennanigans.

Other CBC members — among them New York's Floyd Flake — also offered their support. California Congresswoman Maxine Waters, on the other hand, said through her staff that she did not want "to make trouble" and that Rev should consult his own congressperson if need be.

In London one of Newman's aides, Cathy Salit, and Rev's assistant Jennifer Joseph mobilized students and local activists to lodge a protest with the Home Office. By late in the day on the Thursday before he was due to arrive, the Home Secretary's staff was reporting a deluge of phone calls. Just to be sure, attorney Alvaader Frazier — a founder of the New York City-based International Peoples' Law Institution — accompanied Rev to London as his legal representative.

Meanwhile, back in New York City, Fulani leaned on Mayor David Dinkins, other Black elected officials and progressive leaders to enlist their support in decrying the ban.

By the time Rev, his aide Anthony Charles and attorney Frazier boarded the London-bound Delta Flight #10 in Atlanta, the Rainbow Lobby had been assured by British immigration officials, the Home Office and the US State Department that Rev was free to enter the United Kingdom.

Fred Newman assessed the tempest in a teapot: "The whole thing was a test — the conservatives knew the left wouldn't touch the situation with a ten-foot pole. They wanted to test how we'd do on our own." From the moment that the controversy over the London trip broke, the "official" liberals and leftists on both sides of the Atlantic left them quite alone.

It was no news to Rev, thanks to his voracious appetite for history.

From the days of Garvey, to Adam, to Malcolm and King, he had read about how now and then the left would work alongside Black leaders. But when push came to shove they had been abandoned — often with fatal results.

So here they went again. Maxine Waters' bizarre suggestion that Rev call "his own" congressperson. The refusal of the Socialist Workers Party in England to register an emergency protest to the Home Office (write us a letter asking for our support, advised the SWP, and we'll consider it). The withdrawal of an earlier offer to provide Rev with legal assistance by the British National Council for Civil Liberties. The statement by a grouping of Britain's Black intellectuals asserting that Black Britons were an "observer class" and not prone to action; therefore Rev wouldn't "appeal" to them. The Bishop's cancellation of a scheduled sermon that Rev was to have given at the New Testament Assembly Pentecostal Church.

Safely checked into his hotel, Rev got together with his fellow travelers on the wild and woolly visit, and summed up the scene thus far. "It looks like the international left syndicate won't touch us, because we're not afraid to come in here and deal with domestic issues, like the murder of Rolan Adams. We haven't made any deals so we don't have to keep quiet. It's the issue of independent Black leadership. We're willing to speak out. And we're able to. When it became clear that the left syndicate couldn't stop us, that's when the media went nuts. Since the left couldn't handle it, the media had to try to discourage the Black community from following me."

Without success. Just hours after Rev's arrival in the UK nearly 2,000 demonstrators joined him in southeast London's Thamesmead to protest the murder of Rolan Adams and the free hand given the fascist British National Party, which is held responsible for his death. Rolan's parents joined Rev on the march, thereby undercutting the media's attempt to portray him as an unwelcome interloper and focusing national attention — for the first time since it happened — on the stabbing of the young Black man by a white mob, which attacked him while he waited at a bus stop.

The old left was on hand for the protest as well — including the SWP (after having refused to help Rev get into the country). That tickled the leftist Newman. "They had to be there," he told Rev. "You forced that."

"Yeah, they had to be there," Rev agreed. "And they had to keep their distance, too. Everybody was waving their banners but nobody wanted to get on the front line and have their picture taken with me!"

The two friends laughed at the bizarre happenings here, three thousand miles from home. Their respective home boroughs of Brooklyn and the Bronx suddenly seemed a whole lot closer to each other. Rev told Newman and the rest of the crew about his arrival at the chic hotel where both were staying, cracking everyone up with his mock proper British accent.

Having trailed Rev from the airport, a brigade of reporters, photographers and television camera crews burst into the posh lobby and rushed ahead of him to record his entrance. Two elderly and very elegant hotel guests noticed the commotion. "It must be a rock group," guessed Lady Somebody or Other. Then Rev appeared. "Oh my goodness," gasped her companion. "It's not a rock group. It's the Black power advocate!"

Rev had indeed arrived.

The "Black power advocate" did nothing by the book. He looked straight into the cameras on the live television show "Tonight" hosted by Jonathan Ross and denied tabloid accusations that he had attacked Her Royal Highness, Elizabeth II. "Queen, if you are watching — I did not attack you. I admire you," he said with a straight face. The audience laughed uproariously. "How can you say you admire the Queen?" an outraged SWP "militant" shouted at Rev after his address at Goldsmith College, having missed the point entirely.

Even the queen of New York City trashy tabloids, the *New York Post*, was drawn into the brouhaha. It printed a front-page story — "Royal Pain" — about Rev's prime-time brush with royalty and how the British dailies were having conniptions over Rev's challenge to Buckingham Palace for its failure to condemn the Adams murder. Then the UK tabloids covered the *Post* headline, making that Tuesday's coverage a story about a story about a story.

In fact the virulently racist British media had a field day, churning out one provocative headline after another. The *Sunday Telegraph*: MAYHEM AS THE REVEREND COMES MARCHING IN. *News of* the World: STORM AS BEAST BARGES IN: RACE WAR REV CAUSES CHAOS. The Sunday Mirror: THE REV HATE HITS BRITAIN. The Sunday Express: RACISM SLUR ON QUEEN. The Independent: PASTOR TO PLAY BRIXTON [a working class Black neighbourhood] AND PARK LANE [the fancy hotel where Rev and his entourage put up]. Daily Star: PULPIT BAN ON 'BRONX BEAST.' Today: RACE CRUSADER LIVING IN £550 A NIGHT LUXURY.

But the real story of the Rev in England wasn't told by the tabloids, nor by the ultra-stuffy London Times. The Guardian, a liberal daily, didn't get it either. Only Black papers such as the Voice gave Rev anything approaching sane coverage. But in the end the story was told by the 2,000 students, Black and white, who came out to hear him at Goldsmith, and the 1,500 people who attended a town meeting organized by the Pan African Congress movement, and the hundreds who accompanied Rev on a walking tour through Brixton as he stopped in at beauty parlors, bookstores and groceries to say hello. And it was told by the thousand-plus students who attended the talk given by Rev and Newman on "The Politics and Psychology of Racism" at the London School of Economics.

After his introduction by Newman, Rev began his talk to the standing room only LSE audience with a series of psychological observations. "I think that the media hysteria that was generated by the proposed and actual visit is a case study of some psychotic racists who have gotten loose. To call people a beast and be sitting in an empire that has perpetrated some of the most beastly acts in recorded history is absurd.

"For me to come to a country where a whole building is dedicated to the jewels of Her Majesty that were robbed from Africa, jewels that were stolen from the ground of the continent of Africa, and for them to be lavishly and despicably displayed for tourists while all the media can see is my gold medallion, which is really tarnished brass, shows a psychological madness in this country," Rev continued. "I propose that we give the media in this country free couches and free psychological sessions."

•

In June, Rev and Fulani kicked off a series of marches to Dinkins' Gracie Mansion residence. They brought hundreds of homeless people out to remind the new mayor that although the poverty ravaging the city was not his fault, it *was* his problem.

"We come fresh from the battles that changed the hands of power in the city," Rev roared across the park to the mansion. "David Dinkins didn't win because he was kind and gentle…we come to remind Dave that he is there because we put him there."

And a word of advice to the new mayor from the man who opened the door of City Hall for him: "Racism, poverty, and exploitation must be met with firm, hard leadership…you must not be afraid to make enemies, you must not be afraid to take a stand."

•

In July Rev and Reverend Mitchell were jailed for blocking traffic at LaGuardia Airport in 1988 during a Day of Outrage called to protest Michael Griffith's murder; they had originally been scheduled to begin serving their 15-day sentences in June. But Mandela was visiting New York City at the time and the judge refused to put them in jail while he was in town — apparently fearing that Rev's supporters would have embarrassed the city's Democratic Party as they publicly honored the world's most famous political prisoner while tossing their own political opposition — Rev — in the slammer.

In August came the stunning takeover of the Statue of Liberty to mark the 27th anniversary of Dr. King's historic March on Washington in 1963; thus was launched a campaign to rename the Big Apple "Martin Luther King City," proclaimed that afternoon at the foot of Lady Liberty.

Rev led a crew of homeless women and men in song as they neared the end of their non-violent act of civil disobedience, staying on while panicked park rangers evacuated a mostly amused throng of tourists from the island.

"I want to hereby announce that we will make the dream come true," Rev said as the singing stopped and seaborne police sped toward the island to arrest him. "I'm setting up Dr. King's city right here on Liberty

Island. Whatever happens, listen to your attorneys and remain non-violent. Let's set up our town!"

•

"We don't need Al Sharpton and his brand of leadership to tell us how to do things in this city."

"I suspect he will be roundly rejected in Los Angeles...It is a matter of public record the kind of work Al Sharpton does, the way in which he does it. And it is inconsistent with the way in which we have done work and the way in which we will do work."

"We have had national leaders come to LA to lend their support. Jesse Jackson has been here twice. Reverend Sharpton and Dr. Fulani were not invited on behalf of the coalition of organizations that has come together to support the effort of dumping Chief Gates. They were invited by peripheral elements in the African American community. The coalition should do the inviting. We insist on our right to do the inviting. We hold weekly meetings to plan these things and they were not on the agenda."

The establishment Black leadership in the City of Angels had a fit when Rev and Fulani *dared* to lead a march and rally of over 600 demonstrators from City Hall to the Parker Center police headquarters on Good Friday, 1991 to demand the resignation of the city's police chief, Daryl Gates, in the wake of the videotaped beating of Rodney King nearly a month before.

When Rev and Fulani got to their destination, he was handed a six-foot cross.

"We come to these steps on Good Friday because 2,000 years ago they crucified Christ, and today they're crucifying us," Rev declared. "We're here because we're not afraid to stand up to police brutality."

Although most of the city's religious and political leaders cowered behind their cloak of legitimacy, there were some who joined Rev and Fulani at City Hall. The Reverend Curtis Kelly, who runs the substance abuse program for the West Adams Church, was one. "I was just about the only minister at the rally and there are at least 1,000 Black ministers in this city!" Kelly told a reporter. "They're not here because they've been told that they'll be blacklisted if they stand up with Sharpton. Nobody wants to make trouble. I could care less about what they think. I believe in the brother because what he's doing is right. But one man can't do it alone. Sharpton and Fulani got more media attention than anyone else has ever gotten. That's why it's so important they be here. We have to keep it in the public eye or it will just keep happening."

•

The scene shifts to Raleigh, North Carolina two weeks later. "Though the Rev. Al Sharpton is called a civil rights activist, he is in fact a civil rights opportunist. If Mr. Sharpton were able to see any difference between a mistake with racial overtones and a deliberate racist vendetta, he would never admit it, because recognizing that difference would spoil his game. That game has nothing to do with promoting racial harmony and everything to do with promoting paranoia, division and the continuing celebrityhood of Al Sharpton.

"Raleigh not only has no need for irresponsible itinerant publicity-seekers, it has no use for them — as evidenced by the small crowd he drew in front of City Hall. This city has plenty of its own articulate, effective and responsible Black leaders. They know this community. They have worked for years to make it a better place."

The "mistake with racial overtones" referred to by Raleigh's (white-owned and run) *News and Observer* in this April 3, 1991 editorial was the shooting of an unarmed Black man by a white police officer on January 24, when Detective Jimmy Glover — in plainclothes and without identifying himself — approached the car in which Tony Farrell was sitting and, as a frightened Farrell began to pull away, shot into the car, wounding him in the leg.

After the shooting an organization called Raleigh Citizens for Justice began holding demonstrations outside the municipal building every other week when the City Council was in session to protest the latest eruption of police brutality in the city. But only a handful of people came out each time, and the members of the council — like the city manager and the police chief — stubbornly sat on their hands. A grand jury refused to indict Glover.

Rev traveled to Raleigh on a Tuesday at the invitation of Citizens for Justice and leaders of the New Alliance Party in North Carolina to lead the demonstration (he was in Durham that evening to give an address on "The State of Black America" at Duke University). At least 100 people joined the militant civil rights leader to warn that without justice there would be no peace in Raleigh — a city that had not seen such a large demonstration since the heyday of the civil rights movement a generation ago.

"The newspaper put Sharpton down, and us, because it was so successful," commented the Reverend David Foy, a leader of Raleigh Citizens for Justice. "After this demonstration, the City Council agreed that the first item on the agenda at the next session will be to hear complaints about police brutality. That's not been done before."

•

Meanwhile, the outrages continue: in America when white men with weapons (in or out of police uniform) encounter unarmed Black men (and children) in the night, murderous violence is what comes naturally. The outrages continue. So do the protests. On behalf of the Forgotten Youth of Atlantic City, New Jersey. Against the Ku Klux Klan's brazen launching of a recruitment drive in the hamlet of Schuylerville, a stone's throw from Albany (where Mario Cuomo was too busy to condemn the presence of the cross-burning racists in his own backyard). And every day yet another new name is added to the roll call of casualties, of women and men executed for the crime of being a person of color in white supremacist America.

Mary Mitchell. Ribat Austin. Edwin Torres. Federico Pereira. Jose Cruz. Andrew Gonzalez. The Hillside Massacre.

For those who holler about the presence of Reverend Al Sharpton, in person, in sound bite, or anywhere in their sight, there seems to be a simple way to make him go away: make the *outrages* go away, and perhaps the former wonder boy preacher could return to the dream of a starry-eyed, pudgy four-year-old spellbound by the aura of the Pentecostal Church. If the outrages go away, Reverend Al Sharpton of Brooklyn might just be able to pursue his first love, being a preacher of the gospel.

That is the challenge to America of Reverend Al Sharpton — make him go away by establishing justice.

Don't hold your breath that it will happen any time soon, but the man behind the sound bite will be one happy preacher when that day comes.

Postscript, King's Birthday, 1991

George Bush chose the birthday of America's greatest hero, Dr. Martin Luther King, Jr., as the deadline for the start of the mass destruction of poor Black, brown and white folks in the Persian Gulf. For the first time ever, Rev spent his favorite holiday on the sidelines (and out of jail). January 15 found him lying in the little recovery room at Coney Island Hospital.

But in midtown Manhattan that night the movement was alive, led in spirit by the Rev. Thousands — the "people of the streets, the despised, the voiceless" — marched to the UN.

Adam's people, Martin's people, Malcolm's people.

Rev's people.

Maddox, Mason, Fulani, Newman, Stewart and everyone at the head of this new movement led them down the streets, at the hour of international panic, with a chant that has echoed around the world.

"Yusuf, Yu-SUF!"

Rev didn't have to miss it though; earlier in the day, he videotaped a message to the march from his hospital bed, which in the winter night echoed off the glassy walls of the United Nations to the world.

"Hello to my brothers and sisters. I'm sorry that I could not be with you today. Today is a very important day for all of us. Martin Luther King's birthday should not be used as a deadline for war. Thirty-three percent of those who will be on the front lines will come from neighborhoods that are not even protected in this sovereignty. We must stand up, we must march, we must let our voice be heard. But we must not ever bow in imitation of those beastly forces that we fight. So though I'm not there physically, I'm there in spirit.

"March on. Stand up. Take whatever we got to take. Whatever you do, don't knuckle under. I'll be at your side soon. But more important, righteousness is at your side right now. Thank you. Happy birthday, Dr. King. Let there be peace on earth."

Amen.

APPENDIXES

APPENDIX A

The People's Preacher

The following is a selection of nationally syndicated weekly newspaper columns by the Reverend Al Sharpton.

Despite the Darkness,
the Light of Liberation

In March of 1960, a flamboyant progressive political independent walked into a lower Manhattan courtroom accused of tax evasion, accused of using his political operation for personal profit, but really accused of being independent, progressive, Black and not staying in his place. His name was Adam Clayton Powell; the case was *United States v. Powell*.

Thirty years later to the month, just a few blocks up in lower Manhattan, I walked into court accused of almost the same crimes for the very same reasons. And if one would study the gap between Adam and Al, one would find all of the glory and all of the shame of Black leadership in this country. The fact of the matter is that in the last 30 years there has been an overt attempt by the system to co-opt all Black leadership and to eradicate independent leadership by using the courts, character assassination, vicious media, or outright assassination.

It is ironic that throughout my life, my political hero from age 12 became Adam Powell. My political style has been shaped by my admiration for him, because it was Adam Powell who stood up in the '30s and the '40s and the '50s — alone — teaching the North civil disobedience, boycotts, teaching northern Black leaders how to accumulate power, and then to use power for the *powerless* and not as a passport into the circle of the *powerful*, to use power to change society and not only to rub shoulders. It is a shame that many of them who came down the path of Powell have abandoned the route and the dedication of Powell, and that is to build an audacious independent power and not to become the children or bastions of the status quo.

So here we are again, just like Adam, shunned by the media, shunned by the white liberal aristocracy, but supported by the grassroots, standing before the bar of injustice, waiting for inklings of justice to fall out.

It is not just my trial that is symbolic of this social phenomenon, because just across the street, in three weeks, Central Park will go to trial when seven modern Scottsboro Boys will be faced with no evidence other than video statements they were forced to make.

And then right across the Brooklyn Bridge in two weeks will start the Bensonhurst fiasco, where a DA with no evidence — because no one in the DA's office takes the shooting of Black kids seriously enough to go and get witnesses and get a trial theory together — will go into court and go through a media show. And the result will again be Blacks going home with tears and those in power going home with cheers.

It is clear that we must continue to fight until we can turn it around, because despite the darkness of the hour, I still feel light, and that light stands for liberation. Because I see in the darkness the Alton Maddoxes, the Lenora Fulanis, the Pedro Espadas, the people from different walks of life, different races, who are committed to having one society where justice is not determined by class or race, but where justice is determined by the fact that you are a human being, and you were born with the right to be treated justly. I feel light in Nelson Mandela from Africa, I feel light in people all over Europe screaming "freedom!" I feel light in people all over the African diaspora yelling, "No justice, no peace!"

So even 30 years later, as I walk in Adam's shoes, if Adam can hear me, let him know that I will keep the faith. Let him know that I will not buckle, let him know that I will not bow, and in the words of Jeremiah, I will stand for what is right, and if I perish, let me perish, but let me be on the side of the righteous.

March 29, 1990

Bensonhurst:
Where Are the Decent People?

By the time readers will have seen this column, the jury hearing the evidence against Joseph Fama and the jury hearing the evidence against Keith Mondello will be headed toward the jury rooms to deliberate the fate of two of the most reputed racists in memory. There are some very serious lessons to be learned from the Bensonhurst matter.

The only question that remains unanswered is whether the family of Yusuf Hawkins will gain anything from his untimely and unprovoked murder. Certainly others have unashamedly gained by design or accident from the blood that spilled from the body of this young man.

David Dinkins gained. It was the anger and humiliation of this senseless act that is responsible for him being mayor today. And certainly there are those in radio and TV, not to mention print journalists, who gained by selling newspaper and television stories with the concern of a wrestling promoter and who used the whole unfortunate incident as a way of igniting Blacks who had been ignited too often before to where just getting angry would not now be enough. Certainly the judge — whose now often quotable one-liners will become part of the annals of judicial history long after my body has gone to its grave — has gained.

So the challenge went out to Yusuf Hawkins' parents to find advice and guidance. They stood with the people and chose the people's leaders — Farrakhan, Maddox, Fulani and Sharpton. Grabbed arms with comrades and marched and raised hell, as well as issues, and supported alternatives to the men who hold office today — the independent candidates for the people. Certainly one remembers not long ago while we were being shouted at and called "nigger" and were spat upon how the great phony liberal Bensonhurst State Representative Frank Barbaro joined the others in the *Village Voice* crowd in saying "Don't condemn all Bensonhurst. There are good people out here. This has nothing to do with racism." Etc.

Well, one must look in retrospect and see how one can seriously make that claim when, first, the anniversary march of Mr. Hawkins' death was threatened to be marred by more violence than New York has ever seen. Secondly, we must realize that young Black people are not willing to sit and wait. We've sat for too long and we sat too comfortable. Where are the good people of Bensonhurst? We were told, continually, "Don't condemn them all. There are some good people."

Where are the good people? They weren't in Teaneck marching with us, we so-called outside agitators. They were not with us when we came out 10,000 strong marching on the former mayor's Greenwich Village apartment demanding justice in the Howard Beach case. They have been absent from every move for justice, from Howard Beach to Tawana Brawley, Bensonhurst to James Brown — every move for justice that has moved New York directly or indirectly. And each time, we can expect to be humiliated beforehand, and they come in later and proclaim us crazy for going about the business of making sure Yusuf didn't die unnoticed and didn't die for nothing.

The failure of the Bensonhurst case is the failure of the City of New York to come to grips with racism. The fact of the matter is a lot of Bensonhurst people saw these 30 kids do this vicious act, but none of those decent people will come forward and testify. Tim Minton, the commentator for WABC television, saw what amounted to be a promo bio on me only to ask, "Now can I talk to Moses Stewart first? Can I talk to Diane first?" Eric Shaw of Fox Television — same thing, same spirit. And the list goes on.

Despite the mirage, despite counting and clapping, despite whatever the press will be saying in the next few days — I want you to reflect on what it means to have these young men standing in court and what it will mean if the court sets them free. Yes, the phony liberal is mad because we have stripped him of his emperor's gown and replaced it with nothing but a crown of thorns which appears to be settling in his head. Yes, the phony liberals are angry because they should have brought peace to the Black community, but instead they send the Black community a more profound and shocking lesson. So we say, if there is no justice, there will be no peace.

We mean that from the innermost parts of our souls. Ours is not a cosmetic march and a cosmetic aftermath press conference. We came out because we're serious. There must be justice *for* every one of us or there can never be peace *from* any. I conclude by saying that Bensonhurst shatters the myth of the "decent white man" wherever he may be. As he finishes reading this analysis and this recollection, he can stand and tell the world what I have just told the world. And others will join us in telling the world that had not the people of Bensonhurst been appeased and treated like a baby with a pacifier, but had they instead been challenged, had they been pressured, to give up all they know, give up all those who saw something, maybe the context would have been created for the decency in Bensonhurst to emerge. But that, apparently, is not Mr. Genecin's intent.

But as Fama and Mondello pack up, ready to go home to wait for the jury, Black America looks across the bridge down the column. Still water runs deep, small voices run close, the army is not around at all. Please contact us so we can give them up to get back to the battlefield because the people of Bensonhurst didn't hear us, but they will hear us now. Because we will say it in a way that won't be forgotten. And that is: before I'll be a slave, I'll be buried in my grave and go home to my Lord and be free.

Mr. Fama and Mr. Mondello think they've beaten the rap and that they're on their way home. Be that as it may, I will be there not only for those who have been killed but for every man and woman who lives — I'll be there. I'll be the guy not saying we must wait and see, not saying we must pray with our mayor, not saying that this doesn't make sense, but saying to Jack Newfield and the other phony liberal aristocracy that you can fool some of the people some of the time, you can fool some of the people all of the time, but you can't fool all of the people all the time.

May 10, 1990

Anatomy of a Meeting
with the Mayor

Over the past several weeks Americans in general, and New Yorkers in particular, have been advised by New York Mayor David Dinkins to ignore people like myself because we fan the fires of racial strife and represent no real constituency. We weathered the storm of these attacks and answered them with unprecedented numbers, continuing to march in Bensonhurst, continuing to attend rallies, continuing to seek justice and economic parity in this unbalanced society.

In our pursuit of justice, progressive leadership — including the Reverend William Jones, attorneys Alton Maddox and C. Vernon Mason, Dr. Lenora Fulani — decided to appeal to the moral leadership of the Bensonhurst community to break the cycle of hatred, bigotry and non-communication. We did that by dramatically taking 200 people to St. Dominic's Church for Mass. Surprisingly, we were greeted with no incident and the mass media, which had tried their best to follow the mayor's strange edict, had to report to the nation that we in fact were not anti-racial harmony — we were just pro-racial justice.

A funny thing happened on the way out of St. Dominic's, and that is whites found out that Sharpton didn't have horns in his head, and the Black bourgeoisie found out that we knew how to do more than one strategy. And the public found out that Lenora Fulani has a moral base to her character. And that we are just ordinary people with an extraordinary commitment to what is right.

We must now refocus the views of the public on the issue of justice rather than the issues of aimless racial harmony. We began engaging in closed door meetings with the leadership of Bensonhurst — [State] Senator Christopher Mega, [State] Assemblyman Frank Barbaro, leaders of the Italian-American Civic Association, and Howard Feuer, the Community Board district manager, and others. As we told them, there can never be real peace until we see some modicum of justice. They agreed in private to call on Bensonhurst to give up the guilty; they agreed in private to join us in calling for the governor and the mayor and the state attorney general to attend the sentencing of Joe Fama and Keith Mondello, and for a stiffer sentence to send a signal to racists everywhere.

Those private agreements never saw the light of day. They genuflected, they played curve ball at press conferences, yet we stood up and maintained our dignity and our position to the point where even David Dinkins, who had told the world to ignore us, had to deal with the fact that we had become an issue and a cause whose time had come. Standing on the City Hall steps holding a press conference with the white leadership of Bensonhurst, we came to the knowledge that David Dinkins would be attending the second meeting of that weekend. The news was met with mixed reactions in our circles. Some wanted to not attend at all because they believed it to be an insult that Dinkins would not choose to visit the Hawkins home for a first meeting with the white officials that weekend, but would opt to meet the Hawkins family and the rest of us in Bensonhurst where the tragedy had occurred under the sponsorship of those who knew those who were responsible for the murder of Yusuf Hawkins.

There were those who said we should use it as an opportunity to openly ridicule and chastise him. And then there were calmer voices that said we must keep our eye on the prize and the prize is justice. And even if that means having conversations with those who have chosen to be our enemies rather than our friends, we must pursue that path. And that is the path we pursued.

Having preached in Yonkers at the Messiah Baptist Church that morning, I arrived late picking up the Hawkins family, and subsequently late to the meeting. As we arrived the mayor was leaving. He stopped in the hallway and held a 10-minute meeting with us which he began by explaining why he had to leave. He immediately went into his support for the idea of a citywide effort to have the community cooperate during bias incidents and to turn over those responsible for bias crimes. He agreed to a meeting with Black leaders, to be coordinated by Dr. Jones and Dr. Calvin Butts later in the week.

As I stood there and watched this mayor, a man I've know some 20 years, who rose from a Harlem lawyer to be the mayor of the biggest metropolis in the world, but who has sold so many pieces of himself to so many different people that he will never again own himself without the real threat of ending himself, I thought for the first time to ginger up my attitude against him because I really pitied the man I was looking at. Pitied the weakness of human nature that in blind ambition make a deal with the devil to achieve a place of prominence that really has no meaning since you have agreed to submit to others all of the power inherent in the prominent position. Here is a shell of a mayor, because it is the powers-that-be and the party hacks that really run New York. He only gets the blame, he only gets to make the announcements. And here he's standing, looking at the mother and father of yet another killed young Black male, looking at the advocates of their cause, looking at those who will politically oppose him and question him, like Fulani and others — what can he say to us?

Really, there's nothing to say. The fact that he's standing looking at us at all *is* the statement, and the statement is that truth crushed to earth shall rise again. The statement is that you can ignore whatever you want, but sooner or later you will have been brought into the reality that there is a people's movement which will not be stopped or hampered by anyone or anything. You can say what you want, Dave, but our time as a people has come. And you can ignore the wave, but it will only make you a candidate for drowning.

We must deal with the fact that the people are tired of burying their young. The people are tired of dealing with the abuse of their own. The people are tired of bad education and bad housing, and bad living conditions, of AIDS, of other health epidemics that only press releases from City Hall address but no programs are brought forth to solve. Yes, you thought you were ignoring we who were on the surfboard. It's not the surfboard that you'd better worry about; it's the wave that we're riding on.

June 21, 1990

A Bittersweet Victory

As I sit here writing this column, I realize I should be doing my sixth day in state penitentiary on trumped-up charges by Attorney General Robert Abrams, and the fact that I am not incarcerated and free to continue my work for the time being is in every sense of the word a victory.

Something funny happened to Bob Abrams on the way to incarcerating me — he had an encounter with truth. I'm sure it was a strange encounter for him because never in the lives of politicians — bent as they are on agendas that have nothing to do with fair play or righteousness — do they encounter such intangibles as truth, justice or freedom.

So when someone like me comes along and speaks in terms like those, we are automatically suspected of being frauds or con artists or of having a hidden agenda. It is so far removed from their mentality, they can't really believe that anyone would dedicate their time, let alone their lives, to such an intangible or selfless mission as trying to get freedom and justice for a race, a nation or world.

On June 30, 1989 as I sat in my home talking to a staff person about some business of the United African Movement, the phone rang and I was told the Attorney General's office was downstairs to arrest me. I had known for several months that a grand jury was conducting a witch hunt investigation. I had been phoned by a reporter just that day and told that the grand jury was going to indict me within two weeks.

So it was not a shock when the call came. I merely put my jogging suit on and submitted. I was brought the next day to Albany where I was also indicted. The surprising thing was that in New York County they charged me with 67 counts of fraud, larceny and falsified business actions, the concept being that I had robbed and misused the funds of the National Youth Movement, a civil rights organization that I founded at sixteen years old. In fact, the indictment suggested there was no National Youth

Movement, despite the fact that the Youth Movement could document getting jobs for youth, registering young voters around the country, putting the City of New York against the wall and making them protect Black rights, putting the state against the wall and making them put Black working people on the MTA board, putting the city against the wall on the minority schools chancellor issue, on the Bernhard Goetz issue, on the Howard Beach issue, and the infamous painting of red crosses on crack houses which put the challenge forth to run the crack dealers out of our communities.

Despite all these well-publicized and well-organized things, the attorney general's position was we did not exist. At one level one can say he was misinformed. But at another level, Bob Abrams was trying to wipe out of history an era of movement, an era of rebellion, an era of social mobilization, because to make a fraud out of my participation was to make the whole movement and its effects suspect. It occurred to me that a lot more than me was on trial. It was the Goetz movement and the chancellor movement and the anti-drug movement and the voter registration movement and the independent political movement and the Howard Beach movement. Because had I been convicted, the credibility of the entire effort would have been in question, since I was so visibly a front-line participant in all of these affairs. It astonished me that Abrams' personal vendetta against me for having the nerve to stand up to him for a sixteen-year-old girl whom no one would stand up for, whom no one would believe, whom no one would take the time to make a movement around. But I joined Messrs. Maddox and Mason in saying, "We believe Tawana Brawley. We believe she's not lying," and we got a movement, joined by Lenora Fulani and others, who went all over this country and said that if we had to choose between a fifteen-year-old girl who was found unconscious in a bag with feces all over her body, and a state that has always lied to us, that has always stood for institutional racism, that has always presided over the oppression of our people, we would choose the girl. So I realized the personal vendetta, the roots and the fruit of it, but what astonished me was that there was no balancing, there was no hesitation to discredit the whole world, just to get me.

His ruthless, malicious broad painting was the ultimate downfall of Bob Abrams. Alton Maddox, probably the greatest legal mind of our times, meticulously and carefully picked the jury of our peers. Not of whites working on Wall Street, not even of Black Buppies working around the corporate world, but nine Black average working class persons, a bus driver, office workers, two Asians and one Latino. He knew that they would understand when he told the truth to them. He knew when they heard of us going out every weekend painting crack houses and the attorney general tried to represent that as a publicity stunt that no one risks their life to stand up before men who kill as part of their job descriptions just for a cameo shot on the news; he knew they would know when they heard about the deposits in Black banks that it was the attorney general's office and not my office that should have been negotiating those transactions in the first place; he knew that when they heard about our youth movement choir singing in the streets on a weekly basis, registering new voters to the polls, they would know that it costs money to transport and feed kids so that they would stay and register and do what we had planned to do. Yes, Maddox knew that they would know the truth, and when they heard the truth they would set me free.

The pompous attorney general's office went through a three-and-a-half month case way over schedule with 80 witnesses when they promised only 50. They tried every trick in the book except telling the truth and then, after all of their shouting, after two thousand exhibits put into evidence, after all of their witnesses had finished their song (most of them commending me rather than attacking me) we're standing in the hall, 6:30, July 2. I notice the familiar face of John Ryan the deputy attorney general of the state who conducted the Tawana Brawley grand jury, abruptly walking in with two bodyguards.

I noticed out a window in the hall the judge running across the street to head back in; I saw the TV stations come in and I sensed immediately that it was time. The verdict would be pronounced, and the course of our activism would now be determined. I say "the course" because had I been incarcerated, I would still have been active, so the matter was on which side of the wall I would continue to struggle. I walked toward the defendant's seat with a mixture of excitement and weariness — excitement because I wanted to know what lay ahead. One really doesn't want to leave one's family and friends if it can be avoided. Weariness because the whole process was so tiring, so unnecessary, so humiliating to go through this mindless exercise day after day.

And I sat in the chair and looked as these twelve working class people came out and delivered the most tremendous political blow to the judicial process in memory. *Sixty-seven times* they said not guilty. *Sixty-seven times*, not guilty. The law of averages was on the side of the attorney general. Certainly, they had to find one or two counts, but these people said, "No, he's not the one guilty for the conditions of the oppressed and the working class people; he is not the one guilty for the deception and the deceit of a judicial system in which 85% of those in jail are Black and young; he is not the one guilty for the lack of human rights and civil dignity for people of all races in the state of New York; he is not the one guilty for grandmothers being shot in their own kitchens and no one goes to jail; he is not the one guilty for Michael Stewart being beaten to death on a subway track and his killers walking out of jail and being promoted in their jobs; he's not the one guilty for fifteen-year-old girls being raped and it being called a hoax while a Central Park jogger is allegedly raped with no evidence as to her assailants and yet the accuseds' lives are being held in the balance as they face ultimate time in jail; he is not the one guilty of not being near Howard Beach or Bensonhurst and police brutality marches. No, it is the other side that is guilty; it the other side that thinks that we're dumb enough to read exhibits of nothingness and to send someone away for having the nerve to stand up.

And they said it *sixty-seven times*. "Not Guilty." I immediately felt the excitement of at least being able to spend the next few years at home with my wife and children whom I immediately ran to and hugged. And as I walked to the elevator with well-wishers patting us on the back and shaking hands, I began to get a real spirit of seriousness. I thought about what this really means. I knew the media would be downstairs to hear me interpret in a moment of victory what it really means. It was a bittersweet win even at that moment because I knew that Alton Maddox's license was now gone, and he would not be able to continue to practice. I knew the state would fight harder to stop me; they would still try the trumped-up last three charges in Albany that had really already been tried here since my tax returns were part of this case, and I had been found not guilty of defrauding the state. It would be double jeopardy to try me again in Albany, but I knew it was cynicism because the struggle to progress just didn't digress; I knew that we would have to fight harder because vicious men in defeat only get more vicious; they don't get tame.

But what does this mean? What should I say now that we have won at least this round? And it occurred to me that the real message of this victory was a lot bigger than Al Sharpton or the United African Movement or my friends, the New Alliance Party. The real message I wanted to send was that if some young kid, Black or white, in some depressed or so-called under-privileged area around the country were watching that night as I walked out of that courtroom. I wanted that young kid, whoever he or she may be, to have the courage of his or her convictions and know that you can stand up and win. Don't be afraid to stand up.

The system says if you fight us we can destroy you. The system says you can't beat city hall. The system says it's not with it to go out there. I wanted to send the message to kids — the message that Adam Clayton Powell and Martin Luther King and others sent me — that not only can you stand up but you must stand up and that if you do stand up, all the forces of righteousness in the world will protect you and even in the end goodness and mercy will follow you all the days of your life.

July 19, 1990

Two Symbols Collide

"Give me your tired, huddled masses yearning to be free." This is the engraved statement at the base of the Statue of Liberty. On August 28, 1990, we took her invitation seriously after leading 500 people from City Hall Park to Battery Park to begin a rally commemorating the 27th anniversary of Dr. King's famous speech "I Have A Dream." Rafael Mendez and I, Dr. Lenora Fulani and other UAM and NAP leaders brought about 150 homeless to answer Miss Liberty's invitation.

One of the reasons the invitation has become so important is because the Statue of Liberty is one of the few national monuments that even pretends to invite the masses to come to our freedom. Therefore it was great symbolism for these people to be there while their cousins, nephews, fathers and sons are en route to Iraq and Kuwait to protect the United States government's interests and yet here at home they can't even find shelter to cover their heads — to no one's concern and no one's care.

So they came to Miss Liberty to raise a contradiction: two universal symbols colliding — a gift of the French that has stood in the harbor representing a freedom that was not known to those who were already inhabitants when she got here and a southern Black minister who fought for that freedom. It is noteworthy that Miss Liberty is looking out to the harbor because if she would just turn around, she would be looking at a lot of huddled masses yearning to be free. Turn around, Miss Liberty. 'Cause right behind you is Harlem and Bed-Stuy, streets flowing with drugs sold by policemen, the worst educational facilities in the country, the worst hospitals, homeless people laying up and down the streets. Turn around, Miss Liberty. On the West Side Highway to your right there are the motorists on top who drive furiously toward their Westchester manors, and there are the homeless on the bottom, the victims of society. Those who have had to pay with their natural behinds for Reaganomics and voodoo Bush economics. Turn around, Miss Liberty. If you would just turn around, you would see a nation torn by racial strife, where children are still shot in their backs because of the color of their skins. Where just on the other side of you Phillip Pannell, a hole in his back from a police killing. Turn around, Miss Liberty. There is much more to see if you would look this way rather than just looking at the birds and the steamships in the water. Turn around and see the roaring masses at each other's throats being played off each other by hungry and corrupt capitalists and corrupt and vicious government officials. Turn around, Miss Liberty. You will see a Riker's Island under siege by correction officers and a whimpering mayor, indecisive, trying to be firm with boycotters in Flatbush who respond to injustice while he becomes a patsy to his own military jail force who in fact are the abusers.

The symbol of the great Miss Liberty collided with the symbol of Martin Luther King. It is he who remained on Miss Liberty's island as we gathered and took our tents that day. Here is a man who rose from southern Black obscurity to international world fame. Oh, many write about Dr. King's eloquence and his Ph.D. from Boston University and his Nobel Prize given in Sweden, but none of these are the reason he became world famous. He became world famous because he fought against the powers of oppression. He fought against legal apartheid in the United States. He fought for a young Black woman, Rosa Parks, to have the right to sit at the front of the bus. The only reason she could not was because she had the wrong complexion. He fought the system that went to Viet Nam and dropped billions...that went to the South Bronx and dropped empty promises. He fought and that is why he gained his place in history. Let us not be confused. Neither Dr. King's background nor his style are the reason his story was grabbed and appeared in reporters' notepads. That happened because he took on a monstrous federal system that had never been taken on before. So in a sense we brought our introduction — we introduced Dr. King to Miss Liberty, and that, of course, was too much for America to stand.

We were immediately isolated, the island was sealed off, thousands of tourists were turned back and scores of vendors would make no receipts this day. America couldn't stand for Miss Liberty to talk to Dr. King's children because she would drop her torch if she just heard what we had to say. America couldn't afford for Miss Liberty to sit there and become the shade over the sun for the homeless because that is too much like serving a function. That's too much like making obvious to the world what is already obvious to America — it fits into the economic order to have the poor and homeless and hungry. They just decided at the top to make sure it's not available. As we sat and sang freedom's songs and waited and waited until we were finally arrested, it ran through my mind that if Dr. King were alive, Dr. King would not be somewhere in the Blue Room of City Hall admiring some photo of himself. Nor would he be up in Albany in the governor's mansion. He would be where he left us instructions to be — somewhere building a tent city to dramatize that the poor are still here, the miseducated, uneducated and underemployed are still here, the cast-outs, the rejects, the throwaways of society are still here. That was what his dream was for and that is why we tried to add the torch of Miss Liberty to an already aglow dream. I challenge Miss Liberty to turn around and look our way. I challenge the American government to do likewise. Until then, though, I will bear Dr. King's dream.

September 6, 1990

Where Are the Liberals?

Over the last several weeks New York has been shaken by some appalling revelations. These revelations have simmered for some time now under the surface, in part because of a media white-out that was only recently (and forceably) broken through. As a result, these issues are now rising to the top and becoming inescapable reality to many New Yorkers. One revelation occurred when over 300 Hasidic Jews stormed the precinct in Williamsburg because a rabbi had been arrested by the police, not for marching for Soviet Jews, not for marching against anti-Semitism, not even in a pro-Zionist or a pro-Israeli march, but for soliciting a woman, who happened not to be a prostitute, in a manner in which he clearly identified himself as a potential trick.

This outburst in defense of blatant immorality, which caused the physical injury of 49 police officers, was met with absolutely nothing other than the double standard of preferential treatment that the Hasidics historically enjoy in this metropolis. Despite the police injuries, no one was arrested, no warning shots were fired, nothing was done. And police commissioner Lee Brown immediately entered the competition for Uncle Tom of the Year (with a bullet) award with his boss, Mayor David Dinkins. Brown ran out, not to the wounded policemen, not to the Hispanics who suffer the other, painful part of this double standard, but to the Hasidics. He assured them in private the double standard would remain, while announcing in public an investigation.

Two to three weeks later, after it was apparent that Lee Brown spent his time with the Hasidics kissing the hem of their garments rather than handcuffing the wrists of the culprits, a Latino policeman publicly broke his silence. He revealed to the world that he had made many arrests the night of the riot, but the arrest reports were ripped up in his face and culprits released without question (as long as they were members of the

Hasidic community). He went on to confirm that Hasidics have always been treated differently in the Williamsburg section; policemen would often make good arrests, only to have their superiors mark them invalid and release the suspects.

Aside from being an atrocious, racist, unacceptable act, it raises the question, "Where are the great white liberals of New York?" The last time we saw them they were running around Bensonhurst teaching sensitivity classes to Black and white students, rather than fighting for racial justice in the wake of the brutal murder of Yusuf Hawkins. The last time we saw them, they were condemning people like me, calling us racial racketeers, calling us racial ambulance chasers, while they went and got funded to teach in school what should be taught at home. It seems very strange to me that these liberals only surface when there is a rising up in the Black community, and they only surface to question and condemn Black activist leadership. But they never seem to find their vocal chords, or take off their bedroom slippers and put their running shoes on, when it is whites who are in question. They would have gained a loud and consistent hearing had they condemned the double standard being practiced in Williamsburg. They would have muted critics like me had they brought their wretched sensitivity classes to Williamsburg as they had offered them in Bensonhurst. But it seems that the liberals in New York also operate on a double standard: They say, "We must reprimand and babysit Blacks and turn our heads and ignore the sins of whites."

Which is why the white liberal sector of the Northeast is so totally held in contempt by most Blacks and by most Black leadership, because they see themselves as our overseers rather than moral agents of social change, a role they have played in the past. These liberals have also ignored the fact that over 30 people of Black and Latino descent have been brutally killed by police this year, the last of whom, Mary Mitchell, a 41-year-old Black woman, was killed in her own home. They did not question any of these verdicts because it is their liberal establishment and administration that is in power. They will say, "Well, I cannot work with a Sharpton and that is why I did not join the fight." But isn't it strange that they could work in the past with everyone from Stokely

Carmichael to the Panther Party to Dr. King. The real reason they cannot work today is because the liberals have *come to power*. Mario Cuomo *is* the liberals' choice. So the former outside liberal is today's inside establishment person. It is absolutely hypocritical for them to still pose as liberals when they are in fact in charge; they used every scheme and hustle and means of deceit in the book to get those of us who thought we were reforming things to in fact empower them — and they turned out to be no different from that those who were ahead of them.

Where are the liberals? They've cut down their long hair; they've shaved their beards, taken off vests and hippie beads. They're now in grey flannel suits; they now wear well-groomed hair styles. They no longer write for the *Village Voice* or other Village papers; they now write for the *Observer* or the *Daily News*. They are now part of the Establishment and they hustled, lied and deceived us to make us feel that they had commitments that meant something other than "put me in power." That is where the liberals are; that is where they always have been. They are no longer to be trusted, should never have been paid attention to, and must be removed by any means necessary. Because if there's one thing worse than a straight racist, reactionary fascist, it's one who is using long hair and smiles to cover and deceive those who would be on the lookout for anything other than a fascist in liberal clothing.

December 6, 1990

King's Birthday
in the Persian Gulf

As we near the end of the year and the Christmas season, it is a strange irony that the President of the United States has also chosen this season to begin to loudly beat the war drums. The height of irony is that the cutoff — or the showdown — date given Saddam Hussein to withdraw from Kuwait is January 15, which would have been the 65th birthday of Dr. Martin Luther King, Jr. It is as symbolic as it is ironic, because in many ways, the answer to the Persian Gulf crisis was given by Dr. King before his untimely death 22 years ago. Dr. King, notwithstanding the embracing of his memory by the general American population after his death, was a man who was very much reviled and considered controversial minutes before his death. One of the main reasons was that Dr. King had rightfully pointed out three facts that hold true today in the Persian Gulf crisis, although his observations were on the war in Viet Nam. One, King argued that America was "the greatest purveyor of violence in the world today"; secondly, that America was not the world's policeman and had no moral or legal right to impose its preferences on another nation; and thirdly, that people of color and lower economic ability would bear the unfair brunt of the war at a much higher rate than those who were white and/or wealthy.

It is as true today as it was when King took his Viet Nam position. The strange embracing of Bush's policies by those that claim to come in King's name and plan to walk his path is most confusing and depressing. Mrs. Coretta Scott King, the widow of Dr. King, has chosen General Colin Powell, the chairman of the Joint Chiefs of Staff, as grand marshall for the parade honoring her husband in Atlanta next month, while Rev. Jesse Jackson has appeared on national television condoning Bush's war in Iraq.

History must record that it is a betrayal of the standards and the philosophy of Dr. King for his widow and one of his staff members to in any way salute or praise or condone war-mongering on a platform provided for them by one who courageously stood against the winds of war in his own time. Moreover, Blacks, with only 13% of the US population, already comprise 29% of those in the Persian Gulf, which shows that we can die twice as well as we can live in this country, not to mention that we are fighting for a democratic process in Kuwait that we don't have in South Side Chicago or Brownsville or Miami, Florida; not to mention that now the two options for young Blacks is to die in the Persian Gulf for oil or die in Bensonhurst because of the color of their skin.

It seems a strange mixture of self-hatred and historic deception for Black leaders not to be storming the barricades against this ungodly, unprincipled, immoral and illegal war. It also seems to me very strange that Black and white liberals have spent the last decade preaching to youngsters about refraining from violence, stopping the killing, and now rush them into training camps to learn how to be killers — insensitive cold-blooded murderers of people who have no fight with them. So it is our lot to again begin the solo voice of raising moral issues in an immoral world, knowing from the outset that we will be universally condemned, harassed by those democratic law enforcement agencies that assure a sustained democracy on paper but enforce a real fascism in reality.

But despite all of those clouds that will darken our skies, we must do what is right. We must call upon people not to participate in this orgy of shame that is building up in the Persian Gulf. One: life — flesh and blood — is more important than oil. Two: how can the United States, which invaded Grenada and Panama, turn around and call anyone an aggressor of another nation? And three: how can the United States be the decider of what a just government is when it has institutionalized injustice in its relationship with people of color and of lower economic backgrounds. To think that one would die for such a false and faulty legacy, to think that one could die for such a historic mistake, is unbelievable.

It is time to build an anti-war movement, but this time it should be built with those who will suffer the most, and who will pay the highest price. This anti-war movement will not be led by intellectual elites, or some isolated radicals who sit around preaching to themselves about things that the masses, who they claim to represent, never really understood. This must be an anti-war movement of the masses, because if the masses really get involved in it, it will in fact stop the war, because the soldiers come from the *masses*, not from the intellectual, academic, radical *classes* who try to dominate anti-war movements.

We call on Coretta King to be faithful to her vows to her husband and not to participate in political adultery in his death, by having intercourse with war-mongers when her platform was provided by a peacemaker.

We call on Rev. Jackson and others to become heirs of Dr. King's moral philosophy, not just his media position.

But most of all we call on young Americans to inform their recruitment officers that they're not available to be used as gun fodder for oil barons, to be enforcers of a justice system that they do not have at home, to be the aggressors against Saddam Hussein in the name of the most aggressive international whore of the planet today, the United States government.

And we call on President Bush to be consistent: don't preach to Saddam Hussein what you did not preach to yourself when you headed into Grenada and Nicaragua and Panama. We must not engage in what could be the last war known to mankind, especially not on such non-principles and non-validity as trying to control the world's oil that is not even fairly distributed at home. I shudder to think of young men that leave cold, unheated ghetto tenements to head to the sands of Saudi Arabia to protect an oil that they can't even enjoy at home.

Somebody must speak out. I guess I understand how King felt when he took on the war in Vietnam against the public wishes of the NAACP, the Urban League, and many of his own friends in SCLC. It is in that tradition, the tradition of a little man from Atlanta, Georgia, who had the moral foresight and the courage to stand up, who took me from the back of the bus to the front of the bus. But he just didn't tell us to have a seat in the bus, he told us to act like front riders of a new bus of freedom and justice worldwide. In his name, I say to young America: Don't go, don't participate, STOP THE WAR.

December 20, 1990

Thoughts on the Way to Europe

As we near the summer, I am excited about being able to expand our message on a worldwide level. I'm embarking on a trip to England to share, speak and listen to my people who suffer in Great Britain some of the same indignities, brutalities and murders that we suffer in these United States, the former colonies of Great Britain.

A month ago, the British Broadcasting Corporation decided to do an hour special on our movement in general and me in particular, and began filming certain days in my life and activities of the movement. They were present in fact when I was stabbed in Bensonhurst in January. Since that time, the *London Daily Mail* newspaper and others have chosen to do profiles. Their stand on us has been to expose to the English population — which is only 4% Black — the racial tension that has risen again in the United States, and to accept basically as law what the white media here has said about our movement, our intentions and our goals.

This provoked me to say that maybe we should also go to England and tell our story *ourselves*. My assistant Anthony Charles made a preliminary visit in March and was able to meet with several very credible ministers and activists who, after meeting with him, were very anxious to invite us to come. Striking stories were related to me that sounded so similar to the stories we deal with on a daily basis here in the United States. One of my concerns was that on February 21 of this year a young man named Rolan Adams was killed by a gang of whites who chased him and a companion down and fatally stabbed Rolan. It was reminiscent of Howard Beach over here. There has been no protest, no arrest, no indictments, no prosecution.

We need to share each other's experiences. The Adams family, who invited me to march with them in London, needs to know the strategy used by the Griffith family and the Hawkins family. Police brutality is rampant there. They need to know how we are dealing with Rodney King, and we need to know how they are dealing with their police brutality. The fact of the matter is, given transportation and communication we have become a global village. Those who suffer as a result of exploitation by "allied" nations must have a bond, just like those who profit from it, so we can rise up *together* and challenge the allied nations on their inhumanity, on their barbaric behavior, and the savagery of their policy.

Yes, George Bush has spoken of a new world order, and there will be a new world order, but it will not be the new world order that George Bush offered. It will be a new world order based upon the population of the world. Twenty-five percent of the world is Chinese. *Most* of the world is non-white. So the balance of power in the world cannot be held in the hands of white Europeans in England, Germany and the United States of America. For the masses of those European enclaves and the American Empire to communicate, unite and coalesce, is to establish with Africa and Asia the real new world order, which is the real balance of power based on people population or masses, rather than based on monetary dollars or classes.

It is with that desire that I journey to England and on to Africa at a later date, because we must, at all costs and at all risk, establish a new world order that will challenge people in power who have inflicted the exploitative pain of our day on masses of color around the world. From the Queen at Buckingham Palace to the White House of George Bush we need to organize and display and meticulously execute our outrage, our defiance, our people's revolution for change. We can no longer isolate our struggle. We cannot permit the enemy to make each incident an isolated incident, and therefore an isolated reaction.

When a Winnie Mandela is framed in Johannesburg, South Africa, there must be a global response to such an indignity. When an Alton Maddox is framed by a grievance committee in Brooklyn, New York, there must be a global response. When a Rolan Adams is stabbed to death in London or Rodney King is beaten unmercifully in Los Angeles, there must be a global response. Inter-continental corporations must feel the economic withdrawal. International governmental agencies must feel the tension. The allied states must come to the table to deal with people of color, just like they come to the table to deal with oil and other things of profit.

It is time for the internationalizing of the masses, just as there has been an internationalizing of the classes. This was what Dr. King saw. This is what Malcolm tried to put into place. This is what Mandela had to see as he toured the world. It has now fallen into the laps of the generation coming to bring the struggle into one global village, and we must organize despite our differences of borders, because we all are members and citizens of the Nation of Pain.

May 2, 1991

Reverend Al Sharpton
Year by Year

1951
Rev's older sister, Cheryl "Joy" Sharpton, born.

1954
Alfred Sharpton, Jr., the second child of Ada Sharpton of Dothan, Alabama and Alfred Sharpton, Sr. of Wabasa, Florida, is born in Brooklyn, New York.

Brown v. Board of Education overturns legalized school segregation.

1959
Rev gives his first sermon, "Let not your heart be troubled," at the age of four at Washington Temple Church of God in Christ.

Sharptons move to St. Albans, Queens.

1961
Rev visits paternal grandparents in Florida; first trip south.

1963
Dr. Martin Luther King, Jr. gives "I have a dream" speech after march on Washington.

1964
Rev is ordained as a minister by Bishop Frederick Douglass Washington.

Rev preaches at the World's Fair with gospel great Mahalia Jackson.

Sharptons move back to Brooklyn after sudden departure of Alfred, Sr.

Rev preaches on a 45 rpm record called "Who."

Rev tours Caribbean with Bishop Washington; visits widow of Marcus Garvey.

1967
Rev forms "Youth Committee for Powell" to fight Adam Clayton Powell's expulsion from Congress.

1968
Rev enters Tilden High School in East Flatbush.

1969
Rev becomes part of the Adam Clayton Powell entourage.

Rev is appointed New York City youth director of the SCLC's Operation Breadbasket.

1970
Powell is defeated in Democratic Party primary by Charles Rangel, who will replace him as Harlem's congressman.

1971
Rev forms the National Youth Movement.

1972
Rev attends the National Black Political Convention in Gary, Indiana as the youngest delegate and a member of the platform committee.

Rev is graduated from Tilden High School.

Adam Clayton Powell dies in Bimini.

1973
Rev becomes "surrogate son" to James Brown. For the next eight years he alternates time on the road with James and running the National Youth Movement.

1974
National Youth Movement demands justice in Claude Reese case, the first major police brutality case Rev is involved in.

1978
Rev's first political campaign; he backs an unsuccessful run against State Assemblyman Major Owens.

1979
Rev meets his future wife, singer Kathy Jordan.

1980
Rev records "God has smiled on me" with James Brown.

1981
Rev returns to New York with Kathy Jordan to work full-time with the National Youth Movement.

1983
Fight for a Black schools chancellor in New York City begins.

1984
Jacksons Victory Tour; Rev organizes community relations team that brings community into tour.

Jesse Jackson launches his first Presidential campaign.

1985
Rev leads movement demanding that charges be brought against subway vigilante Bernhard Goetz.

1986
Rev takes lead in fight against crack. War on Crack Celebrity Dinner at Waldorf-Astoria Hotel.

Michael Griffith killed in Howard Beach.

Daughter Dominique is born.

1987
Rev leads movement that results in conviction of three of Michael Griffith's killers.

Tawana Brawley abducted and raped.

Daughter Ashley is born.

"Day of Outrage" shuts down Brooklyn subway. Rev among 73 arrested.

1988
Brawley case sparks coming together of new independent Black leadership, including Rev, Minister Louis Farrakhan, Dr. Lenora Fulani, attorney Alton Maddox, Jr. Protests at Democratic National Convention in Atlanta.

New York State grand jury issues report claiming Tawana fabricated her story.

New York State begins investigation of Rev and National Youth Movement.

Disciplinary action is begun against Maddox and C. Vernon Mason.

Rev, Maddox and Mason form United African Movement in New York.

Fulani receives quarter-million votes in independent Presidential run.

Death of Bishop Frederick Douglass Washington.

1989
Yusuf Hawkins is killed in Bensonhurst.

10,000 youth march on Brooklyn Bridge in memory of Yusuf.

Rev leads first of 29 marches through Bensonhurst.

Rev is indicted on tax charges.

David Dinkins defeats Ed Koch in Democratic Party primary for mayor and squeaks by Rudolph Giuliani in general election to become New York City's first African American mayor.

1990
Bensonhurst trials result in only one murder conviction.

Rev's trial begins; he's acquitted on all 67 counts.

Alton Maddox's law license suspended.

Phillip Pannell, Jr. is killed by police in Teaneck, New Jersey.

Demonstrations in Teaneck result in indictment of Officer Gary Spath on manslaughter charges.

APPENDIX C

The Howard Beach Case: A Chronology

December 20, 1986
Michael Griffith is killed after he is run down on the Belt Parkway in Queens while fleeing a white mob; Cedric Sandiford, Griffith's stepfather, is also severely beaten by the same mob; a third man, Timothy Grimes, escapes without physical injuries.

Dominick Blum, the court officer who hit Griffith, continues his trip home to Brooklyn without stopping. He claims that he thought he hit a tire. Blum later returned to the scene with his father, a police officer, in his father's car.

Police find Sandiford in Howard Beach but treat him as a murder suspect rather than as a crime victim.

Michael Griffith's mother Jean Griffith and Sandiford retain Alton Maddox.

New York City Mayor Edward Koch posts a $10,000 reward, describing

Griffith's killing as a "lynching."

December 21, 1986
Reverend Sharpton's National Youth Movement posts $5,000 reward and challenges Black churches to match Koch's offer.

Maddox charges that New York City is unprepared to prosecute a white mob for murdering a Black man.

December 22, 1986
Maddox thwarts the police effort requiring Sandiford to view a lineup while he wears a patch over his right eye and has lost vision in his left eye.

Police arrest four white teenagers.

To demonstrate the rights of Blacks to travel freely throughout New York City, Reverends Al Sharpton, Herbert Daughtry and Jerry West visit the New Park Pizza shop where the three victims were first confronted by the white mob.

December 24, 1986
Maddox publicly discusses the case for the first time on WLIB and demands a special prosecutor.

Sandiford refuses a subpoena which requires him to appear at the district attorney's office to discuss the case.

December 26, 1986
Attorney C. Vernon Mason and Reverend Calvin Butts join Maddox at a Queens press conference. Maddox accuses police of a cover-up and fingers Blum as one of the mob members.

Michael Griffith is eulogized at Our Lady of Charity Catholic Church.

December 27, 1986
Led by the NAACP's executive director Benjamin Hooks and Reverends Sharpton and Daughtry, thousands march in Howard Beach to protest racial violence.

December 29, 1986
A Queens judge dismisses murder-manslaughter charges against Jon Lester, Jason Ladone and Scott Kern at a seldom used preliminary hearing. Sandiford and Grimes refuse to testify at the hearing.

Maddox, Mason, Sharpton and James Bell begin daily meetings at District 65 of UAW to coordinate strategies.

Police department admits errors in its investigation of Blum.

December 30, 1986
Police Commissioner Benjamin Ward characterizes Maddox as an ambulance chaser and a mercenary. Bill Lynch, who was chief of staff for Manhattan

Borough President David Dinkins, calls Maddox a "people's lawyer."

Congressman Charles Rangel questions Maddox's strategy.

The New York Court Officers Association calls for Maddox's disbarment for alleging that Blum was a suspect.

Brooklyn activist Jitu Weusi urges Black elected officials and clergymen to boycott a meeting called by Koch with Black leaders.

December 31, 1986
A spokesperson for Governor Cuomo says that Maddox has "zero credibility" in the Black community.

Black leaders meet with Koch but refrain from criticizing Maddox after intervention by Reverend Sharpton, who characterizes the City Hall meeting as "a coon show."

Federal law enforcement officials announce a civil rights probe of the Griffith murder.

The district attorney of Queens County considers abandoning his criminal investigation and referring it to federal authorities for possible civil rights violations.

Maddox and Mason, who represents Timothy Grimes, petition the governor to appoint a special state prosecutor.

January 2, 1987
Sharpton and Bell scrap plans for a school boycott and call for a "Day of Mourning and Outrage."

Special State Prosecutor Charles Hynes calls for the production of any evidence of official misconduct and is rebuffed by Maddox and Mason, who charge that Hynes has no authority to prosecute.

January 3, 1987
At Abyssinian Baptist Church, Sandiford in his first press conference states that police mistreatment and prosecutorial indifference are the reasons for his non-cooperation.

Mason calls for a boycott of pizza shops. Brooklyn activist Sonny Carson asserts "Maybe we can take a page from the [ANC's] book. There are a lot of tires around this city."

January 6, 1987
Two thousand rally at Boys and Girls High School in Brooklyn.

January 7, 1987
Jon Lester, a defendant in the Howard Beach racial attack, is sentenced as a youthful offender and given five years' probation for illegally possessing a handgun when he was apprehended in a stolen car.

Queens District Attorney John Santucci announces that he is considering granting immunity to eight members of the mob to prevent criminal prosecutions.

Governor Cuomo announces the establishment of a racial task force.

January 8, 1987
Police Commissioner Ward denounces charges of a police cover-up and renews his criticism of Maddox.

Federal authorities say they will take no action until the state completes its investigation.

January 9, 1987
Maddox and Mason receive support from trade unions.

January 10, 1987
Reverend Sharpton leads a picket line in front of police headquarters calling for Ward's resignation.

New Alliance Party calls for community rallies with only the Black press in attendance.

January 11, 1987
Timothy Grimes is falsely arrested on charges of loitering for the purpose of prostitution. The arrest was voided.

January 12, 1987
Cuomo and Santucci meet to discuss the possibility of appointing a special prosecutor.

Koch meets with 200 clergy and calls for racial harmony.

At Governor Cuomo's direction Manhattan Borough President David Dinkins and a group of Black officials meet with Maddox and Mason.

January 13, 1987
Governor Cuomo, after meeting with Black officials and clergy, names Charles Hynes as New York's first special prosecutor in a racial case.

January 15, 1987
Hynes interviews Sandiford and Grimes.

January 20, 1987
Hynes assembles a grand jury panel.

January 21, 1987
Ten thousand protesters march from mid-town Manhattan to Koch's home in Greenwich Village in a "Day of Outrage."

January 28, 1987
Sandiford appears before state grand jury panel.

February 9, 1987
Grand jury hands up indictments against 12 members of the white mob.

February 10, 1987
Mob members arraigned in Queens Supreme Court.

Hynes announces that Robert Riley, one of the gang members, has cooperated with the prosecution.

March 1, 1987
State and local officials propose laws against hate crimes.

March 6, 1987
Riley agrees to cooperate with the prosecution throughout court proceedings in exchange for lenient treatment.

March 13, 1987
Maddox files a civil suit against city on behalf of Sandiford.

April 14, 1987
Pre-trial suppression hearings commence in Queens Supreme Court.

May 18, 1987
William Bollander, a Howard Beach defendant, is charged with assaulting a student and security guards at a high school.

May 22, 1987
A Queens grand jury votes to clear Blum.

June 19, 1987
Justice Thomas Demakos rules that there will be two trials.

September 8, 1987
Jury selection commences in the trials of Jon Lester, Scott Kern, Thomas Pirone and Jason Ladone. All are charged with murder except Ladone, who is charged with manslaughter.

September 21, 1987
Justice Thomas Demakos proscribes defense lawyers from using peremptory challenges in a racially discriminatory manner.

October 20, 1987
Reverend Sharpton files disciplinary complaint against defense lawyer Stephen Murphy.

December 5, 1987
A coalition including Sharpton, Maddox, Carson and Father Lawrence Lucas calls for a "Day of Outrage" to protest racial violence.

December 9, 1987
Reverend Sharpton leads a prayer vigil in front of courthouse.

December 10, 1987
Jury deliberations begin.

December 12, 1987
Mason praises Hynes for his handling of the case.

December 20, 1987

A memorial service and mass are held at Our Lady of Charity Catholic Church for Michael Griffith.

December 21, 1987

"Day of Outrage" in downtown Brooklyn shuts down bridges and subway lines in defiance of a court order prohibiting civil disobedience in any form. Seventy-three people are arrested.

Lester, Kern and Ladone are convicted of manslaughter in the second degree and assault in the first degree. Pirone is acquitted of all charges.

December 23, 1987

Maddox files civil actions against Howard Beach defendants.

January 22, 1988

Justice Demakos imposes the maximum sentence of 10 to 30 years on Lester.

February 5, 1988

Justice Demakos imposes the maximum sentence of 6 to 18 years on Kern.

February 9, 1988

The district attorney's office dismisses charges against 52 of the 73 "Day of Outrage" demonstrators, but Reverend Sharpton, Reverend Timothy Mitchell, Charles Barron and 18 others must stand trial.

February 11, 1988

Justice Demakos imposes a sentence of 5 to 15 years on Ladone.

February 24, 1988

Blum is found guilty in an administrative hearing into his role in the hit-and-run death of Michael Griffith. The judge finds his testimony at the hearing incredible.

March 11, 1988

Justice Demakos rules that seven remaining defendants must be tried in a single trial with two juries.

May 19, 1988

Defendant Harry Buonocore appears in a closed court proceeding and pleads guilty. He is sentenced as a youthful offender to five years' probation.

May 24, 1988

Salvatore DeSimone pleads guilty to riot charge. He is given five years' probation and is sentenced as a youthful offender.

June 8, 1988

Jury selection is completed for trial of remaining defendants.

July 14, 1988

Jury acquits Thomas Gucciardo.

August 7, 1988

A jury convicts William Bollander, James Povinelli and Thomas Farino of misdemeanor riot charges. Defendant John Saggese is acquitted.

September 23, 1988
Robert Riley, who testified for the prosecution, is sentenced as a youthful offender and given six months.

August 29, 1989
Robert Riley begins his sentence at Brooklyn House of Correction.

December 11, 1989
An intermediate appellate court reverses the conviction of William Bollander, James Povinelli and Thomas Farino and orders new trials.

March 29, 1990
New York's highest court upholds the convictions of Lester, Kern and Ladone.

September 4, 1990
Retrial of Bollander, Farino and Povinelli commences before Justice Thomas Demakos in Queens Supreme Court.

October 2, 1990
Bollander, Farino and Povinelli are convicted of lesser charges.

November 28, 1990
Bollander, Farino and Povinelli are given youthful offender treatment.

The Tawana Brawley Case: A Chronology

February 27, 1987
Hildegarde Smith, an African American woman, is attacked by a gang of white men in Newton, NJ who smear feces over her body, crop her hair and mark an "X" on her head, nine months before Tawana's abduction. There are no arrests.

November 24, 1987
Tawana Brawley, 15 years old, is kidnapped and sexually abused in Dutchess County, New York.

Harry Crist, a part-time police officer in Fishkill, New York, fails to report for evening duty.

Crist and New York State Trooper Scott Patterson admit to being at the location where Tawana was abducted.

November 28, 1987
While riding together in a car Assistant District Attorney Steven Pagones, Patterson and Crist talk about a girl "in a bag of shit" — hours

before Tawana is found. Crist allegedly threatens to shoot Pagones and Patterson in his car.

A white mailman observes Crist's automobile near the site where and when Tawana was found.

Tawana is found unconscious, smeared with feces and "KKK" and "nigger" scrawled on her body.

At the hospital, Tawana refuses to speak to white policemen, but tells a Black police officer that a white police officer who fits Crist's description was among her abductors.

December 1, 1987
Crist is found dead, having allegedly committed suicide.

Brawley family retains attorney Alton Maddox.

Tawana scribbles a note while in a doctor's office in response to question about identity of perpetrator: "I want him dead. I want [Dutchess County Sheriff Frederick] Scoralick — dead."

December 2, 1987
New York State NAACP president Hazel Dukes accuses local officials of participating in a cover-up.

December 12, 1987
Minister Louis Farrakhan, Reverend Al Sharpton, C. Vernon Mason, Sonny Carson, Viola Plummer and others address rally in Newburgh, New York.

December 21, 1987
Reverends Al Sharpton, Timothy Mitchell and Charles Barron and hundreds of protesters stage "Day of Outrage" in Brooklyn, shutting down all trains.

January 5, 1988
Tawana, her mother Glenda Brawley and Juanita Brawley, Tawana's aunt, receive subpoenas to appear before a local grand jury.

January 13, 1988
Tawana, Glenda and Juanita refuse to appear before grand jury.

January 14, 1988
Pagones reveals to the Dutchess County District Attorney that he was with Crist and Patterson when Tawana was found. Pagones admits, then later denies, that Crist talked about a "girl in a bag of shit."

Dutchess County DA's office prevents a grand jury witness, the mailman, from placing Crist's car near the location and time of Tawana's discovery.

Maddox accuses the DA's office of refusing to allow Tawana to view photos of policemen in Dutchess County and calls for a special prosecutor.

January 20, 1988
Dutchess County DA William Grady cites an undisclosed conflict of interest in withdrawing from grand jury investigation.

January 21, 1988
Judge Judith Hillery of county court names Poughkeepsie attorney David Sall as special prosecutor.

January 22, 1988
Sall steps down as special prosecutor, stating that no local attorney can conduct the investigation.

January 25, 1988
Judge Hillery asks Governor Cuomo to appoint a special prosecutor.

January 26, 1988
Cuomo appoints New York State Attorney General Robert Abrams.

January 27, 1988
Reverend Sharpton and Mitchell lead a protest march at LaGuardia Airport in Queens, resulting in arrests and convictions.

February 5, 1988
Maddox charges that the state has names of Tawana's assailants, which is the basis for the district attorney's undisclosed conflict of interest.

February 9, 1988
A judge in Brooklyn Criminal Court

drops charges against 52 protesters arrested during the December 21 "Day of Outrage."

February 10, 1988
Bill Cosby and Ed Lewis, the publisher of *Essence* magazine, announce a $25,000 reward.

February 11, 1988
Alton Maddox, C. Vernon Mason and Reverend Sharpton meet with Cuomo.

February 13, 1988
Mike Tyson and Don King meet with Tawana. Tyson leaves her his watch as a present.

February 16, 1988
Maddox, Mason and Reverend Sharpton meet with Abrams.

February 22, 1988
Charles Hynes, then the New York State deputy attorney general, denounces Sharpton.

February 23, 1988
Samuel Evans, an employee in Abrams' office, is arrested for the theft of the Dutchess County grand jury minutes.

February 24, 1988
Evans attempts suicide.

February 27, 1988
One thousand people march in Poughkeepsie to protest Abrams' handling of Brawley case.

February 29, 1988
Abrams convenes a nearly all-white grand jury in Dutchess County.

March 1, 1988
Brooklyn Assemblyman Roger Green blasts Reverend Sharpton in the media for his defense of Tawana.

March 9, 1988
Conrad Lynn, an NAACP attorney, blasts Maddox, Mason and Sharpton in the media, and demands that Tawana be placed in foster care.

March 14, 1988
Maddox calls on Abrams to arrest Pagones.

March 17, 1988
Photos of Tawana's naked torso in Abrams' possession are released and shown on national television.

March 18, 1988
Tawana's textbooks, which she was carrying when she was abducted, are found at her former high school.

March 21, 1988
Dr. Lenora Fulani leads a 300-strong women of color march in Poughkeepsie in support of Tawana and her advisors, urging the removal of Abrams from the Brawley case.

March 22, 1988
Reverends Sharpton and Mitchell lead a march in Poughkeepsie protesting Abrams' handling of grand jury.

March 23, 1988
Coolidge Miller, who is legally blind, is arrested in Poughkeepsie during a protest of Abrams' grand jury probe. Miller and other witnesses charge that he is assaulted by Deputy Attorney General John Ryan, who was appointed

by Abrams to handle the Brawley case.

A State Supreme Court justice denies Tawana's motion seeking to block Abrams' access to her medical records and photographs.

March 27, 1988
Queens State Assemblywoman Cynthia Jenkins calls for a nationwide boycott of NBC for televising Tawana's hospital photographs.

April 5, 1988
William West, a state investigator assigned to the Brawley investigation, is arrested in Brooklyn after selling cocaine to an undercover narcotics officer.

May 24, 1988
Glenda Brawley defies Abrams' grand jury subpoena.

June 6, 1988
Justice Angelo Ingrassia sentences Glenda to 30 days in jail for contempt of court.

June 8, 1988
Glenda is given sanctuary by Ebenezer Baptist Church in Queens.

June 9, 1988
Abrams states that no arrest will be made within Ebenezer Baptist Church but that he is contemplating the initiation of disciplinary charges against Maddox and Mason.

June 10, 1988
Glenda is given sanctuary by Bethany Baptist Church in Brooklyn.

June 14, 1988
Perry McKinnon, a former security guard employed by Reverend Sharpton, tells the media that Brawley's claim is a "pack of lies" after he is fired by Sharpton.

Cuomo exonerates Crist, Pagones and Patterson in the abduction and sexual abuse of Tawana.

June 15, 1988
Jitu Weusi and Elombe Brath inform the media that Perry McKinnon is a credible witness.

June 16, 1988
McKinnon appears before Abrams' grand jury.

June 17, 1988
Alvin McKinnon, Perry's first cousin, states that Perry is a "basket case."

Perry McKinnon meets with federal investigators.

Abrams concedes that Perry McKinnon was under psychiatric care while in the Army but condemns Maddox, Mason and Sharpton for exposing McKinnon.

June 18, 1988
Aljetta McKinnon of Reidsville, Georgia, who is married to Perry McKinnon, comes to New York and states that Perry McKinnon "wants to be a bigshot and should have been in a hospital a long time ago."

Reverend Sharpton reveals that McKinnon must be a bigamist since he attended the wedding of McKinnon to another woman early in 1987.

June 20, 1988
Samuel McClease tells the media that Reverend Sharpton hired him to bug his telephone, and claims to have tapes proving that the Brawley case is a hoax.

June 21, 1988
McClease surrenders to federal authorities on a material witness warrant.

June 22, 1988
McClease demands immunity for his criminal past, including any possible cocaine trafficking-related crimes, before he discloses the tapes.

June 23, 1988
McClease is given immunity for his prior criminal conduct.

June 24, 1988
Manhattan Borough President David Dinkins defends Cuomo and Abrams in their handling of the Brawley case and accuses Maddox, Mason and Sharpton of damaging the civil rights movement.

June 25, 1988
Federal authorities arrest McClease for giving them blank tapes.

July 12, 1988
The body of an African American woman, Anna Kithcart, is found near Tawana's home with "KKK" carvings on it.

July 14, 1988
Abrams states that Tawana may have engaged in forgivable, consensual sex despite her being a minor and despite applicable statutory rape laws.

Cuomo states that Sharpton-led protests in Atlanta may alter his travel plans to the Democratic National Convention.

July 16, 1988
Maddox, Mason, Reverend Sharpton, the Brawleys and their supporters join Minister Louis Farrakhan and Dr. Lenora Fulani at the 1988 Democratic National Convention in Atlanta.

July 29, 1988
Reverend Sharpton and 11 others are convicted of engaging in civil disobedience in Albany, New York.

August 2, 1988
Pagones appears before the grand jury.

August 17, 1988
Maddox, Mason and Sharpton establish United African Movement (UAM).

August 29, 1988
UAM marches on Gracie Mansion demanding Koch's ouster; Sharpton and 15 others are arrested.

September 26, 1988
Abrams' employee Samuel Evans is sentenced for stealing grand jury minutes.

October 6, 1988
Abrams issues a grand jury report charging that Tawana fabricated the story of the rape and was responsible for putting herself in the condition in which she was found. All law enforcement officials named as her assailants are exonerated. Abrams

simultaneously files disciplinary complaints against Maddox and Mason.

October 28, 1988
Court officers riot in a Brooklyn courtroom and beat scores of Sharpton and Mason supporters. Seventeen people are arrested in the riot, including Sharpton, Mason and William Kunstler. The incident is videotaped by Minister Clemson Brown.

November 17, 1988
Pagones commences a $600 million civil action against Tawana, Maddox, Mason and Sharpton in Supreme Court, Dutchess County seeking damages for defamation, conspiracy and intentional infliction of mental and emotional distress.

December 15, 1988
"Day of Outrage" trial begins in Brooklyn Criminal Court before Judge Albert Koch.

January 6, 1989
The trial abruptly stops after city refuses to divulge its list of informants.

February 7, 1989
Judge John Turner dismisses appeals and orders Sharpton, Pete Seeger and ten other persons jailed to finish a sentence for protesting in Albany against statewide racism and official foot-dragging in the Brawley investigation.

February 28, 1989
Judge Ralph A. Beisner grants

Maddox's motion to dismiss Pagones' complaint, in part by dismissing more than 60% of his causes of action against Maddox, Mason and Sharpton.

June 30, 1989
Reverend Sharpton is arraigned on a 67-count indictment in Manhattan Supreme Court.

July 1, 1989
Reverend Sharpton is arraigned on a three-count indictment in Albany Supreme Court before Judge John Turner.

November 13, 1989
Maddox refuses to appear before grievance committee for the Second and Eleventh Judicial Districts rather than be forced to divulge confidential attorney/client information.

November 20, 1989
Pagones obtains a restraining order which allows him to avoid giving a deposition in his civil lawsuit against Maddox, Mason and Sharpton.

November 22, 1989
Appellate Division, Second Judicial Department orders Maddox to appear before the grievance committee within 30 days and divulge confidential information or face immediate suspension.

December 13, 1989
Maddox refuses to appear before the grievance committee.

January 8, 1990
Maddox again refuses to appear before

the grievance committee.

March 12, 1990
Maddox appears before the grievance committee with Dr. William A. Jones of Bethany Baptist Church in Brooklyn, but refuses to be sworn in, citing, among other things, the grievance committee's refusal to provide him with a copy of Abrams' complaint.

March 19, 1990
Sharpton's grand larceny trial begins in Manhattan Supreme Court before Judge Joan Carey.

May 7, 1990
Maddox appears before the grievance committee with Reverend Jones but refuses to be sworn in, citing, among other things, a conflict of interest arising out of his current defense of Reverend Sharpton.

May 21, 1990
The Appellate Division, Second Judicial Department suspends Maddox from the practice of law without a hearing and without any conditions for reinstatement.

July 2, 1990
After six hours of deliberations, a jury in Manhattan Supreme Court acquits Reverend Sharpton of all 67 counts of the indictment.

July 5, 1990
The New York Court of Appeals denies Maddox's application for leave to appeal to the state's highest court.

September 27, 1990
Chief Judge Thomas C. Platt of Brooklyn Federal Court informs Maddox that he cannot be suspended from practicing law in federal court without a hearing.

The Bensonhurst Case: A Chronology

August 23, 1989
Yusuf Hawkins is fatally shot in Bensonhurst, where he and two friends had gone to look at a used car and were attacked by a white mob.

August 25, 1989
Steve Curreri, Keith Mondello, James Patino, Pasquale Raucci and Charles Stressler are arrested in the killing and arraigned in Brooklyn Criminal Court.

August 26, 1989
Reverend Charles S. Fermeglia of Bensonhurst deplores the killing in a Sunday sermon at St. Dominic's Church.

August 27, 1989
Three hundred people march through Bensonhurst to protest the killing. Neighborhood residents hold up watermelons and shout racial slurs.

Joseph Serrano is arrested. Joseph Fama, wanted as the gunman, is suspected of having fled the country.

August 29, 1989
The late Bishop Francis J. Mugavero of Brooklyn joins Mayor Ed Koch in charging that the marches in Bensonhurst have inflamed racial tensions by blaming the entire Bensonhurst community for the crime.

The FBI begins what is described as a routine inquiry into possible civil rights violations in the killing of Yusuf Hawkins.

August 30, 1989
Yusuf is buried following his funeral at Glover Memorial Baptist Church, where Reverend Al Sharpton and Minister Louis Farrakhan are among those in attendance. Koch, Governor Mario Cuomo and other politicians are heckled and forced to wait outside the church.

Mondello is charged with murder.

August 31, 1989
Ten thousand youth march on the Brooklyn Bridge in a memorial protest for Yusuf and slain former Black Panther Huey Newton. Dozens of police are injured after they attack marchers, who defend themselves on the bridge.

Mondello and Raucci are indicted on second-degree murder charges. Fama surrenders in Oneonta, New York and pleads not guilty in Brooklyn Criminal Court.

September 2, 1989
Sharpton and Lenora Fulani lead 300 marchers into the heart of Bensonhurst, with 400 policemen on duty to serve as a barrier against another hostile response. Sharpton vows to keep marching "until the whole gang is in jail."

September 3, 1989
Bensonhurst clergy lead a march of 200 people, nearly all white, through Bensonhurst. A wreath of flowers is laid at the murder site.

September 6, 1989
Sharpton announces he will lead a march through Bensonhurst despite opposition from some Black ministers, who worry that the march could hurt David Dinkins' primary campaign for mayor.

September 8, 1989
Serrano is indicted on second-degree murder charges.

Three hundred march in Bensonhurst.

September 9, 1989
Fama is indicted for murder.

September 12, 1989
David Dinkins "dumps Koch" and becomes the Democratic nominee for the mayoral election in November.

September 14, 1989
Patino indicted for murder and manslaughter.

November 7, 1989
Amidst highly charged racial tensions, and in an overwhelmingly Democratic town, Dinkins barely beats Republican Rudolph Giuliani in the mayoral race. Voting is heavily split along racial lines.

January 1, 1990
David Dinkins is inaugurated as the first African American mayor in the history of New York City.

January 15, 1990
In commemoration of Martin Luther King's birthday Reverend Sharpton, Moses Stewart, Fred Newman, and Lenora Fulani lead the first of many multi-racial marches through the heart of Bensonhurst demanding racial justice. They launch a campaign to rename 20th Avenue in Bensonhurst Yusuf Hawkins Boulevard.

February 28, 1990
Brooklyn District Attorney Charles Hynes meets secretly with Moses Stewart, the father of Yusuf Hawkins, Sharpton and attorney Alton Maddox in an attempt to ease racial tensions and assure them that the Bensonhurst murder case would proceed on time.

Hynes admits losing a key witness, 21-year-old John Vento, who had told

then-Brooklyn DA Elizabeth
Holtzman that he had seen Serrano
pass a gun to Fama moments before
the shots were fired. Vento had agreed
to testify if he wasn't indicted, but
vanished in December. Hynes pleads
for public support in finding Vento.
Nobody — including Moses Stewart
— knew about Vento's deal with the
DA or his subsequent disappearance.

March 1, 1990

In a radio interview originating from
Harlem's Apollo Theater, Stewart
steps up an attack on city officials
following news of Vento's
disappearance. Stewart says that the
death of his son was responsible for
Dinkins' election.

Sharpton calls for a march on March 3
in Bensonhurst, and asks Dinkins and
Bensonhurst Assemblyman Frank
Barbaro to lead an appeal to the
Bensonhurst community to bring forth
witnesses.

Rally at Brooklyn Supreme
Courthouse.

March 3, 1990

Sharpton leads a march through the
streets of Bensonhurst to protest a
possible delay in the trials of seven
defendants and to demand community
support in finding the witnesses.

March 5, 1990

On the day the trial is scheduled to
begin, the Brooklyn DA's office asks
for a 30-day postponement, citing the
disappearance of their key witness,
Vento. Judge Thaddeus Owens
reluctantly grants the request and
orders the trial to begin on April 2.

March 10, 1990

Sharpton leads march in the streets of
Bensonhurst to protest the
mishandling of the case by Hynes.

March 19, 1990

Yusuf Hawkins' birthday. He would
have been 17. A small group of family
and friends gather at the gravesite to
mourn the slain youth and pray that
his killers are brought to justice. Rev.
Wayne Stokeling of St. John's Baptist
Church in Brooklyn conducts a brief
ceremony.

April 2, 1990

Rally at Brooklyn Supreme Courthouse.

Jury selection begins in trial of Fama
and Mondello. Judge Owens rules that
there will be separate juries.

April 5, 1990

Vento surrenders to FBI in Ohio.

May 2, 1990

March in Bensonhurst.

May 3, 1990

Sharpton brings 200 supporters to St.
Dominic's Church.

May 8, 1990

Courthouse rally.

May 11, 1990

Courthouse rally.

Dinkins appears on all local TV and
radio stations pleading for racial
tolerance in response to Sharpton's
warning that if the juries in the
Bensonhurst case bring back anything
less than murder convictions the city
might explode.

May 12, 1990
Sharpton leads a Mother's Day march demanding justice; an exceptionally hostile crowd marches alongside on sidewalk.

May 17, 1990
Jury finds Joseph Fama guilty of murder.

May 18, 1990
In a separate trial the jury finds Keith Mondello not guilty. African American community is outraged while Bensonhurst celebrates.

May 19, 1990
Brooklyn's top federal prosecutor says he is considering a civil rights prosecution of Keith Mondello after his unexpected acquittal of homicide charges.

Sharpton leads the largest march to date, with 1,000 supporters marching through Bensonhurst. Barbaro works the sidelines appealing for calm.

May 20, 1990
Sharpton and Dinkins meet.

May 21, 1990
Newsday devotes full page editorial to argument that the media are giving Sharpton too much coverage. A *Daily News*/ABC poll on Mondello conviction shows New Yorkers agree (by a 2 to 1 margin) with Sharpton (as opposed to Dinkins) that Mondello was guilty of murder.

May 22, 1990
Dinkins mobilizes city's social service unions to bring busloads of union members out for a "unity" rally at St.

John the Divine Church following split verdicts in Bensonhurst murder trials. Cuomo and Dinkins are among speakers. Rally calls on New Yorkers to wear blue ribbons and turn on car headlights. Sharpton responds that they should save the ribbons for "Elsie the Cow" and deliver justice.

May 23, 1990
Ad hoc clergy group called Coalition for Harmony holds news conference in Bensonhurst calling for an end to the marches led by Sharpton, while local clergy, politicians and the leaders of Italian community groups meet at St. Dominic's Church to discuss how to stop the marches. The group distributes 10,000 fliers in the neighborhood urging residents to stay home during the marches.

May 24, 1990
In response to a reporter's question, Sharpton says that anything less than a murder verdict will light a match to the powder keg that could burn New York City down. Media respond with cartoons, sharply criticizing him for his single-minded passion to see justice done. Dinkins denounces Sharpton on TV. Police and Bensonhurst community leaders invite Sharpton to meet in the hope of avoiding another confrontation.

May 25, 1990
Courthouse rally.

May 26, 1990
For the second week in a row, Sharpton leads a march through Bensonhurst to protest the acquittal of Mondello on murder and

manslaughter charges. Bensonhurst community remains behind closed doors.

June 2, 1990
March in Bensonhurst.

June 3, 1990
Two hundred marchers go to St. Dominic's with Rev. Sharpton, precipitating a meeting with Bensonhurst leaders. It is agreed that marches will stop if leaders ask the community to make an honest effort to produce strong sentences.

June 7, 1990
Attorney C. Vernon Mason announces that Bensonhurst community leaders and march organizers agreed to end the marches after discussions this week. Under the agreement the negotiators call on elected officials to attend the sentencing of defendants Fama and Mondello; they demand maximum sentences for Fama and Mondello and cooperation from Bensonhurst community leaders to seek out the roughly 30 other attackers who were never arrested. Upon failure to fulfill these demands, the marches will resume.

June 10, 1990
Dinkins — on his way to meet Bensonhurst community leaders — and Sharpton meet at St. Dominic's.

Dinkins meets with Bensonhurst elected officials and community leaders — including State Assemblymen Frank J. Barbaro and Peter J. Abbate, Jr. and Jack Spatola,

president of the Federation of Italian-American organizations — in his crusade to "ease the racial tensions" on the eve of the sentencing of Joseph Fama and Keith Mondello. Bensonhurst community leaders meet with Moses Stewart and Diane Hawkins, Yusuf's parents.

Community leaders rally.

June 11, 1990
Judge Owens gives Joseph Fama and Keith Mondello maximum sentences for the charges against them in the murder of Yusuf Hawkins. Fama receives 32 2/3 years to life in prison for second-degree murder, riot, unlawful imprisonment, weapons possession and other crimes. Mondello is sentenced to 5 1/3 to 16 years in prison for his conviction on riot, unlawful imprisonment, discrimination and several lesser charges.

Start of jury selection for John Vento, who was charged with murder after reneging on deal to cooperate with prosecution.

Judge Owens sets trial dates for five other young men accused in the murder.

Courthouse rally.

June 16, 1990
Sharpton and Fulani lead rally at Gracie Mansion calling on Dinkins to join "people's alliance for justice."

June 18, 1990
Vento case begins.

June 25, 1990
Vento jury begins eight days of deliberations.

July 3, 1990
Vento is acquitted of intentional murder and convicted of two lesser charges. He is sentenced to 2 2/3 to 8 years. Jury fails to reach a verdict on second murder charge and on riot charge, and Judge Owens sets new trial date on unresolved charges.

July 15, 1990
Gracie Mansion rally.

August 23, 1990
Memorial service and rally at Hawkins gravesite.

October 11, 1990
Trial of Charles Stressler ends in a mistrial after an outburst by a juror, who yells that Stewart was staring at her throughout the proceedings.

November 19, 1990
Patino and Serrano trials begin. Second Vento trial begins.

December 4, 1990
Serrano is convicted only of carrying a baseball bat, while Patino is acquitted of all charges.

December 6, 1990
In his second trial, Vento is acquitted of murder and manslaughter charges and convicted on riot charges.

January 11, 1991
Vento receives sentence of 1 1/3 to 4 years. Serrano receives three years' probation. Sharpton vows to resume marches in Bensonhurst the next day.

January 12, 1991
Sharpton is back in Bensonhurst to lead a march to protest recent court setbacks in Bensonhurst case. Four hundred police officers are there to protect the 500 marchers who congregate in an enclosed school yard, as police instruct them to do for their own safety. At the rally, 27-year-old Michael Riccardi of Bensonhurst gets past 300 officers in a "frozen" zone and stabs Sharpton in the chest.

January 13, 1991
Fulani leads rally through Bensonhurst to protest police negligence in Sharpton stabbing.

Bibliography

Books

Baldwin, James. *Notes of a Native Son*. Boston: Beacon Press, 1957.
____. *The Fire Next Time*. New York: Dell Publishing Co., Inc., 1962.
Caro, Robert A. *The Power Broker: Robert Moses and the Fall of New York*. New York: Vintage Books, 1975.
Essien-Udom, E.U. *Black Nationalism: A Search for an Identity in America*. New York: Dell Publishing Co., Inc., 1964.
Farrakhan, Louis, Lenora Fulani, and Al Sharpton. *Independent Black Leadership in America*. New York: Castillo International, 1990.
Grand Jury of the Supreme Court. *Report of the Grand Jury of the Supreme Court State of New York County of Dutchess issued pursuant to criminal procedure law section 190.85 subdivision (1)(b)*, 1988.
Holiday, Billie, and William Dufty. *Lady Sings the Blues*. New York: Lancer Books, 1956.
Hynes, Charles J., and Bob Drury. *Incident at Howard Beach: The Case for Murder*. New York: Putnam Publishing Group, 1990.
King, Martin Luther, Jr. *Stride Toward Freedom: The Montgomery Story*. New York: Ballantine Books, 1960.
____. *Where Do We Go from Here: Chaos or Community?* New York: Bantam Books, 1968.
Lomax, Louis. *The Negro Revolt*. New York: Harper & Row, 1962.
Malcolm X. *Malcolm X Speaks*. New York: Pathfinder Press, 1989.
Malcolm X, and Alex Haley. *The Autobiography of Malcolm X*. New York: Ballantine Books, 1973.
McFadden, Robert D., Ralph R. Blumenthal, M.A. Farber, E.R. Shipp, Charles Strum, Craig Wolff. *Outrage: The Story Behind the Tawana Brawley Hoax*. New York: Bantam Books, 1990.

Morris, Charles R. *The Cost of Good Intentions: New York City and the Liberal Experiment*. New York: McGraw-Hill, 1981.

Pinkney, Alphonso. *The Myth of Black Progress*. Cambridge: Cambridge University Press, 1984.

Reynolds, Barbara A. *Jesse Jackson: America's David*. Washington, DC: JFJ Associates, 1975.

Articles

Barricklow, Denise. "Big Al." *The Face*. (May 1990):68-70.

Bastone, William, Joe Conason, Jack Newfield, and Tom Robbins. "The Hustler: How Al Sharpton Conned the Movement, the Media, and the Government." *Village Voice*, February 2, 1988.

Blauner, Peter. "King on the Ropes: Boxing's Promoter Fights for his Professional Life." *New York*, March 18, 1991.

Dannen, Fredric. "The Born-Again Don." *Vanity Fair*, February, 1991.

Drury, Bob, Robert E. Kessler, and Mike McAlary. "The Minister and the Feds." *New York Newsday*, January 20, 1988.

_____. "Black Leader: Probe FBI. Activist Hits Feds over Sharpton Case; Minister Brands Report as 'Ludicrous.' " *New York Newsday*, January 21, 1988.

Drury, Bob, Robert E. Kessler, Bob Liff, Mike McAlary, Paul Moses, and Manny Topol. "The Minister and the Mob. Feds' Data Ties Sharpton to Reputed Crime Figures." *New York Newsday*, January 22, 1988.

Farber, M.A. "A 'New' Sharpton: Maturing of a Maverick." *The New York Times*, January 21, 1991.

_____. "Sharpton: Champion or Opportunist?" *The New York Times*, February 2, 1988.

Friedman, Dan, and Frank Solomon. "The Cops Stood By." *Probe* (Spring 1991):2-6.

Getlin, Josh. "Al Sharpton, Media Star." *The Los Angeles Times*, September 27, 1989.

Howell, Ron, with Robert E. Kessler. "The Rev and the Fugitive: Sharpton Tried to Set Up Chesimard, Activists Say." *New York Newsday*, October 21, 1988.

Kilson, Martin. "Adam Clayton Powell, Jr.: The Militant as Politician." In *Black Leaders of the Twentieth Century*. Edited by S.H. Franklin and A. Meier, 259-75. Urbana University of Illinois, 1982.

Klein, Michael. "Abrams Must Resign." *National Alliance*, April 19, 1990.

_____. "The Leader They Can't Bury." *National Alliance*, March 8, 1990.

_____. "Justice in the Streets." *National Alliance*, March 15, 1990.

_____. "Three Leaders Who Won't Be Destroyed." *Probe* (Spring 1991):10-13.

Kurtz, Howard. "Al Sharpton, in His Own Image." *The Washington Post*, September 5, 1990.

Lee, Spike. "The Gospel According to Reverend Al." *Spin* (Oct. 1990):39-45.

Newman, Fred. "Liberalism: An Ahistorical Prescription. An Analysis of Cuomo's Victory." *Practice* 2-3 (Fall, Winter 1983):225-230.

Richardson, Clem. "A Dialogue with Al Sharpton." *Emerge* (Nov. 1990):11-12.

Sager, Mike. "The Sharpton Strategy." *Esquire* (Jan. 1991):23-24, 112-115.

Walton, Anthony. "Who Needs Al Sharpton?" *7 Days* (Oct. 11, 1989):15-18.

Index

Photo Credits